JEAN MCNIFF AND JACK WHITEHEAD

ALL YOU NEED TO KNOW ABOUT
ACTION RESEARCH

SECOND EDITION

SAGE

Los Angeles | London | New Delhi
Singapore | Washington DC

First published 2005

This edition 2011

Reprinted 2012

SAGE Publications Ltd
1 Oliver's Yard
55 City Road
London EC1Y 1S

SAGE Publications Inc.
2455 Teller Road
Thousand Oaks, California 91320

SAGE Publications India Pvt Ltd
B 1/I 1 Mohan Cooperative Industrial Area
Mathura Road, New Delhi 110 044
India

SAGE Publications Asia-Pacific Pte Ltd
3 Church Street
#10-04 Samsung Hub
Singapore 049483

British Library Cataloguing in Publication data

Library of Congress Control Number: 2010935730

A catalogue record for this book is available from the British Library

ISBN 978-0-85702-582-1
ISBN 978-0-85702-583-8

Typeset by C&M Digitals (P) Ltd, Chennai, India
Printed and bound in Great Britain by TJ International Ltd, Padstow Cornwall
Printed on paper from sustainable resources

ALL YOU NEED TO KNOW ABOUT
ACTION
RESEARCH

SAGE has been part of the global academic community since 1965, supporting high quality research and learning that transforms society and our understanding of individuals, groups, and cultures. SAGE is the independent, innovative, natural home for authors, editors and societies who share our commitment and passion for the social sciences.

Find out more at: **www.sagepublications.com**

Contents

Introduction

This book is a complete guide to action research. It is written to help you to undertake an action enquiry in your own workplace, and to produce a high quality report for publication and further dissemination. It explains how to identify a research question, map out an action plan, use appropriate methodologies and generate evidence from the data to test your findings against the most stringent critique. It also explains why you should do action research and the potential benefits for your own learning and the learning of others.

There are two main reasons for doing action research. First, you can improve learning in order to improve workplace practices. Second, you can advance knowledge and theory, that is, new ideas about how things can be done and why. All research aims to generate knowledge and theory. As a practitioner-researcher, you are aiming to generate theories about learning and practice, your own and other people's.

This is a key point. Most of the action research literature talks about improving practice, but talks less about improving learning as the basis of improved practice, and even less about how this should be seen as new theory and an important contribution to the world of ideas. The literature tends to reinforce the portrayal of practitioners as doers, those who are competent to be involved in improving practice, rather than thinkers, those who are competent to be involved in debates about knowledge, or who have good ideas about what is important in life and how we should live. Consequently, in wider debates, including policy debates, practitioners tend to be excluded, on the assumption that they are good at practice, but perhaps they should leave it to official theorists to explain what, how and why people should learn, and how they should use their knowledge. So strong is this discourse that many practitioners have come to believe it themselves, and collude in their own subjugation by refusing to believe that they are competent theorists, or by dismissing 'theory' as being above their heads or irrelevant.

We authors, Jean and Jack, do not go along with this. We believe that practitioners can, and should, get involved. We also believe that theory itself needs to be reconceptualized, not as an abstract, seemingly esoteric field of study, but as a practical way of thinking about social affairs and how they can be improved. This is why doing action research is so important. You can show how you have learned to improve practice, in terms, say, of achieving better working conditions or increased opportunities for learning, and also how this has enabled you to produce your own personal theory about why it worked (or did not, if that is the case, and what you need to do differently next time). Theorizing your practice in this way shows that you are producing ideas that can influence the learning of others. Your practice is the grounds for your own theory.

This view of theory is barely evident in the mainstream literatures, which largely maintain that theory should be expressed as sets of propositions, or statements, produced by official knowledge-creators in universities and think tanks. Such propositional theories do exist, of course, and are important, for example, for predicting social trends and keeping track of national economies. However, this is not the only kind of theory available or recognized. People's living theories are just as important as propositional theories, but they tend not to be seen as such in the mainstream literatures. There should be room enough for both kinds, and discussions about how one can contribute to the development of the other.

We authors subscribe firmly to Foucault's idea that knowledge is power. We urge you to regard yourself as a researcher, well capable of creating your own theories by studying your living practice. You have important things to say, both in relation to workplace practices, and also in relation to the world of ideas and theory. We have written this book to help you to say those things in such a way that others will listen and want to hear more. The book aims to help you take your rightful place as a publicly acknowledged competent professional and as a brilliant knower.

Reading this book

The book is organized as seven parts, which deal with what you need to know and why you need to know it, how you learn and test your learning, and how you disseminate your knowledge for public use. The chapters follow a coherent sequence, and each deals with a separate issue. The material is organized like this so that you can see action research as a whole, and also focus on particular issues as needed. The chapters are reasonably short and snappy, with case studies throughout. We have expanded the number of case studies in this second edition, with relevance to many workplaces outside mainstream education. We emphasize consistently that whenever we present ideas as free standing, this is for analysis only. Action research is an integrated practice, comprising multiple practices, all of which contribute to everything else, so it is important to see the holistic connections and their potential for generating further connections.

You should note the form of the book as you work with it. We have presented it as an example of the generative transformational nature of living systems, which is one of the key themes that underpin our work. This idea, which is a recurrent theme throughout the history of ideas, is that each living organism has its own internal generative capacity to transform itself into an infinitude of new forms.

Each new form is a more fully realized version than the previous one. Caterpillars metamorphose into butterflies, and acorns into oak trees. Here we explain how values can turn into practices, and inexperienced action researchers into doctoral candidates. The organization of the ideas in the text also reflects this idea of relentless and unstoppable growth. 'How to do action research' turns into 'Why do action research?' and 'What can you achieve for social good?' We do not stop at how to do action research, but develop into how your action can transform into the grounds for your own and other people's new learning, and what the implications of your work may be.

This transformational process mirrors our own commitments as professional educators. We believe, like Habermas (1975) that people cannot not learn in processes of social evolution. We all learn, potentially every moment of every waking day. What we learn is at issue, and what we do with that learning. Do we transform our learning into new learning and new practices that will benefit ourselves and others? In other words, what educational influences do we exercise in our own learning, in the learning of others, and in the learning of social formations? Do we celebrate our living, in the certainty that one day we will be gone? What kind of legacy will we leave? What do we do, to try to ensure a better world today for tomorrow?

Working with the text itself can be seen as you engaging in your action enquiry about how you can learn about action research and generate your own ideas about how to do it and what some of the implications may be for your own practice. On pages 8–9 we explain that doing action research involves asking a range of questions, such as the following:

- What is my concern?
- Why am I concerned?
- How do I gather evidence to show reasons for my concern?
- What do I do about the situation?
- How do I test the validity of my claim(s) to knowledge?
- How can I check whether any conclusions I come to are reasonably fair and accurate?
- How do I modify my practice in the light of my evaluation?
- How do I explain the significance of my work? (see also Whitehead, 1989)

In the introduction to each part we draw your attention to where you are in this action-reflection cycle. As you read and work with the ideas, you may become aware of your own process of becoming increasingly critical, and more aware of the values base of what you are doing in your real-life contexts.

We invite you to engage with these ideas, and to transform your own understanding about how you can make your contribution. While you may read the book initially to learn more about how to do action research, we urge you to think about what you can achieve through your own enquiry, and how this can benefit yourself and others.

Writing the book

The book is part of our own writing and dissemination programme, as we pursue our research into how we can encourage practitioners to believe in themselves as they produce their descriptions and explanations (their theories) of practice and produce accounts that will contribute to new learning. We believe passionately in the right of all to speak and be listened to, and we believe in the need for individual practitioners, working collectively, to show how they hold themselves accountable for what they do. We aim to do the same. Although we do not appear much in this book as real persons, you can easily contact us and access our work via our websites, which show how we also test our ideas against public critique. If you contact us, we will respond, perhaps not immediately, but we will.

We hope that this book speaks to your experience.

Jean McNiff and Jack Whitehead

You can contact Jean at jeanmcniff@mac.com. Her website is http://www.jeanmcniff.com.

You can contact Jack at jack@actionresearch.net. His website is http://www.actionresearch.net.

PART I

What Do I Need to Know?

This part is about the key issues in action research. It explains that action research is about practitioners creating new ideas about improving their work, and putting those ideas forward as their personal theories of practice. This is different from traditional social science research, in which official researchers produce theory, which they then expect practitioners to apply to their practice. Given the power-constituted nature of these issues, therefore, we are immediately into issues of power and politics, about what counts as knowledge and who counts as a knower.

Part I discusses these ideas. It contains the following chapters.

Chapter 1 What Is Action Research?
Chapter 2 Who Does Action Research?
Chapter 3 The Underpinning Assumptions of Action Research
Chapter 4 Where Did Action Research Come From?

We said in the Introduction that you could regard working with this book as your action enquiry into how you can learn about action research and how to do it. At this point in your action–reflection cycle you are asking, 'What is my concern?' You are saying that you need to find out what the core ideas of action research are, so you have a firm grasp of the basics in order to begin your action enquiry from an informed position.

ONE

What Is Action Research?

The action research family is wide and diverse, so inevitably different people say different things about what action research is and what it is for, and who can do it and how. You need to know about these issues, so you can take an active part in the debates. Taking part also helps you appreciate why you should do action research and what you can hope to achieve.

This chapter is organized into four sections that deal with these issues.

1 What action research is and is not
2 Different approaches to action research
3 Purposes of action research
4 When and when not to use action research

1 What action research is and is not

Action research is a form of enquiry that enables practitioners in every job and walk of life to investigate and evaluate their work. They ask, 'What am I doing? Do I need to improve anything? If so, what? How do I improve it? Why should I improve it?' They produce their accounts of practice to show: (1) how they are trying to improve what they are doing, which involves first thinking about and learning how to do it better; and (2) how they try to influence others to do the same thing. These accounts stand as their own practical theories of practice, from which others can learn if they wish.

Action research has become increasingly popular around the world as a form of professional learning. It has been particularly well developed in education, specifically in teaching, but is now used widely across the professions. A major attraction of action research is that everyone can do it, so it is for 'ordinary' practitioners as well as principals, managers and administrators. Students also can and should do action research (McNiff, 2010a). You can gain university accreditation for your action enquiries, as the case studies in this book show.

Action research can be a powerfully liberating form of professional enquiry because it means that practitioners themselves investigate their practices as they find ways to live more fully in the direction of their educational values. They are not told what to do. They decide for themselves what to do, in negotiation with others. This can work in relation to individual as well as collective enquiries. More and more groups of practitioners are getting together to investigate their collective work and put their stories of learning into the public domain. Your story can add to this collection and strengthen it.

This is what makes action research distinctive. Practitioners research their own practices, which is different from traditional forms of social science research, where a professional researcher does research on practitioners. Social scientists tend to stand outside a situation and ask, 'What are those people over there doing? How do we understand and explain what they are doing?' This kind of research is often called outsider or spectator research. Action researchers, however, are insider researchers. They see themselves as part of the context they are investigating, and ask, individually and collectively, 'Is my/our work going as we wish? How do we improve it where necessary?' If they feel their work is already reasonably satisfactory, they evaluate it and produce evidence to show why they believe this to be the case. If they feel something needs improving, they work on that aspect, keeping records and producing regular oral and written progress reports about what they are doing.

Here are some examples of social science (outsider) questions and action research (insider) questions to show the difference between them.

Social science (outsider) questions

- What is the relationship between nurses' practice-based knowledge and the quality of patient care?
- Does management style influence worker productivity?
- Will a different seating arrangement increase audience participation?

Action research (insider) questions

- How do I study my nursing practice for the benefit of the patients?
- How do I improve my management style to encourage productivity?
- How do I encourage greater audience participation through trying out different seating arrangements?

Action research aims to be a disciplined, systematic process. A notional action plan is:

- take stock of what is going on;
- identify a concern;
- think of a possible way forward;

- try it out;
- monitor the action by gathering data to show what is happening;
- evaluate progress by establishing procedures for making judgements about what is happening;
- test the validity of claims to knowledge;
- modify practice in light of the evaluation. (This is a modified version of the plan in McNiff and Whitehead, 2010)

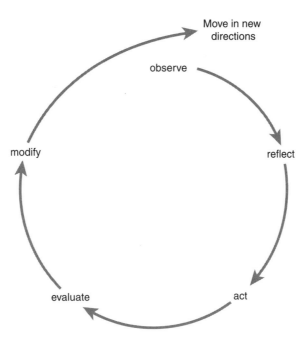

Figure 1.1 An action–reflection cycle

This can be turned into a set of questions, as follows:

- What is my concern?
- Why am I concerned?
- How do I show the situation as it is and as it develops?
- What can I do about it? What will I do about it?
- How do I test the validity of my claims to knowledge?
- How do I check that any conclusions I come to are reasonably fair and accurate?
- How do I modify my ideas and practices in light of the evaluation? (Adapted from Whitehead, 1989)

In practical terms, this means you would identify a particular concern, try out a different way of doing things, reflect on what was happening, check out any new understandings with others, and in light of your reflections try a different way that may or may not be more successful. As a nurse, for example, you would monitor and evaluate how you were relating to patients, and how they were responding to you (Higgs and Titchen, 2001). This would help you find the best way of working with patients to encourage their self-motivation towards recovery. As a sales person you would experiment with different seating arrangements to find the best ways of selling your product (see Varga, 2009, for ideas).

The process of 'observe – reflect – act – evaluate – modify – move in new directions' is generally known as action–reflection, although no single term is used in the literature. Because the process tends to be cyclical, it is often referred to as an action–reflection cycle (Figure 1.1). The process is ongoing because as soon as we reach a provisional point where we feel things are satisfactory, that point itself raises new questions and it is time to begin again. Good visual models exist in the literature to communicate this process (Elliott, 1991; McNiff, 2002).

2   Different approaches to action research

The action research family has been around for a long time, at least since the 1930s, and has become increasingly influential. As often happens, however, different family members have developed different opinions and interests, some have developed their own terminology, and some have formed breakaway groups, which have in turn become mainstreamed. You need to decide which kind of action research is best for you, which means developing a critical perspective to some key issues. These are as follows.

- Different views of what action research is about and which perspective to take.
- Different forms of action research and different names and terminology.

Different views of what action research is about and which perspective to take

There is general agreement among the action research community that action research is about:

- *action*: taking action to improve practice, and …
- *research*: finding things out and coming to new understandings, that is, creating new knowledge. In action research the knowledge is about how and why improvement has happened.

There is disagreement about:

- The balance between taking action and doing research: many texts emphasize the need to take action but not to do research. This turns action research into a form of personal-professional development but without a solid research/knowledge base.

- Who does the action and who does the research, that is, who creates the knowledge.

Furthermore, because knowledge contributes to theory, that is, explanations for how and why things happen, it becomes a question of who does the action and who generates the theory (explanations) about the action. Take the example of a film set (this will remind you of issues already raised).

On film sets, some people are positioned, and frequently position themselves, as actors and agents (doers), while others see themselves as directors and producers (thinkers). Practitioners in workplaces are usually seen as actors whose job is to do things, while researchers in research institutions such as universities are seen as directors and producers whose job is to direct what the practitioner-actors do. They produce explanations about what the actors are doing and why they are doing it. The hidden assumptions are that the actors are good at acting but are not able to theorize what they are doing; while the directors are good at theorizing what the actors are doing and writing reports about it. Theory and practice are seen as separate, and theory is generally seen as more prestigious than practice. This attitude is normal in the world of social science research (see above), where a researcher writes reports about what other people are doing. Ironically it is also commonplace in certain forms of action research. The difference between a social science scenario and an action research scenario is that in social science the aim is to demonstrate a causal relationship ('If I do this, that will happen'), whereas in action research the aim is to improve practice. However, the power relationships between actor and theorist remain the same.

These issues have given rise to different perspectives and terminologies in the literatures. Furthermore, another issue about the type of theory enters the debate.

Different forms of action research and different names and terminology

Broadly speaking, the action research family falls into two groups, sometimes looking like dynasties or clans, and these also sub-divide.

The first group was founded by John Elliott, Stephen Kemmis, Clem Adelman and others (see Chapter 4). It contains people who believe that the proper way to do research is for an external researcher to watch and report on what other practitioners are doing. This is generally referred to as interpretive action research. It is probably still the most common form of action research around.

The second group was founded by Jack Whitehead (Chapter 4), and contains people who believe that a practitioner is able to offer their own explanations for what they are doing. This is referred to variously as self-study action research, first-person action research, living theory action research, or just plain action research.

However, the differences between outsider and insider groupings are often not clear, because people sometimes tend not to take a definitive stance, but position themselves somewhere between the two.

What is different, however, is the *form* of theory (explanations) used. Externalist forms of theory are about what 'they' are doing, and tend to speak about action research as a 'thing' to be implemented. Person-centred forms of theory are about what 'I' am doing as a living person. 'I' speak about action research as something I do, part of 'my' experience. 'My' theories take on a living form: the explanations the person offers for their life and practices are within the way they live and practise. So it is usual nowadays to understand the word 'theory' in two ways: as an abstract propositional form about what is happening for other people; and as an embodied living form about what is happening for me. This latter view has given rise to the term 'living theory', which is seen as distinct from ordinary 'theory'.

More cousins

To complicate matters, the two main groups have given rise to different sub-groups who have given themselves different names. The following is a rough guide, as the situation changes rapidly and allegiances shift.

Within the group who espouse propositional forms of theory

Here are some of those groupings in question, and some definitions of action research.

Reason and Bradbury (2008) have developed a useful typology, which they call 'first-, second- and third-person action research'. They (2008: 6) say:

> 'First-person research is the kind of research that enables the researcher to foster an inquiring approach to his or her own life, to act choicefully and with awareness, and to assess effects in the outside world while acting. …' Second-person research is when the practitioner can 'inquire face-to-face with others into issues of mutual concern …' Third-person research looks at influencing wider social systems, and to create '… a wider community of inquiry involving persons who, because they cannot be known to each other … have an impersonal quality.'

Others speak about participatory action research: this term was first used when action research came to prominence in the 1940s and 1950s and referred to groups who wished to reclaim lands taken from them; it was associated with the work of Orlando Fals Borda and shares the same heritage as scholars such as Paulo Freire. Today, participatory action research has the same undertones as the original version, but tends to be used as emphasizing the participative nature of action research: however, this could be seen as tautological because action research is by default participative. Similarly, some people speak about 'collaborative action research', which again would appear to be unnecessary, because action research is always collaborative.

Then you have Feminist Participatory Action Research (Reid and Frisby 2008), Educational Action Research and Practitioner Action Research (all tautological). At a tangent you have action learning, which emphasizes the actions of work-based learning rather than theory-generation (though action learning is shifting more and more towards action research these days), and action science, which takes a more scientific stance towards demonstrating causal relationships. Furthermore, many of these different groupings cross over or draw on other movements such as narrative inquiry, appreciative inquiry and complexity theory; so it is difficult to see where one piece of scholarly territory ends and another begins.

The same is happening in the other camp.

Within the group who espouse living forms of theory

Since the 1970s Jack Whitehead has been promoting the idea of individuals studying their practices and offering descriptions and explanations for what they do. This view is well established in the literatures under the broad names of self-study action research, or living theory action research (which is technically inaccurate but has caught on). Jack and Jean McNiff began working together in the 1980s and they have had significant influence in contemporary thinking. The book you are reading comes out of this perspective.

In 1993, at the American Educational Research Association annual meeting in San Francisco, a group of action researchers inclined towards self-study met to discuss which directions action research should take. The group included Jean Clandinin, Gaalen Erickson, Stefinee Pinnegar, Tom Russell and Jack Whitehead. They felt that action research should be about the self studying the self, the living 'I' studying their own practices. Out of this meeting a new perspective and a new Special Interest Group (SIG) was born: the Self-Study of Teacher Education Practices (S-STEP). However, over the nigh-20 years of its existence, many in the S-STEP group seem to have broken away from the idea of action research, and some see self-study as mainly about improving practice without the need to do research in order to generate theory, a situation that returns us to the same hierarchical power relationships that the SIG was originally set up to challenge.

Added to this, many people within these groupings prefer to speak only about reflective practice. However, taken on its own, reflective practice could be seen as people reflecting on what they are doing without necessarily taking action to improve it. You can sit all day reflecting on what you are doing but this is no use when trying to improve social situations with justification, which means drawing on a research base that demands personal accountability.

So there we are: a wonderful rich tapestry of people, all working with the same purposes of finding better ways of creating a better world, from their different values perspectives and methodological commitments. It would be difficult for any novice to enter this world and immediately make sense of who is doing what and why, because there is no clearly delineated route map, and people who are active in the field move around and change perspective. Perhaps the best advice for beginning action researchers is to read as much as possible, and keep a level head when dealing with different terminology. Keep in mind that the key issues are about the politics of theory – who counts as a knower, who is able to offer explanations, about what, what counts as knowledge, and who makes decisions about these things.

This brings us to ideas about the purposes of research in general and action research in particular.

3   Purposes of action research

The purpose of all research is to generate new knowledge. Action research generates a special kind of knowledge.

We said above that 'action research' contains the words 'action' and 'research'. The action piece of action research is about improving practice. The 'research' piece of action research is about offering descriptions and explanations for what you are doing as and when you improve practice. Another word for 'descriptions and explanations' is 'theory'. Like all research, the purpose of action research is (1) to generate new knowledge, which (2) feeds into new theory. When you generate new knowledge, you say that you know something now that you did not know before: for example, 'I now know more about car mechanics', or 'I understand better how to dance properly'. You need this knowledge in order to explain what you are doing and why you are doing it (to theorize what you are doing). You say, 'I can describe and explain how and why I have learned about car mechanics' or 'I can describe and explain why it is important to dance properly'. Being able to explain what you are doing and why you are doing it also enables you to be clear about its significance for your field, which is important when it comes to saying why your research should be believed and taken seriously by others, especially peers (see Part V).

By doing your action research you are hoping, therefore, to make knowledge claims such as the following:

- I have improved my practice as a nurse, and I can describe what I have done and explain why I have done it.
- I am a better manager than before because I have studied what I am doing, and I can explain how and why I have improved it.

Action research has always been understood as people taking action to improve their personal and social situations, and offering explanations for why they do so. Some see its potential for promoting a more productive and peaceful world order (Heron, 1998; Heron and Reason, 2001). New work is emerging about ecoliteracy (Sinclair, 2010) and sustainable improvement (Scott, 2010; Tattersall, 2010).

Educational action research is widely seen as a methodology for real-world social change. People communicate their ideas as theories of real-world practice, by explaining what they are doing, why they are doing it and what they hope to achieve. These personal theories are also living theories, because they change and develop as people themselves change and develop. In the perspective adopted by us authors, the aims of action researchers are to generate living theories about how their learning has improved practice and is informing new practices for themselves and others.

The best accounts show the transformation of practice into living theories. The individual practitioner asks, 'What am I doing? How do I understand it in order to improve it? How can I draw on ideas in the literature and incorporate them into my own understanding? How do I transform these ideas into action?' Asking these questions can help practitioners to find practical ways of living in the direction of their educational and social values. The examples throughout this book show how this can be done.

4   When and when not to use action research

You can use action research for many purposes, but not for all.

When to use action research

Use action research when you want to evaluate whether what you are doing is influencing your own or other people's learning, or whether you need to do something different. You may want to:

Improve your understanding

- Patient waiting time in the hospital is too long. How are you going to find out why, so that you can do something about it?
- Your students are achieving remarkably high scores. Why? Is it your teaching, their extra study, or a new classroom environment?

Develop your learning

- How do you learn to encourage people to be more positive?
- How do you learn to improve your own timekeeping?

Influence others' learning

- How do you help colleagues to develop more inclusive pedagogies?
- How do you encourage your senior management team partners to listen more carefully to employees?

When not to use action research

Do not use action research if you want to draw comparisons, show statistical correlations or demonstrate a cause and effect relationship. For example:

- You want to see whether adults who are accompanied by children are more likely to wait at pedestrian crossings than those who are not accompanied by children, so you would do an observational study and include statistical analyses of a head count.
- You want to see why some male teachers seem reluctant to teach relationships and sexuality education, so you would probably do a survey and analyse the results. You may also possibly do a comparative analysis of results from your survey and another survey you have read about in the literatures, which aims to find out which subjects teachers find most attractive.
- You want to show the effects of good leadership on organizational motivation. You could interview a sample of employees and analyse their responses in terms of identified categories. You would probably also interview a sample of business leaders and get their opinions on the relationship between their leadership and the quality of employees' motivation.

These are social science topics where researchers ask questions of the kind, 'What are those people doing? What do they say? How many of them do it?' Action research questions, however, take the form, 'How do I understand what I am doing? How do I improve it?', and place the emphasis on the researcher's intent to take action for personal and social improvement.

A point to remember is that these kinds of social science topics can be included within practitioner researchers' living theories. Questions that ask 'How do I ...?' need to identify a clear starting point for the research, what Elliott (1991) calls a reconnaissance phase, and they often incorporate questions of the form 'What is happening here?'. However, it is necessary to go beyond fact-finding and into action if real-world situations are to be improved.

Here is an example of how 'How do I ...?' questions can incorporate 'What is happening here?' questions.

'How do I ...?' questions	'What is happening here?' questions
How do I stop the bullying in my office?	How many colleagues are being bullied? Who is bullying whom? Why are they bullying them?
How do I encourage my students to read?	What kind of books do my students read at present? How many categories of books are in the college library? How much time is given to independent reading in the curriculum?

─────────────────── Summary ───────────────────

This chapter has set out some core issues in action research. It has explained that, unlike social science, action research places the individual 'I' at the centre of an enquiry. Different forms of action research have emerged over the years, which prioritize different aspects. Action research can be useful when investigating how to improve learning and take social action. It is inappropriate for investigations that aim to draw comparisons or establish cause and effect relationships.

The next chapter deals with the interesting and contested question of who can do action research, and who says.

Further reading

A range of books is available that explain what action research is and is not. Among the most useful are the following.

McNiff, J. (2002) *Action Research: Principles and Practice*. London: Routledge.
A seminal text that established new principles of thinking and a tradition of academic writing for everyday practitioners. About to go into its third edition, the book remains a practical work-based textbook.

McNiff, J. (2010) *Action Research for Professional Development: Concise Advice for New (and Experienced) Action Researchers*. Poole: September.
A developed version of the ubiquitous booklet to be found at http://www.jeanmcniff. com/ar-booklet.asp (still available free and for downloading), this new book covers a lot of ground in a succinct and easily accessible way.

McNiff, J. and Whitehead, J. (2010) *You and Your Action Research Project*. Abingdon: Routledge.
New and updated in its third edition, this book takes you through the entire process of doing an action research project.

Reason, J. and Bradbury, J. (2008) *The SAGE Handbook of Action Research: Participative Inquiry and Practice*. London: Sage.
An action research classic, the Handbook covers the territory of action research from a more academic perspective. Excellent as a reference book, but not for light reading.

Whitehead, J. (1989) 'Creating a living educational theory through questions of the kind, "How do I improve my practice?"', *Cambridge Journal of Education*, 19 (1): 137–53.
A seminal paper that remains relevant for all professions, and that was influential in establishing self-study action research as a major tradition.

TWO

Who Can Do Action Research?

Anyone and everyone can do action research. You do not need any specialized equipment or knowledge. All you need is curiosity, creativity and a willingness to engage. You can do action research virtually anywhere, in institutional settings, in homes and on safaris.

Investigating your work and finding ways to improve it means that you now become a knowledge creator. This idea has implications for the politics of knowledge, because not all people would agree that practitioners should be knowledge creators. Some people think that practitioners should concern themselves only with workplace practice, and not get involved in research or generating knowledge. Others think that practitioners should credit themselves as working with their intellects and contributing to policy debates. These differences of opinion can be traced back to differences of interests (see page 253). The question arises: whose interests are served by perpetuating the mythology that practitioners cannot do research or think for themselves, or that those currently positioned as knowledge workers should not see themselves also as practitioners?

This chapter is organized into four sections, which address the following issues.

1 Who is a practitioner?
2 Why is practitioner knowledge important?
3 What is special about practitioners' theories?
4 How can practitioners contribute to new practices and new theories?

1   Who is a practitioner?

The contested nature of the territory is illustrated by a famous metaphor by Donald Schön about the topology of professional landscapes.

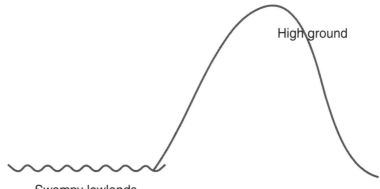

High ground

Swampy lowlands

Figure 2.1 The topology of professional landscapes

The topology of professional landscapes

In 1983, and later in 1995, Schön developed a metaphor that was to become an enduring theme in the social sciences and practitioner research. He wrote about the topology (the contours and different heights) of professional landscapes, where there is a high ground and a swampy lowlands. The high ground is occupied mainly by those whom Schön calls 'intellectual elites', such as university and organizational researchers, who produce 'pure' conceptual theory about disciplines such as nursing, education, management and other matters. This theory is regarded as legitimate both by themselves and by practitioners. Practitioners, such as nurses, teachers and shop-floor workers, occupy the swampy lowlands. They are involved in everyday practices and so create the kind of knowledge that is valuable for conducting everyday lives. However, it is held both by elites and by practitioners that practitioner knowledge should not be regarded as theory, nor should practitioners regard themselves as legitimate knowledge creators. In this metaphor, Schön returns us to the issues addressed earlier. The entire research community, including practitioner-researchers, have been persuaded to believe that there are 'real' theorists, desk-workers designated by higher institutional rank, who produce abstract conceptual theory, and there are shop-floor practitioners in workplaces, who create practical knowledge, which is useful knowledge but not 'real' theory. The irony for Schön is that the knowledge produced in the swampy lowlands is the kind of knowledge that is of most benefit for everyday living, while the knowledge produced on the high ground is often far removed from the practicalities of everyday living, and so often does not touch ordinary people in a meaningful and relevant way. Its remoteness is accentuated by the kind of language used. Professional elites tend to use their own language to talk to one another. This language can often be obscure and in code, and, in Schön's opinion (which is shared by other researchers such as Jenkins [1992] and Thomas [1998]), the elites deliberately keep it that way.

Schön maintained that practitioners in the swampy lowlands should create their own knowledge through investigating their practice, and submit their emergent personal theories to the same rigorous processes of testing and critique as happens in the creation of high-ground theory. This would be important if practitioners wanted to demonstrate the validity of their arguments, and have their ideas accepted as bone fide theory by the high-ground research community and the wider public.

Schön's ideas were definitely appropriate for former times, and still hold true for some quarters today, but things have changed considerably with the advent of action research. The topology is beginning to level out. Many people working in higher education and managerial positions now perceive themselves as practitioners in a workplace with the responsibility of supporting people in other workplaces, while also generating their living theories of practice about how they do this. Self-study action research as a recognized practice has legitimized their positioning as practitioners who are supporting other practitioners, and who are creating democratic communities of practice committed to a scholarship of educational enquiry (Whitehead, 1999). Here are some examples.

Mary Hartog (2004) tells how she regards herself as an academic in a higher education setting, whose work was to support the enquiries of others, while she was herself a part-time PhD candidate. What she learned from her doctoral studies informed her practice with practitioners and higher degree candidates, and what she learned from them informed her doctoral studies. She saw her professional identity not in terms of a formal role but in terms of how she understood her relationships with others.

You can access Mary's PhD abstract from http://www.actionresearch.net/living/hartog.shtml

Jane Spiro (2008) arrived at a notion of knowledge transformation, through understanding the story of herself as creative writer, creative educator, creative manager and educational researcher. In her thesis she tells stories of how she arrived at a living theory of creativity which she calls 'knowledge transformation'. She explores this theory through story as a methodology that connects both the creative writer and action researcher, and raises questions about self, reflective process and voice that are central to her enquiry. ... Jane's premise is that 'knowledge transformation' involves the capacity to respond to challenge, self and other, and is central to the notion of creativity. She considers how far this capacity can be transferable, teachable and measurable in educational contexts, arriving at a notion of 'scaffolded creativity' which is demonstrated through practice in the higher academy.

You can access Jane's PhD abstract from http://www.actionresearch.net/living/janespirophd.shtml)

The changing topology has highlighted the need for all to regard themselves as practitioners and to study their practice collaboratively, in a disciplined and scholarly way, and to make their accounts of practice public, so that others in their communities and elsewhere can learn and benefit.

The implications for recognition and accreditation are considerable. Those who are not seeking accreditation for work-based learning come to be regarded as competent professionals. Those who are seeking accreditation come to be seen as practitioner academics whose studies are supported by academic practitioners. Any previously existing hierarchies of power between academics and practitioners are demolished, and power is shared among equals for the benefit of others.

2 Why is practitioner knowledge important?

Practitioner knowledge is central to practical and theoretical evolution.

Practical evolution

Evolution refers to the idea that living systems have the internal capacity for independent and interdependent self-renewal. Reliance on any external agency means that a system may collapse if the agency is withdrawn, whereas internal capacity implies the independent and interdependent creation of renewable resources for growth.

Practitioners' personal theories constitute these renewable resources. All are free to stake their claim about what needs to be done to enable themselves and others to grow in ways that are right for them. This was the idea that first inspired action research. Lewin (1946), one of the originators of action research (page 41), believed that if all members of a workforce were involved collaboratively in implementing and testing strategy, the organization itself would grow. This view is developed elsewhere. Amartya Sen (1999), winner of the 1998 Nobel Prize in Economic Science, distinguishes between an economic theory of human capability and theories of human capital. He talks about the need to move from seeing capital accumulation in primarily physical terms to seeing it as a process in which human beings are integrally involved in the production of their own futures. Through education, learning and skills formation, people can become more productive over time, which contributes greatly to the process of economic expansion.

Theoretical evolution

Practitioners' theories of practice are also core to sustainable theoretical evolution, in the sense that practice-based educational research needs to show its own capacity for self-renewal. It can do this by developing new forms that increasingly demonstrate their capacity for internal transformation. Grand theory, that is, the idea of a body of knowledge that deals with eternal truths, is now complemented by local forms of theory that celebrate individual narratives. 'Movements' such as postmodernism explain how researchers need to regard themselves as influenced by, and influencing, the situation they are investigating. Some researchers such as Law (2004) explain that the stories people tell about research actually come to inform how they do research in the future. The reality of this story can be seen in the following examples.

Jean tells stories of how teachers in Qatar and Israel saw possibilities of how they could work together through sharing their research, and did so as real-life projects (see also McNiff 2011c). Her description of this process can be accessed at http://www.jeanmcniff.com/qatar.asp

Jack has demonstrated this capacity for internal transformation in the evolution of his epistemologies from propositional, to dialectical, to inclusional. His transformation from dialectics into inclusionality was inspired by Alan Rayner, who originated the idea of natural inclusionality. His description of this transformation can be accessed at http://www.actionresearch.net/writings/jack/arjwdialtoIncl061109.pdf

---

Action research has this self-transforming capacity. Practitioners can show how they have contributed to new practices, and how these new practices can transform into new theory. When researchers claim that they have generated new theory, they are saying that they have created knowledge that never existed before. Perhaps pieces of knowledge existed, but what practitioners do with that knowledge and how they have reconfigured it in relation to their own contexts can be seen as their original theorizing. This capacity for ongoing creativity contributes greatly to theoretical evolution.

3   What is special about practitioners' theories?

The basis for many practitioners' research is that they are trying to live in the direction of their educational values (see page 28). If they hold values of justice and compassion, they try to live in a way that is just and compassionate. They make practical judgements about the extent to which they can show that they are living in the direction of these values.

Jill Wickham, a physiotherapist and university lecturer in physiotherapy, has strong commitments to the capacity of practising physiotherapists to celebrate their practical work-based knowledge. She found that many trainee physiotherapists could not see the relationship between the practical knowledge they gained on placements in the workplace and the disciplines-based knowledge communicated at the university. This situation denied Jill's values of epistemological and social justice, and she works hard to encourage trainees to appreciate how the theory-practice gap has been perpetuated and can be demolished. By encouraging them to see their knowledge as integrated, and

---

to learn how to incorporate disciplines-based knowledge into their practical theorizing, Jill is contributing to new discourses both in placement contexts and in the University. Furthermore, she is influencing colleagues in the University to appreciate that different forms of knowledge can be integrated within professional education curricula, and she is actively influencing a reconceptualization of physiotherapy education for a curriculum for higher education within the university. You can read her work at Wickham 2009 and 2010 (see http://www.jeanmcniff.com/york-st-john-university.asp).

Like Jill, many practitioners work in contexts where their values of social and epistemological justice and compassion are denied in practice. Nor are external forces the only sources of this denial. Most of us often deny our own values by acting in a way that is contrary to what we believe in. Then we put our best efforts into trying to practise in a way that is consistent with our values, and we assess the quality of our work in those terms. We gather data and generate evidence that we believe show instances of ourselves at work with others in ways that can be understood as in keeping with our values, such as justice and compassion, and we invite critical feedback on our perceptions. If other people agree that we are acting in accordance with our values, we can claim that we now know better, and put forward our claims for public consideration.

This is a rigorous and stringent research process that can be seen as systematic enquiry and an uncompromising testing of the validity of claims to knowledge. The account that a practitioner produces contains descriptions of the research (what was done) and explanations (why it was done and what was aimed for). This account then constitutes the practitioner's own living theory of practice.

4   How can practitioners contribute to new practices and new theories?

Many people believe that 'theory' is something mysterious, which it is not. We often say things like, 'I have a theory about cats', or 'This is my theory about the way things work'. A theory is a set of ideas about what we claim to know and how we have come to know. If we can show that what we know (our theory) stands up to public scrutiny in relation to agreed criteria and standards of judgement, we can claim that our theory has validity (has truth value and is trustworthy).

By doing your research, you can claim to have generated your living theory of practice, that is, you can say with confidence that you know what you are doing and why you are doing it. You are showing that you are acting in a systematic way, not *ad hoc*, and that you are developing a praxis, which is morally committed practice.

Your living theory of practice may contain other theories, such as a theory of learning or a theory of management. Mary Hartog (2004, cited above), a tutor in higher education in the UK, created her own theory of learning – her own living theory of education – by showing how she supported teachers who were studying for their masters degrees in a way that enabled them to learn effectively. Pip Bruce Ferguson (1999), also a tutor in higher education in New Zealand, created her living theory of educational management by showing how she ensured equal opportunities for Maori and white practitioners. Moira Laidlaw (2002), a volunteer worker supporting teachers and administrators in China, has shown how she is creating a living theory of sustainable development by enabling teachers to engage in new practices that encourage people to take control of their individual and collective lives for social benefit. All these theories are valid theories, because the explanations have been demonstrated as having truth value through a rigorous process of stringent public critique. They are not just a matter of their authors' opinions. They are now established as social facts. Social situations have changed for the better because of these practitioners' committed interventions.

Jack suggested to the masters and doctoral researchers he is supervising to frame their writings in relation to a discussion on the significance of generating and sharing living theories started by Pip Bruce Ferguson in *Research Intelligence*, a newsletter of the British Educational Research Association. They could access the live URLs below, short two-page contributions that focus on the importance of bringing the embodied knowledge of practitioners into the public domain. The entries below appear in chronological order.

Bruce-Ferguson, P. (2008) 'Increasing inclusion in educational research: Reflections from New Zealand', *Research Intelligence*, 102: 24–25. Retrieved 11 January 2008 from http://www.actionresearch.net/writings/bera/24&25RI102.pdf

Whitehead, J. (2008) 'Increasing inclusion in educational research: a response to Pip Bruce Ferguson', *Research Intelligence*, 103: 16–17. Retrieved 11 January 2008 from http://www.actionresearch.net/writings/bera/16&17RI103.pdf

Adler-Collins, J.K. (2008) 'Creating new forms of living educational theories through collaborative educational research from eastern and western contexts: a response to Jack Whitehead', *Research Intelligence* 104: 17–18. Retrieved 11 January 2008 from http://www.actionresearch.net/writings/bera/16&18RI104.pdf

Laidlaw, M. (2008) 'Increasing inclusion in educational research: a response to Pip Bruce-Ferguson and Jack Whitehead', *Research Intelligence*, 104: 16–17. Retrieved 11 January 2008 from http://www.actionresearch.net/writings/jack/2829RI105.pdf

Whitehead, J. (2008) 'An epistemological transformation in what counts as educational knowledge: responses to Laidlaw and Adler-Collins', *Research Intelligence*, 105: 28–9. Retrieved 11 January 2008 from http://www.actionresearch.net/writings/jack/2829RI105.pdf

Huxtable, M. (2009) 'How do we contribute to an educational knowledge base? A response to Whitehead and a challenge to BERJ', *Research Intelligence*, 107: 25–6. Retrieved 11 January 2008 from http://www.actionresearch.net/writings/huxtable/mh2009beraRI107.pdf

Rayner, A. (2010) 'The inclusional nature of living educational theory: a receptive response to Whitehead', *Research Intelligence*, 109: 26–7. Retrieved 17 February 2010 from http://www.actionresearch.net/writings/jack/alanraynerRI10926-27opt.pdf.

These writings are also accessible from http://www.bera.ac.uk/blog/category/publications/ri/

Summary

This chapter has set out a debate about the politics of knowledge, in relation to who should be regarded as a practitioner or a member of an elite, and who decides; and whether such divisive language should be re-thought so that it reflects the evolving, non-partisan nature of human interactions. It has addressed the questions:

- Who is a practitioner?
- Why is practitioner knowledge important?
- What is special about practitioners' theories?
- How can practitioners contribute to new practices and new theories?

The point has been made that all should regard themselves as practitioners, regardless of role or setting, who are involved in learning and influencing the learning of others.

The next chapter develops some of these ideas as we consider the main features of action research and its underpinning assumptions.

Further reading

The issue of whether practitioners should be recognized as researchers remains at the heart of debates about the politics of knowledge and theory generation. The debate has spread to most fields, especially health care and nursing, teaching, and business and management studies.

Koch, T. and Kralik, D. (2006) *Participatory Research in Health Care.* Oxford: Blackwell.
A useful guide to practitioner research in health care.

Noffke, S. and Somekh, B. (2009) *The SAGE Handbook of Educational Action Research.* London: Sage.
The fields of practice are expanded in this other Handbook, written for practitioners. A great reference book and more accessible than Reason and Bradbury (2008) (Chapter 1, Further reading).

Schön, D. (1983) *The Reflective Practitioner: How Professionals Think in Action.* New York: Basic Books.
The classic text for raising issues about work-based professional learning, and the need to see practice as grounded in reflection, not just about doing things. A must for any dissertation or thesis.

Winter, R. and Munn-Giddings, C. (2001) *A Handbook for Action Research in Health and Social Care.* London: Routledge.
A highly recommended book, full of thoughtful advice, this book is a great addition to the field, setting out the principles and practices of action research within the field of health and social care. Lots of case study examples to show you how it can be done.

THREE

The Underpinning Assumptions of Action Research

In order to see how action research is different from other kinds of research, it is useful to look at its underpinning assumptions, and to see how these can transform into different kinds of practices. Doing this also reveals the main features of action research.

Action research is one form of research among many. You can use different forms of research to achieve different goals, in the same way as you can use different vehicles for different purposes. You use a tractor to plough a field and a fast car to get somewhere quickly. You use traditional research when you want to show an 'if … then …' relationship between variables, and you use action research when you want to find ways of taking action to improve learning with social intent.

All kinds of research, including action research, share common features, which distinguish them as research and not just activity. When you do any kind of research you should aim to do the following:

- Identify a research issue.
- Identify research aims.
- Draw up a research design (plan).
- Gather data.
- Establish criteria and standards of judgement.
- Generate evidence from the data.
- Make a claim to knowledge.
- Submit the claim to critique.
- Explain the significance of the work.
- Disseminate the findings.
- Link new knowledge with existing knowledge. (McNiff and Whitehead, 2010: 8–9)

Where research traditions differ is how they perceive the values-based positioning of the researcher (ontological commitments), the relationship between the knower and what is known (epistemological commitments), the processes of generating knowledge (methodological commitments) and the goals of research in terms of how the knowledge will be used (social and political commitments). It is not only action research that is different from other kinds of research. All research methodologies are different from one another according to these underpinning assumptions. However, self-study action research has made a gigantic leap from other research methodologies, in that the researcher is placed at the centre of the enquiry, and accepts the responsibility of showing how they account for themselves.

This chapter sets out these underpinning assumptions. It is in four sections.

1 Ontological assumptions
2 Epistemological assumptions
3 Methodological assumptions
4 Social purposes of action research

1 Ontological assumptions

Ontology is the study of being, and is strongly linked with values: for example, you can say, 'My ontological commitments are that I value the environment.' Our ontologies influence how we view ourselves in our relationships with others. The ontological commitments that underpin action research include the following.

- Action research is value laden.
- Action research is morally committed.
- Action researchers perceive themselves as in relation with one another in their social contexts.

Action research is value laden

To appreciate the value-laden nature of action research it can be helpful to consider other research methodologies. One particularly influential approach is positivism. This means that explanations can be offered about the way things work by establishing a cause and effect between variables: 'If I do this, that will happen.' Positivist forms of research are notionally value free. The researcher stays out of the research, so as not to 'contaminate' it, and reports are written in the third person ('the researcher did'), which is supposed to reduce bias in the claim to objectivity. You would use a positivist approach, using a traditional 'scientific method', if you wanted to test the effectiveness of a particular plant food. You would apply the plant food to an experimental group of tomato plans to see if they yielded bigger, better and more tomatoes in comparison with a control group. Some social science adopts this perspective, but not all.

Action research is done by people who are trying to live in the direction of the values that inspire their lives. For example, you may be passionate about justice, or about people being free to run their own lives. If you are a doctor, your commitment to justice may inspire you to see your patients as real people who can make decisions about their treatments. Your values come to act as your guiding principles. Action research often begins by articulating your values and asking whether you are being true to them. But be aware that you can have different kinds of values. An anti-social value such as cruelty is a value as much as kindness. It is up to you to decide which values you want to live by and be accountable for.

Action researchers often experience themselves as 'living contradictions' (Whitehead, 1989), in that they can hold a set of values, yet not live according to them. You may believe in justice but act in an unjust way. You set out to find ways of living in the direction of your values. This can be difficult, because investigating your practice involves other people who have values of their own, and these may not be commensurable with yours. It is then a case of negotiating meanings and practices, which is easy to say but difficult to do.

Abdullah is a nurse. He believes that patients have a right to get out of bed when they wish, provided they are well enough to do so, yet normative hospital practices are that patients get out of bed only at certain times. Abdullah's values of patient choice and care are denied by the hospital regimes. He finds that he is also denying his own values because he has to abide by the hospital rules. What does he do?

Action research is morally committed

Action researchers choose which values they subscribe to, and they explain how they hold themselves accountable for their choices. Doing your action enquiry involves explaining what inspires you to do things as you do, and what you hope to achieve. If you are aiming to improve some aspect of your practice, you are doing it for a reason, consistent with what you believe to be better practice, which involves explaining what you understand as 'good' and 'better', to avoid being seen as imposing your values on others. This can be tricky, because people hold different views of 'good'. We live and learn in different cultures, which have their own values system. You have to decide which values system to live by, within your own culture. You may sometimes try to influence the culture because you find that your values are in conflict with it.

Lina lives in an Arab country, and abides by Islamic traditions, so she wears traditional dress. She works in-country with a European company, and her women colleagues urge her to wear western dress in the office, on the basis that she represents the company. She, on the other hand, urges them to wear traditional Arab dress, or at least dress modestly, out of respect for the customs of her country. Who lives according to which values?

Whatever you decide, you will aim to make yours a purposeful, morally committed practice, that is, praxis.

Remember that you cannot hold yourself responsible for other people's decisions. They decide for themselves, just like you. It is your responsibility to hold yourself accountable for yourself, and how you try to influence other people's learning. This has big implications. Do you do it in a coercive way, insisting that people listen to you, or in a more educational way, respecting others' points of view but inviting them to consider other options?

Holding these views can get you into trouble within established contexts. For example, Mary Roche (2007), a primary teacher, encouraged her four- and five-year-old children to think critically and to ask questions about the status quo. When the children were instructed to form straight lines in the playground during a fire drill, one of them asked, 'What's so good about straight lines anyway?' Critical pedagogies that encourage such questions can often get researchers into trouble if they work in institutions that are run according to bureaucratic values.

Action researchers perceive themselves as in relation with one another in their social contexts

An increasingly important perspective in action research is the development of relational and empathetic values (Dadds, 2008). The idea of establishing empathetic relationships refers not only to the social world, where we see ourselves in relation with others, but also to the mental world, where we see how ideas are in relation with other ideas. The core idea of transformational capacity enables us to incorporate the insights of others and transform them as we create our living theories of practice.

Action researchers always see themselves in relation with others, in terms of their practices and also their ideas, and with the rest of their environment. They do not adopt a spectator approach, or conduct experiments on others. They undertake enquiries with others, recognizing that people are always in company. Even when we are alone, we are still in the company of others, who are perhaps absent in time and space, but their influence is evident. The pen or computer you are using was created by someone else for someone's use (yours) at some time. The ideas you express began as other people's ideas. What is special is that you have made the equipment and the ideas your own. You have mediated them through your own unique capacity for creativity, perhaps using your computer in special ways, or reconfiguring other people's ideas in your own original way. Your beginnings, however, were in other people. You have transformed those beginnings into new opportunities and practices.

The idea of never being alone is key. Although the focus of the enquiry is you, as you ask, 'How do I improve what I am doing?', your question automatically assumes that any answer will involve other people's perceptions of your influence in their learning. You are also in company with others who are asking the same question, and who also assume that their answers will involve other people's perceptions of their influence in learning. It is not a case of you as a free-standing 'I', in the company of other free-standing 'I's', because each one of you recognizes that you are in company, and that you form a community of 'I's', all of whom understand that their claims to educational influence will be evaluated by others within their range of influence.

Action researchers therefore aim to develop the kind of methodologies that nurture respectful relationships. This does not mean that everyone has to agree on how we should live in terms of social practices. Differences of opinion are understood as the basis for creative engagement. It does, however, mean that everyone recognizes the uniqueness of the other, even though the other may act and think in ways that are sometimes radically different from themselves, and this attitude informs their practices. Habermas (2002) speaks about 'the inclusion of the other', but this view is grounded in a hope, not a requirement, that the other will hold the same view. If all agree to live according to a shared ethic, difficulties can be reduced. The task for action researchers is especially demanding when the other does not agree to share the same ethic, which means that they have to find ways of living in the direction of their values within a context of being with others who do not share the same underpinning ethic of empathy and a willingness to develop understanding relationships.

Dan is a newly-appointed manager in a firm in the North of Wales. He is recently arrived from a Gulf State, where the working day is from 7am until 2pm, because the temperature rises dramatically during the day, so people do as much work as possible while it is still reasonably cool. He sees other benefits of an early start to the day for increased productivity, and suggests to his co-managers that they review the work schedule, but his suggestions are met with resistance. What should he do?

Summary: ontological assumptions at a glance

Given the emphasis on relational values:

- Action research is value laden and morally committed, which is a transformation of the assumption that research can be value free.
- It aims to understand what I/we are doing, and not only what 'they' are doing. This demonstrates a shared commitment towards 'we–I' forms of enquiry.
- It assumes that the researcher is in relation with everything else in the research field, and influences, and is influenced by, others. The research field cannot be studied in a value-free way, because the researcher brings their own values with them.

Now let us look at some epistemological assumptions.

2   Epistemological assumptions

Epistemology is to do with how we understand knowledge, and how we come to acquire and create knowledge. The epistemological assumptions underpinning action research include the following.

- The object of the enquiry is the 'I'.
- Knowledge is uncertain.
- Knowledge creation is a collaborative process.

The object of the enquiry is the 'I'

'The object of enquiry' (some people call it the 'unit of enquiry') refers to the focus of the research. In self-study action research, the focus of the research is you. You study yourself, not other people. The questions you ask are of the kind, 'What am I doing? How do I improve it?', not of the kind, 'What are they doing? How do they improve it?' You aim to show how you hold yourself accountable for what you do.

This idea of personal accountability has big implications. One is, as noted earlier, that you cannot accept responsibility for what others do and think, but you must accept full responsibility for what you do and think. This can be difficult, because it sometimes means being prepared to let go of favourite positions, which may even have become entrenched prejudices, and it also means interrogating things that we may take for granted. For example, say you are convinced of the rightness of your opinions. Then why do conversations stop when you say something? Are people so impressed with what you say that they are awe-struck, or could it be that they resist the imposition of your ideas?

Another implication is that you always need to recognize that you may be mistaken. Testing your ideas rigorously against the feedback of others is not a sufficient safeguard. Public approval does not necessarily mean that practices and their underpinning assumptions are socially beneficial, or that what people say is always believable. Take the case of Galileo. Galileo was shown instruments of torture as if they were to be used on him to make him recant what he knew to be true. The most stringent safeguard against the hubris of believing that one is right beyond a reasonable doubt is to take into account the opinions of all whose lives are involved. In your case, this refers to your research participants. In the case of governments, it refers to all citizens of the world.

Ariela is a foster parent. She constantly evaluates her practice to ensure that she is doing her job well and to provide feedback for her monthly report to her managers. She is convinced that she is right in insisting that the children she fosters should be at home in the evening at a certain time. A new foster child resists her wishes, and stays out longer than she has said. What should she do: impose her wishes, or reason with the child? What will she do if they cannot come to an agreement? How does she find a way to negotiate with the child?

Knowledge is uncertain

Traditional researchers tend to believe that knowledge is certain, and assume the following (Berlin, 1998).

- There is an answer to everything. Knowledge is certain and true, and is 'out there', waiting to be discovered.
- Knowledge can be discovered using specific methodologies such as the 'scientific method', which aims to predict and control outcomes.
- Answers to questions are fixed for all time. All possible answers are compatible and commensurable.

This perspective may be valuable when it is a case of genetic engineering or weather forecasting, but it does not necessarily work in relation to real human practices, because humans are unique and unpredictable, and make their own choices.

Action researchers, in contrast, tend to assume the following (Berlin, 1998).

- There is no one answer. Knowledge is uncertain and ambiguous. A question may generate multiple answers.
- Knowledge is created, not only discovered. This is usually a process of trial and error. Provisional answers, and the process itself, are always open to critique.
- Any answer is tentative, and open to modification. Answers are often incommensurable and cannot be resolved. People just have to live with the dissonance and do the best they can.

This means that action researchers do not look for a fixed outcome that can be applied everywhere. Instead they produce their personal theories to show what they are learning and invite others to learn with them. They judge their work not in terms of its generalizability or replicability, which are social science criteria, but in terms of whether they can show how they are living in the direction of their educational and social values, using those values as their living standards of judgement (see Chapter 14). It also means that it is legitimate for action researchers to have different aims. In some participatory action research, for example, researchers usually act to resolve a common problem, whereas other researchers may wish to find ways of living in situations where people disagree, often fundamentally, about how they should live.

Knowledge creation is a collaborative process

Although the 'I' is central, the 'I' should never be understood as in isolation. We all live and work in social situations. Whatever we do in our professional practices potentially influences someone somewhere. Action research means working with others at all stages of the process. At the data gathering stage you (singular or plural) are investigating your practice in relation with others; at the validation stage you negotiate your findings with others. It is definitely not a solitary activity. As well as this, the people you are working with are also possibly doing their action research into their practice, so the situation becomes one of collectives of individuals investigating their practices, a question of the 'I/we' investigating the

'I/we' in company with others who are also investigating their individual or collective practices.

Innovative practices have developed recently, where groups of action researchers have undertaken their joint enquiries. In this case the focus shifts from 'I' to 'we'. This is particularly helpful when the aim of the research is to improve whole organizational practices (Marshall, 1999, 2004). Underpinning such initiatives is the understanding that groups share certain collective values that they wish to realize.

The staff and children of the Nave Bamidbar School (Oasis in the Desert) in Hazerim Kibbutz near Beer Sheva have been engaged in their collective action research for several years. This initiative is led by Deputy Principal Galit Arzi, who did her Masters degree at the Ben Gurion University in 2005, using an action research methodology. She was so excited by the possibilities that she introduced action research to her school immediately, and the ideas were warmly embraced by Principal Ruthy Rubin. Together with another teacher, Tamar Golan, Galit conducted a collaborative survey in the school to identify what the staff and children saw as key challenges and areas for action. These emerged as improving relations in the family, taking care of the environment, taking better care of animals, road safety and, one of the most important topics, improving relationships with neighbouring Arabs (Bedouin) who live in the Negev. Currently, all the children (7–12 years old) undertake their action enquiries into one of these areas, as they choose, within a broad focus of how they can live in peace with their Arab neighbours. This is especially important, since Beer Sheva is near Gaza, so the school is involved in issues of international importance. Each teacher and child is fully committed to their chosen area of research. Some children are studying how they can overcome their fear of an uncertain life style (such as living with the constant fear of rocket attacks); others are finding better ways of cherishing their desert environment, under threat of erosion. A key issue for Galit and her colleagues as Israelis is to respect the traditions and perspectives of their Arab neighbours, and not impose Israeli traditions and values on them. Their main desire is to live in peace with one another while respecting their different viewpoints. Jean is now working with the school out of her own commitments to developing mutual understanding locally and internationally. Some of Galit's writings will soon be available at http://www.jeanmcniff.com/israel.asp

---

Summary: epistemological assumptions at a glance

Given the emphasis on relational values:

- In action research the object of enquiry is not other people, but the 'I' in relation with other 'I's'.
- Knowledge is uncertain. Answers are created through negotiation. Often answers cannot be negotiated, so people have to learn to live with the situation. Answers can be communicated through how we live as much as in what we say.
- Knowledge is a property of individuals, so it is often subjective and biased. Individuals have to negotiate their meanings with other knowing individuals.

3   Methodological assumptions

Methodologies refer to the way research is conducted. The main methodological assumptions of action research include the following.

- Action research is done by practitioners who regard themselves as agents.
- The methodology is open-ended and developmental.
- The aim of the research is to improve learning with social intent.

The idea of agency is that people are able to, and should, take an active part in decisions about how they and others should live. An agent, says Sen, is 'someone who acts and brings about change, and whose achievements can be judged in terms of her [sic] own values and objectives, whether or not we assess these in terms of some external criteria as well' (1999: 19). In his book *The Irish Diaspora in Britain, 1750–1939,* Don MacRaild (2010) makes the point that many Irish emigrants to Britain did not see themselves as lacking agency, as if often implied, but set about creating new lives for themselves, in spite of frequent hostility from British nationals.

The main responsibility of agents is to ask questions, and not accept complacency or self-righteous justification, their own or anyone else's. In this sense, they act as public intellectuals (Said, 1994) whose job is to interrupt and question the status quo. Why are things as they are? Are they satisfactory? If not, how can they be changed? For action researchers this means that they need always to ask questions and not accept final answers.

Traditional forms of research assume that the researcher is a neutral, value-free operative who observes, collects data and generates evidence to support their findings, but should not influence or be influenced by the research itself. Action researchers accept full responsibility for exercising influence. This involves taking action and considering what influence they may be having in their own and other people's learning. Therefore, when you ask, 'How do I improve what I am doing?' you raise questions about two related processes. The first process refers to what is going on 'out there', in the social situation you are investigating. The second process is about what is going on 'in here', in relation to your own learning. You ask critical questions about why things are as they are. Why do you think as you do? Do you think for yourself, or what someone else tells you? Who writes your script? Further, how can you show that your own capacity for critique influences other people's capacity also to critique?

Jo works with paedophiles in a prison. Her job is to counsel the offenders so that they can be rehabilitated into society on their release. When she first started doing this work she found a resistance in herself to the offender. She had to work with her own prejudices to understand why they did the things they did; not to be judgemental; and to focus on finding ways of enabling them to live successfully in society. One of the most difficult aspects for her to learn was to accept that there is no 'cure' for paedophilia. The most she

---

could do was work with the offender to try to persuade them not to offend again. Every time a paedophile goes back into mainstream society, Jo feels high levels of anxiety, knowing that there are no answers to the dilemma, and it is a matter of faith in the human capacity for self-governance.

The methodology is open-ended and developmental

Unlike traditional social science, action enquiries do not aim for closure, nor do practitioners expect to find certain answers. The process itself is the methodology (Mellor, 1998), and is frequently untidy, haphazard and experimental. Richard Winter (1998) talks about 'improvisatory self-realisation in action research', where a certain degree of entrepreneurialism is involved; and Marian Dadds and Susan Hart (2001) talk about 'methodological inventiveness', where we try multiple innovative ways until we find the one that is right for us. We look out for what might be a useful way forward, and try it out. One step leads to another, and one cycle of action–reflection leads to another. Answers are held as provisional because any answer already has new questions within itself. This emphasizes the value of being open to new possibilities, and understanding learning as never complete. Traditional ways of doing research offer a completed story. Action researchers let their own story evolve. It is as much about the storyteller as about the story.

> In a story of the growth of his educational knowledge Whitehead explains how his educational enquiry moved through four social science methodologies of the analytic scientist, the conceptual theorist, the conceptual humanist and the particular humanist (Mitroff and Kilman 1978) before he evolved an educational research methodology for his educational enquiry, 'How do I improve what I am doing?' (Whitehead 1985).

As well as being exciting, this way of working is also risky. Action researchers constantly stand on the edge. The next moment is unknown. They commit to the risk of creating a new future. This is a different mental set from traditional assumptions that knowledge is given. Action researchers anticipate new problematics. Concrete answers do not pre-exist but are created by real people, in negotiation with others. This can be destabilizing for people who are used to being told what to do. Instead of beginning with a hypothesis, which they aim to accept or reject, action researchers start with an idea and follow it where it leads them.

The aim of the research is to improve learning with social intent

Traditional research tends to try to show a cause and effect relationship. It works on the assumption that if people do this, that will happen. It also insists that things should be 'either this, or that', even though the situations that people are in may be full of contradictions and irresolvable dilemmas. This view can be seen in many workplace and education programmes that work on the principle of cause and effect, which can make thing difficult for people. Sometimes managers or principals are expected to ensure that specific inputs are arranged to produce certain outputs, which often appear as targets. Many curricula are organized to generate learning outcomes consistent with official policy. Learners are expected to internalize messages. They are expected not to think for themselves but to do as they are told.

Conversely, if all people have agency, they can, and should, think for themselves and make decisions. Managers and educators need to provide appropriate conditions for this. They should not be overly concerned with behavioural outcomes, unless of course the behaviours in question prevent others from thinking for themselves. Their task is to enable people to work with their new knowledge in ways that are right for them, and help them to create their own new futures.

This idea, however, carries conditions. If people wish to create their own futures, they have to accept responsibility for the present. This means generating their living theories of practice to show whether the practice is consistent with their values. They generate theories to explain how they are improving their own and other people's learning with social intent, and they subject these theories to stringent critique, before putting them into the public domain for further testing and wider consideration about how new practices can be developed.

Summary: methodological assumptions at a glance

Given the emphasis on relational values:

- Action researchers do not do research on others, but do it on themselves, in company with others. Action research is participatory and collaborative in the sense that it takes place in social contexts and involves other people.
- Action research begins with the experience of a concern and follows through a developmental process which shows cycles of action and reflection. It aims to demonstrate relationships of influence.
- Action researchers aim to investigate their practice with a view to improving it. They aim for new beginnings. The idea of closure is transformed into the idea of one state metamorphosing into another. Change is understood as people improving learning to improve practices.

4   Social purposes of action research

Social purpose refers to why we do research in relation to informing and improving its social contexts. The main social purposes of action research include the following.

- It aims to improve workplace practices through improving learning.
- It aims to promote the ongoing democratic evaluation of learning and practices.
- It aims to create good social orders by influencing the education of social formations.

It aims to improve workplace practices through improving learning

Action research is increasingly workplace-based (Williams and Dick, 2004; Garnett et al., 2009), not exclusively higher education-based, as traditional research tends to be. It is generally for practitioner-researchers who may or may not be supported by higher education personnel or by people in the workplace acting as university tutors and professional mentors. Some workplaces now award their own forms of accreditation.

The aim is consistently to improve practice through improving learning. Improved practices do not just happen; they happen if people think about what they need to do differently in relation to others. They then produce their explanatory accounts that show the processes involved, and make these public. These accounts constitute practitioners' theories of practice, which have arisen from within the practice. By relating their personal accounts and living theories with those of others, practitioners produce a respectable body of theory that clarifies what is involved in understanding work as a living practice. Their living theories are different from the conceptual theories of spectator researchers. This is why it is important for you to put your story of practice into the public domain, because you can show how you are contributing to new discourses about how practice should be seen as a living form of theory.

It aims to promote the ongoing democratic evaluation of learning and practices

Action research is such a common-sense approach to personal and professional development that, when people first meet the idea, they often say, 'That's what I do in any case. What's different?'

What is different is that action research insists on justifying claims to knowledge by the production of authenticated evidence, and then making the claims public in order to subject them to critical evaluation in order to test their validity.

However, evaluation itself is a problematic concept, because different people have different views about what it entails. Most would agree that evaluation aims to establish the value of something; yet what is valuable for one person is not necessarily valuable for another. Consequently different views exist about who should do evaluation and why, and what they are supposed to be evaluating.

Traditional perspectives regard evaluation as evaluating a thing or a product from an outsider's perspective: an outsider evaluator makes judgements on an insider's practice. Doing action research, however, is the responsibility of individuals, an ongoing process of developing learning and action, and reflection on the learning and action. The process is generative and transformational, because the end of one thing becomes the beginning of something else. All organic systems have their own internal generative capacity to transform into ever more fully developed versions of themselves (McNiff, 2000; McNiff et al., 1992). It is not a case of working towards a notional perfect end state, because a living system always has the potential to transform into even more fully realized states. Action research is this kind of generative transformational process, where claims to improved learning and practice generate further learning to improve practice.

The question therefore arises, who evaluates what? In traditional outsider/spectator approaches, an external researcher makes judgements on what other people are doing. From a self-study perspective, the researcher evaluates their own work. If action research is a process in which the 'I' studies the 'I' in company with other 'I's', then evaluation can be seen as the 'I' making judgements about what the 'I' is doing in relation to others. This calls for considerable honesty, and the capacity to listen to and act on critical feedback. It also calls for the articulation of standards of judgement that, consistent with the idea of Sen (1999), draw on the practitioner's own values and objectives.

It aims to create good social orders by influencing the education of social formations

In action research, the situation changes from an external person studying 'them', to an individual studying 'me', or a collective of individuals studying 'us'. Each person asks, 'How do I improve what I am doing for my own and others' benefit?' Each person is seen as an agent with the capacity for influencing their own and others' practices, with the potential to influence wider social change.

In Part VII we discuss fully the idea of the education of social formations and how this can be a contributing factor in the creation of good social orders, to do with how social groupings learn to work together. This tends to be more difficult than it sounds, because working together means working in a way that regards all as legitimate participants whose different traditions and ways of thinking need to be valued. This may be straightforward in contexts where all share more or less the same values and come from more or less the same tradition, but can be problematic in contexts in which parties hold different values perspectives and come from radically different traditions. Further, in politically contested contexts, where one party is dominant, that party may mobilize their resources to continue subjugating the other. The subjugated party then comes to be seen, and sometimes to believe, that they are not worthy of being regarded as a legitimate participant, but remain as peripheral and subservient. In many cases, the oppression leads to such frustration that feelings spill over into violence. How, then, do social groupings learn to see the other as a valuable participant whose opinion and voice may be different, but who needs to be listened to if the dialogue is to go forward? How do the Democratic Unionist Party and Sinn Féin learn to understand the other's point of view? How do Palestinians and Israelis learn to listen, so that they can talk as equals?

July sees the height of the marching season in Northern Ireland. Parades are held, mostly by Protestants, who sometimes choose to exercise their right to march through Catholic communities. Some see this as symptomatic of the historic dominance of British rule, largely Protestant, that aimed to stamp out the Irishness of people in Ireland, mostly Catholic.

---

12 July marks the official anniversary of the victory of William of Orange (Protestant) over King James (Catholic) at the Battle of the Boyne in 1690. It is the day when some Orangemen still parade through what have often been designated no-go areas, such as along the largely Catholic Garvaghy Road leading to Drumcree Church, though these days things are much more peaceful than before and less confrontational. At the time of writing this book (July 2010), reports tell of new outbursts of violence as 12 July sparks off old hatreds. Europe has largely overcome the legacies of its wars of the last 100 years yet some factions in Northern Ireland continue to celebrate a war that is over 400 years old.

In action research, people begin by holding themselves accountable. They do not make judgements on others without first making judgements on themselves, and they do not expect others to do anything they are not prepared first to do themselves. The education of social formations begins with each participant learning to recognize themselves as other to the other (McNiff, 2005), and subject to the same conditions of entry to a community that they wish others to agree to.

Summary: social purposes of action research assumptions at a glance

Given the emphasis on relational values:

- Action research can be workplace based, which raises questions about who is seen as a worker, and what is seen as a workplace. It can also take place within non-work based relationships in the family and community.
- Practitioners evaluate their own work in relation to their values. They do not need 'external' evaluation, but they understand the need for stringent testing and evaluation at all stages of the research, which involves the critical insights and judgements of others.
- Practitioners constitute their own social orders, and need to learn how to change their thinking in order to improve their practices. The capacity of individuals to think for themselves and to hold themselves accountable for their educational influence can act as the grounds for the creation of good societies.

―――――――― Summary ――――――――

This chapter has set out some of the main features of action research and its underpinning assumptions. The assumptions are ontological, epistemological, methodological and to do with social purpose.

The main ontological assumptions are that action researchers see themselves as trying to live in a way consistent with their values. These are to do with seeing

(Continued)

(Continued)

oneself as in relation with others, and how empathetic relational practices can strengthen those relationships.

The main epistemological assumptions are that knowledge is always in process, so it is impossible to create final answers. Processes of knowledge creation involve social processes; while knowing may be a property of the individual knower, all answers should be regarded as provisional and subject to social critique.

The main methodological assumptions are that action research is done by practitioners who perceive themselves as agents, regardless of their social and institutional contexts. Their methodologies are open-ended and developmental as they ask how they can learn to improve social practices.

The main assumptions underpinning the social purposes of action research are that learning can be improved in relation to all social practices, and that the way societies operate can be improved if their members reflect on what they are doing and explain how they hold themselves accountable for their thinking and actions.

We now turn to an outline of the historical development of action research, which provides a context for what action research is about. Part VII sets out what its achievements are and where it may be going.

Further reading

Carr, W. and Kemmis, S. (1988) *Becoming Critical*. Lewis: Falmer.
An evergreen, this book explains the foundations of action research. Dealing with the history of the political philosophy of action research, it provides a sound theoretical base for developing arguments about its validity and legitimacy.

Polanyi, M. (1958) *Personal Knowledge*. London: Routledge and Kegan Paul.
A life-changing book that should be compulsory reading on all courses. Polanyi explains, in his own poetic style, how personal knowledge should be regarded as the grounds for rational forms. A classic for all.

Scott, D. and Usher, R. (1996) *Understanding Educational Research*. London: Routledge.
One of the best books to provide a critical discussion on the underpinning epistemological and methodological assumptions, this book is not easy reading but you will be rewarded if you stick with it. Read Chapter 1 'A critique of the neglected epistemological assumptions of educational research' for a stringent critique of different methodological approaches.

Winter, R. (1989) *Learning from Experience*. London: Falmer.
Another evergreen that aids understanding of the methodological and philosophical foundations of action research. Winter brings his usual thoughtful approach to explaining how quality in action research may be assessed, especially in identifying six criteria for successful action research.

FOUR

Where Did Action Research
Come from and Where Is it Now?

This chapter traces the emergence of action research from its beginnings in the 1930s and 1940s to its current position of world importance. It discusses the historical journey of action research through social science and educational research, and places it within the emergence of different paradigms. It also discusses the positioning of action research within the increasingly popular approach of mixed methods. The chapter is organized into three sections, which discuss these questions.

1 Where did action research come from?
2 Where is action research located in different research paradigms?
3 How can action research be integrated within a mixed methods design?

This chapter has implications for the question, 'Where is action research going?', which is dealt with fully in Part VII.

1 Where did action research come from?

Action research has been around for some 80 years. It has always been linked with social change for social justice. Noffke (1997) says that the term 'action research' appeared in a 1961 speech by Martin Luther King. An emphasis on learning by Whitehead (1976) shows how people can learn to act in ways that improve learning while connected to democratic processes of evaluation.

It is generally understood that action research began with the work of John Collier in the 1930s, acting as commissioner for Indian affairs, and Kurt Lewin in the 1940s. Lewin, a Jewish refugee from Nazi Germany who worked as a social psychologist in the USA, believed that people would be more motivated about their work if they were involved in decision making about how the workplace was run. He researched what happened when people did become involved (Lewin, 1946).

Lewin's original ideas have remained influential, and, following his ideas, many researchers organize their work and reports as a cycle of steps: observe – reflect – act – evaluate – modify. This cycle can turn into another cycle. Figure 4.1 shows this process.

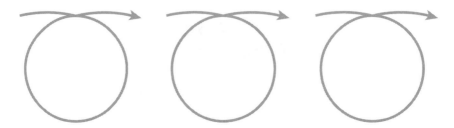

Figure 4.1 A cycle of action–reflection cycles

In the 1950s action research was taken up in education, specifically by the teaching profession, and Stephen Corey's (1953) book *Action Research to Improve School Practices* became influential in the USA. This could also be seen in the context of the free schools and progressive education movements of the 1960s (Miller, 2002), in which the emphasis was on education for the promotion of democratic practices that would enable all people to take a full and active part in political life. Education came to be seen as concerning the production of thoughtful and responsible citizens.

Action research went into decline in the USA during the late 1950s because of the focus on the need for technical excellence after the launch of Sputnik and the emergence of new research and development models. It did, however, begin to take hold in the UK, mainly through the influence of Lawrence Stenhouse, who was working in contexts of teacher education. Departing from the previously dominant disciplines approach to education, in which teachers studied the psychology, sociology, history and philosophy of education, Stenhouse advocated a view of teachers as highly competent professionals who should be in charge of their own practice. He maintained that professional education involved:

> The commitment to systematic questioning of one's own teaching as a basis for development;
>
> The commitment and the skills to study one's own teaching;
>
> The concern to question and to test theory in practice by the use of those skills. (Stenhouse, 1975: 144)

Stenhouse believed that teachers in classrooms should be supported by higher education personnel: 'fruitful development in the field of curriculum and teaching depends upon evolving styles of co-operative research by teachers and using full-time researchers to support the teachers' work' (1975: 162). Full-time researchers should therefore continue to have primary responsibility for reporting the research. This situation was ironic, because the same power relationships that action research sought to combat thus became evident within contexts of the professional education of teachers.

The work of Stenhouse was developed by a group of action researchers who were situated in and around the Centre for Applied Research in Education, some of whom later went their separate ways and developed ideas in other contexts. Stephen Kemmis, for example, became active in Australia, and has had worldwide influence by developing ideas with a critical and participatory focus.

This theme of teachers being in charge of their own practice was developed specifically by two prominent researchers, but from different perspectives. John Elliott, a colleague of Stenhouse's at the University of East Anglia, developed an interpretive approach, and Jack Whitehead, at the University of Bath, developed a self-study perspective. These different perspectives had implications for how professional education should be understood and conducted, and also for how action research itself could be seen as fulfilling its own values of social justice. In general terms, action research became known as a form of practical research that legitimated teachers' attempts to understand their work from their own point of view. Instead of learning about the disciplines and applying theory to themselves, teachers were encouraged to explore what they were doing and propose ways of improving it. This would mean they could generate new theory while incorporating the theories they were learning from the disciplines into their own processes of theorizing. In this way, the practical wisdom of teachers was awarded greater status, as well as their professional standing. Action research is now widely accepted as a form of professional learning across the professions, with potential for contributing to new forms of theory generation.

Creating your own living educational theories

The issue remains, however, about who is competent to research practice and make judgements about it. It would seem that, if action research is about social justice, action research itself should promote just practices, that is, do away with hierarchies of power in relation to who knows, and recognize that practitioners themselves should be acknowledged as the creators of their own knowledge. We authors, Jack and Jean, have relentlessly pursued this idea in company with thousands of other practitioner-researchers. We have said consistently that all practitioners, including teachers, should both study their own practice and regard their practice as the grounds for the generation of their own personal theories of practice (Whitehead, 2003; McNiff and Whitehead, 2005). They then make their theories available for public critique and testing. Action research should be seen as not simply about problem solving, but also about learning and creating knowledge. The kind of knowledge created can contribute to personal and social well-being.

This is a powerful stance. A living theory perspective places the individual practitioner at the heart of their own educational enquiry. Individuals undertake their research with a view to generating their personal living educational theory, which would be an account containing the descriptions and explanations of practice that individuals offer as they address the question, 'How do I improve my practice?' (Whitehead, 1989). It is the responsibility of the individual researcher to explain how they hold themselves accountable for their potential influence in the learning of others.

Jack and Jean both began working separately in action research in the 1970s, and then together in the 1980s, sharing and developing ideas. Each of us has made special contributions to the literature in the form of our individual original ideas. Jack has contributed the ideas of trying to live one's values in one's practice, and, drawing on the work of Ilyenkov (1977) among others, of experiencing oneself as a living contradiction when one's values are denied in one's practice. These ideas have had far-reaching influence and have been adapted by many people (for example, Loughran et al., 2004). Jean's major original contribution, drawing on the work of Goethe (Bortoft, 1996), Chomsky (1965) and Bergson (1998), has been the idea of the generative transformational nature of evolutionary processes, within an ecological framework. In this view, all living systems are in constant transformation, connected with one another, and each new transformation holds within itself its next potential transformation.

These combined ideas have had significant implications for the extended development of relational practices, which are part of the foundation of social justice. Although the individual researcher is placed at the heart of their own enquiries, the researcher is seen as in company with others in the research and in the wider community. People are always in relation with other people and with the rest of their environment. The quality of the relationship is important for ecological improvement, because this depends on the freedom of the individual to make decisions about their own lives. Freedom, however, comes with responsibility. The individual action researcher has to accept that they have a responsibility to others, and, in their educational relationships as professional educators, to place the interests of the other above their own. Action research therefore may be undertaken by individuals, singly or collectively, but it is always a participative and collaborative exercise, not individualistic. The methodologies of living enquiry are both rigorous and scientific, and always grounded in care and consideration for the other, while still maintaining the integrity and unique capacity of the individual to know and make judgements about the validity of claims to knowledge.

These ideas have had significant influence in a range of international contexts. Jack has worked extensively in China, Japan and elsewhere, including the USA, where a recent contribution took the form of a keynote presentation to the Seventh Annual Action Research Conference at the University of San Diego School of Leadership and Educational Science. This was on the theme 'Empowerment and action research: Personal growth, professional development, and social change in educational and community settings' (see http://www.actionresearch.net/writings/jack/hwsandiego10.pdf). He has also worked with the Durban Institute of Education in South Africa. Jean is also active in South Africa. She has worked with a number of universities, including the Nelson Mandela Metropolitan University (NMMU), and the University of Pretoria, as well as

---

with teachers in Khayelitsha (McNiff, 2011b). The development of the Action Research Unit at NMMU, which Jean and Ana Naidoo (former dean of education) established, is now thriving under the leadership of Professor Lesley Wood (Wood, 2010): a brilliant example of the generative transformational power of people who share the same values and the commitment to realize them. Jean and Jack regularly present workshops for teachers and university faculties (see http://www.jeanmcniff.com/items.asp?id=93). See also http://www.jeanmcniff.com/ for Jean's presentation at the NMMU conference 'Action Research: Exploring its Transformative Potential' (August 2010).

Practitioners in all these contexts have taken the ideas of experiencing oneself as a living contradiction as the basis for their action enquiries. You can access many of these narratives in the *Educational Journal of Living Theories* at http://www.ejolts.net – see for example page 22 of Jacqueline Delong's (2010) contribution on 'Engaging educators in representing their knowledge in complex ecologies and cultures of inquiry' (pp. 1–38): available at http://ejolts.net/node/174.

---

2   Where is action research located in different research paradigms?

If you are studying for higher degree accreditation, you need to know where action research is located within different methodological and epistemological developments.

Most research methods texts draw on different theories of scientific and social progress to explain the emergence of new paradigms. A paradigm is a set of ideas or theories appropriate to a specific context. These different theories see progress in different ways. The work of Kuhn and Lakatos, for example, is often cited when discussing models of progress. Kuhn (1970) maintained that paradigm change was often a case of replacement, whereas Lakatos (1970) saw progress as the incorporation of old ideas into new ones (see Losee, 2004, for a useful overview). You should make up your own mind about how processes happen, but try to avoid assuming a cut and dried sequential process, because paradigm shifts often involve a good deal of overlap, repetition and back-tracking. Also one paradigm may borrow from another, and sometimes it is difficult to see where one paradigm begins and the other leaves off.

Many research methods texts (see, for example, Hitchcock and Hughes, 1995; Usher, 1996) explain that understanding educational research means understanding that it involves different paradigms. A common approach is to identify the following.

- technical rational (often called empirical) research;
- interpretive research;
- critical theoretic research.

Each of these paradigms, or approaches, has different views about the nature of knowledge, how it is acquired and how it is used. (Each also has sub-categories, which we will not go into here.)

Technical rational (empirical) research

This form of research assumes that:

- The researcher stays outside the research field to maintain objectivity. Knowledge generated is uncontaminated by human contact.
- There is a cause and effect relationship throughout: 'If I do this, that will happen', more generally, 'if x, then y'.
- Results are generated usually through statistical analysis, and remain true for all time.
- The results can be applied and generalized to other people's practices, and will be replicable in similar situations.

Technical rational research is used throughout scientific enquiry, and has led to major developments in technology, medical care and space travel. However, many rational researchers assume that the methodologies of the natural sciences can be applied to human practices, so they tend to view humans as machines, or as data. Stringent critiques say that rational research is a myth (Thomas, 1998), and objectivity is unattainable. Some ask what is so special about objectivity anyway.

Interpretive research

This form of research assumes that:

- Researchers observe people in their natural settings, and offer descriptions and explanations for what the people are doing.
- Analysis of data tends to be qualitative, in terms of meanings of behaviours.
- The people in the situations offer and negotiate their own understandings of their practices with the interpretations of external researchers, but it is still the external researcher's story that goes into the public domain.

Interpretive research is used widely in the social sciences and educational research, often taking the form of case study (Yin, 2009). The aim is to understand what is happening in social situations and negotiate meanings.

Critical theoretic research

This form of research assumes that:

- It is important to understand a situation in order to change it.
- Social situations are created by people, so can be deconstructed and reconstructed by people.
- Taken-for-granted situations need to be seen in terms of what has brought them into existence, especially in terms of relationships of power.

Critical theory emerged as a critique of existing forms of research, on the basis that research is never neutral, but is used by a researcher for a specific purpose, which is often linked with the desire to predict and control. It is important, in this tradition, to understand the human interests involved both in social situations (page 253) and in the means used to find out about them.

Box 4.1

Important Note! Form of Theory

The chapter so far has set out what different approaches say. It is important also to note how they say it, that is, the form of logic used, and to consider the form of theory generated.

The stance of researchers working in these traditions remains external. They speak about research and ideas as things 'out there'. What is known is assumed to be separate from a knower. Reality, and ideas about reality, are turned into free-standing things, which can be studied, taken apart, and put back together in new ways. Many researchers working in these traditions do not seem to appreciate that they are part of the same reality they are studying.

This tendency has been exported also into many forms of action research. People talk about action research, but do not always see themselves as living participants, doing action research.

Some implications are developed in the next section.

Action research

Action research developed out of critical theory, and went beyond it. Critical theory asked, 'How can this situation be understood in order to change it?' but aimed only for understanding, not for action. Action research went into action and asked,' How can it be changed?' Some researchers, however, still like to locate action research within a broad framework of critical theory, emphasizing its participatory nature to combat relations of power.

What distinguishes a living theory form of action research is that it is grounded in the ontological 'I' of the researcher, and uses a living logic, that is, researchers organize their thinking in terms of what they are experiencing at the moment. While many research approaches still tend to adopt an externalist stance, using a form of thinking that sees things as separate from one another, action researchers working with a living theory approach use a form of thinking that sees things as in relation with one another. The researcher's goal is to explain how they hold themselves accountable for their learning and their influence in the learning of others.

This has important implications for how action research is conducted in the world, and also how it is theorized. Currently a lot of work goes on that is called action research, but is actually social science research, when an official researcher observes, describes and explains what other people do. Adopting this stance does not do much to move people to develop empathetic or relational practices. Instead, it reinforces a view of aristocrats and servants, and asymmetrical relationships of power.

Power sharing happens when all parties perceive the other as powerful, potentially able to speak for themselves and exercise their own agency, and agree to talk with one another on those terms. It happens because people see themselves as in relation with one another, as participants who are creating their life world. They may even sometimes feel that they are in a combative relationship with the other, but at least the recognition of a relationship is a start, which can be developed. The worst position is when one party perceives the other party as a non-person, which is no basis at all for the development of life-affirming human practices.

Recently Jean became connected with the National Zoological Gardens in Pretoria. There she met Elizabeth du Plessis, an amazing young woman whose work involves caring for spiders. Initially, Elizabeth was not so keen on the idea, but began to appreciate that spiders are much-maligned animals, and have feelings of their own. Spiders understand what is going on in their own way. Elizabeth has researched spiders extensively, and has turned the spider house into a world-class research centre. In a recent conversation, she explained to Jean how she had moved from a position of seeing spiders as objects to seeing them as animals with emotions, who made their own decisions about how they wished to behave. Elizabeth communicates these ideas to the general public, as part of her mission to help people appreciate spiders as beautiful creatures, who contribute much to the evolution of the planet. She helped Jean understand and engage with her own reactions to spiders, with the result that Jean has changed her perceptions and behaviours. You can see a video of Jean's encounter with spiders at http://www.youtube.com/watch?v=smiKLAwWd-Y

---

3   How can action research be integrated within a mixed methods design?

Mixed methods research is an increasingly popular approach, and researchers often speak about how action research may be integrated with other methods. This instantly raises problematics because action research is not so much a method, as the mixed methods literatures suggest, but a methodology. So, we ask, what is the difference between a method and a methodology?

- A **methodology** is the overall approach to a research programme, including research topic, research question, conceptual frameworks, intents and purposes, values-orientation, data collection, interpretation and analysis, validation procedures, and so on.

- A **method** is a specific technique, such as using a questionnaire to gather data, interpreting video data through the use of content analysis, or validating a claim to knowledge through the critical feedback of a validation group.

However, and returning to the debates about what counts as research, many writers see action research only as a method among other methods – hence the suggestion that it may be part of a mixed methods approach. So, if this were the case, which we do not think is an accurate perception, action research may be seen as one method among many, and the methods may be easily linked. Yin, for example, speaks about the possible nested relationships between a main strategy and a case study. He says: 'For instance, a study could employ a survey to describe certain conditions, complemented by an experiment that tried to manipulate some of those conditions (e.g., Berends and Garet, 2002)' (2009: 63). He then presents a diagrammatic view of how methods may be related:

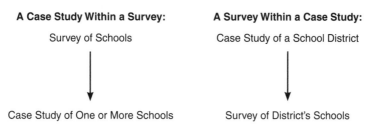

A Case Study Within a Survey:

Survey of Schools

Case Study of One or More Schools

A Survey Within a Case Study:

Case Study of a School District

Survey of District's Schools

Figure 4.2   Mixed methods: two nested arrangements

Source: Yin, R. (2009) *Case Study Research: Design and Methods* (4th edn). Thousand Oaks, CA: Sage. Reproduced with permission.

We authors take the view that action research, as a methodology, takes a different stance from other research methodologies, in that, as noted earlier in this chapter, the form of theory arising from the research is different. Action research generates living theories ('Here is my explanation for what I am doing') while social science research generates propositional theories ('Here is an explanation for what other people are doing').

However, we fully endorse the idea that propositional theories can, and should, be incorporated into individuals' living theories, and that the processes of individuals' action research can and should incorporate a range of methods from other approaches. For example, practitioners' living theories can include both quantitative and qualitative analyses of data, as found for example in James Finnegan's (2000) PhD thesis 'How do I create my own educational theory in my educative relations as an action researcher and as a teacher?', available at http://www.actionresearch.net/living/fin.shtml. Similarly, they draw on theories in the literatures. Accounts such as Jane Spiro's (2008) PhD thesis 'How I have arrived at a notion of knowledge transformation, through understanding myself as a creative writer, creative educator, creative manager, and educational researcher' contains a chapter on her creative engagement with ideas from, for example, Senge (1990) and Senge et al. (2000) (see http://www.actionresearch.net/living/janespirophd.shtml; while Mary Hartog (2004) engages critically with Belenkey et al.'s (1986) ideas about 'women's ways of knowing' (see http://www.actionresearch.net/living/hartog.shtml). We explore ideas about engaging with the literatures further in Chapter 10.

So, where is action research now?

In response to the question in the chapter heading 'Where did action research come from and where is it now?', a brief answer would be that action research is about to ride the crest of a wave: not quite there yet but about to reach its zenith. Action research is fully acknowledged as a coherent research methodology, with its own criteria and standards of judgement, as well as a powerful means of personal and professional education. What holds it back is the perhaps inevitable squabbles within the broad family of action researchers, some of who are precious about positions and wish to keep people out. These debates, however, say less about research methodologies and more about the personalities of the people involved.

As always, it is your personal decision where you position yourself. The only requirement is that you inform yourself of what is going on in the field so that you can make rational decisions out of accurate knowledge.

──────────── **Summary** ────────────

This chapter has given a brief summary of where action research has come from. We have traced its development from its beginnings in social science in the 1930s and 1940s, through its use in the work of Lawrence Stenhouse and his idea of 'teacher as researcher', and on to its most up-to-date position in the work of Jack Whitehead and Jean McNiff, in our idea of 'practitioner as theorist'. We have set out its location within different research paradigms, while emphasizing that living theory approaches have made a leap into new forms of thinking about research and its underpinning logics and values.

As well as considering where it has come from, it is also important to ask, 'Where is it going?' Where it is going can be seen in the reality of multiple interconnected branching networks of communication, all of which recount stories of action researchers using their best efforts to ask, 'How do I improve my learning?' 'How do I improve my work?', and holding themselves accountable to themselves and one another for what they are doing. Action research has gone into many new places, including war zones and zoos, and is being communicated using innovative forms of representation through the use of new technologies. These themes are developed in Part VII.

Further reading

Carr, W. and Kemmis, S. (1986) *Becoming Critical*. London: Falmer.
Carr and Kemmis provide excellent historical outlines for theoretical frameworks in action research. See also,

Carr, W. (1995) *For Education*. Buckingham: Open University Press.
Carr focuses on the philosophical aspects of educational enquiry: similarly,

Carr, W. and Hartnett, A. (1996) *Education and the Struggle for Democracy*. Buckingham: Open University Press.
Cresswell, J. (2007) *Qualitative Inquiry and Research Design: Choosing Among Five Approaches* (Second Edition). Thousand Oaks, CA: Sage.
A wonderfully comprehensive and readable book that communicates the author's sheer love of his subject. See a living theory response to Cresswell's text at http://www. actionresearch.net/writings/arsup/Cresswellqualitativemethods.pdf

Clandinin, J. (ed.) (2007) *Handbook of Narrative Inquiry: Mapping a Methodology*. Thousand Oaks, CA: Sage.
Jean Clandinin was one of the founders, with Michael Connelly, of narrative inquiry as a genre. Here she maps out the territory, with chapters that set out what, why and how and how to do it.

PART II
Why Do I Need to Know?

Part II sets out why you should do action research. The emphasis shifts from what action research is to why it is important. It contains the following chapters.

At this stage in your action enquiry you are asking, 'Why am I concerned?' By asking the question, you show how you are engaging with the underpinning values and commitments of action research (Chapter 5), to do with freedom, democracy and accountability. You exercise your creative capacity as you learn to improve your practice (Chapter 6); you show your capacity for collaborative and negotiated forms of working as you contribute to new forms of theory (Chapter 7); and you demonstrate your accountability as you evaluate your own research (Chapter 8).

FIVE

Why Do Action Research?

We said in the Introduction that action researchers undertake their enquiries for two main purposes:

- to contribute to new practices (this is the action focus of action research);
- to contribute to new knowledge and theory (this is the research focus of action research).

Both aspects are intertwined and interdependent.

Many practitioners would probably feel at ease with the idea that they are contributing to new practices, but perhaps fewer would immediately see their work as contributing to theory or new ideas or new knowledge. In fact, practitioners are often suspicious of the idea of theory and research, some having had the experience of being researched on by officially appointed researchers. However, it is vital that practitioners do see themselves as both practitioners and researchers. The public acknowledgement of practitioners as practice innovators and theory creators is a key factor if practitioners are to be seen as legitimate participants in public debates about what is worth striving for in life, and which lives are important. However, public acknowledgement begins with the private acknowledgement of practitioners themselves. It is no good expecting someone else to value your work if you do not value it yourself. You need to appreciate the importance of your work in relation to your capacity to generate both new practice and new theory, and see how this ties in with policy formation and implementation.

This chapter deals with these aspects. It is in two sections.

1 The importance of seeing yourself as a capable practitioner
2 The importance of seeing yourself as a capable theorist

1 The importance of seeing yourself as a capable practitioner

In Chapter 2 we set out Donald Schön's ideas about the topologies of professional landscapes. Schön was, as we are here, making the point that practitioners should be regarded as competent professionals whose practical knowledge is key to developing human capabilities, their own and other people's.

This idea of developing human capability is core to action research. Sen (1999) describes capabilities as people's ability to think for themselves, and to make their own decisions about how they wish to live their lives. He also makes the point that realizing these capabilities requires people to be free, and to exercise their freedom to ensure the continued development of their own capabilities and the capabilities of others. This is done, he says, by 'support in the provision of those facilities (such as basic health care or essential education) that are crucial for the formation and use of human capabilities' (1999: 42). The task for practitioners then becomes how they can learn to think for themselves and make decisions about their own lives, and encourage others to do the same. Because practitioners are also professionals, they do not assume that this is just happening, but carry out stringent tests to see whether it is. They check whether they really are living in the direction of their values of freedom of thinking and the capacity of all to make informed decisions.

These ideas can provide a useful background context form which to start an action enquiry.

Starting an action enquiry

People have different reasons for starting an action enquiry. You may feel that your current practice is already really good, and other people can learn from you. You evaluate your work to explain how and why you can show this to be the case. Sometimes you have a hunch and you ask, 'I wonder what would happen if …?' Perhaps something could improve, and you may want to try out a new style or strategy. This means evaluating what happens. Is it working? Should you change something? This involves asking, 'How do I understand what I am doing?' 'How do I improve it?', and generating evidence to support any claim that you have improved practice by studying it systematically.

Roual and Maria work in the same restaurant, and are both registered for masters programmes in business management. This includes a module that requires them to undertake an action enquiry. The focus of their enquiries is as follows.

Roual is a chef. He wants to see how customers are responding to a new menu, so he gathers data about numbers of initial and repeat orders for different meals. His data archive shows him which meals customers prefer, and he adjusts the menu in relation to this feedback, and continues to monitor customers' choices. In this way he ensures that business remains buoyant by catering for customer choice.

Maria is the floor manager in the restaurant. She is interested in seating arrangements for customers, and any extra incentives for them to visit the restaurant. She leaves a little extra space between tables to give customers a feeling of private space. This means losing one table across the entire seating area, but her feedback shows greater customer satisfaction with the new arrangement, which means greater income generation. She also arranges for warm bread to be served to each table prior to the main meal (instead of the previously cold bread rolls), and this also improves customer satisfaction.

These are simple strategies that world-famous people have used, such as Sir Stuart Rose of Marks & Spencer. He arranged for the entire appearance and 'feel' of stores to be made more open, light and airy. Over the course of a few years, he raised the fortunes of the firm to world-class status (see http://uk.ibtimes.com/articles/24769/20100525/marks-spencer-pretax-profits-beats-consensus.htm).

Experiencing oneself as a living contradiction

Many action researchers begin their enquiries because they want to improve certain aspects of their work or work situation, so they can live more fully in the direction of their social and educational values. Sometimes, in Whitehead's (1989) words, they experience themselves as 'living contradictions' when their values are denied in their practice. By this he means that we hold values about what is important in life, which act as our guiding principles, and try to live accordingly. Sometimes we do, and sometimes we do not. For example, many people are guided by the principles of fairness and equity, and try to work in a way that is fair and equitable. Often they succeed, but sometimes not. Perhaps we lose courage and energy; perhaps external circumstances get in the way.

Here are some examples, from real-life practices, of successes and failure. Often, you have to compromise and focus on winning the war while being prepared to lose a battle or two.

Caroline Muir (2004) showed how she involved people in credit unions in workplace decision making. This participative working influenced people's economic and personal-social well-being and contributed to the success of their small businesses. In this case, she showed how living her values of participative working enabled other people to succeed.

Perhaps, like Mary Geoghegan (2000), a principal and manager, you find that you tend to run business meetings yourself, even though you believe in participative working. You experience yourself as a living contradiction because you deny your values of democratic participation. Mary introduced a rotating chair system, which meant everyone had the chance to lead, and they developed confidence in their capacity for leadership, even to the extent of questioning Mary's decisions.

Margaret Cahill (2007), a special needs resource teacher, worked in an education system that espoused the rhetoric of equity and entitlement, yet these values were consistently denied when some children were labelled by terms such as having 'special educational needs'. These children were bright and articulate, many with significant visual or kinaesthetic intelligence (Gardner, 1983). However, verbal and kinaesthetic intelligences were less valued in the education system than numerical and verbal intelligences, so the children were relegated to lower status. In her doctoral thesis, Margaret shows how she managed to live in the direction of her values in her own class context, yet was prevented from doing so in wider contexts. The conflict of values (Sowell, 1987) that such situations create can lead to emotional dissonance for the people involved.

What goals do action researchers wish to achieve?

Traditional social science tends to describe and explain what is happening in the existing social order, to maintain and reproduce it. Social science researchers ask, 'What is happening here?' 'How can we predict and control future outcomes?' Their ideas make up a body of theory that practitioners can apply to their practices, if this is what they want to do.

Action researchers also describe and explain the status quo, often drawing insights from the social sciences, and show how and why they are changing it. They ask, 'What is happening here?' 'How do we ensure that it communicates our commitments to the capacity of all to think and act responsibly?'

Action research is rooted in the ideas of social and intellectual freedom. These are that people can think for themselves and make their own life decisions, and will come together on an equal footing to negotiate their life plans. Action researchers therefore support public institutions that aim to safeguard people's social and intellectual freedom and the exercise of those freedoms for personal and social benefit. They generate their theories of human capability (Sen, 1999) that encourage innovative forms of personal and social evolution, rooted in freedom, and they use that freedom to support new freedoms. They make their theories public through their research accounts, which others can access and learn from.

Winnie Hignell (2004) explains how she and others worked collaboratively to enable so-called 'disabled' people with physical and mental trauma to be part of the social economy. She ensured that those who were labelled 'disabled' were included in other people's activities, and also developed their own capacity for creative work. She tells how she and her colleagues supported groups to decide for themselves how to set up their own businesses to produce texts and videos designed to inform the public about disability. They explained that disability should be reconceptualized not as a property of people with trauma but as a social practice of people, including those who construct disabling terms such as 'disability'.

2   The importance of seeing yourself as a capable theorist

When you tell other people about your work, whether orally or in a written report, you are showing two things. First, you are showing how you have developed innovative practices. Second, you are showing how these ideas about practice are brand new. You may have adopted, or incorporated, other people's ideas into your own work, but the work is yours, an original contribution. Other people can now learn from you, and adapt or incorporate your ideas if they wish. You explain that you are contributing to the practical life world by adding your story of practice, and you are contributing to the intellectual life world by offering your explanations for practice, your theory of practice. The idea of contributing to the intellectual life world is important. Edward Said (1994) talks about practitioners as public intellectuals. Perhaps all practitioners should be seen as potentially public intellectuals. Many shopkeepers and pop singers have as worthwhile contributions to make as professional elites. The fact remains that as a professional you are in a privileged position where you can use your voice. Unless you use your voice and profess your status as a public intellectual, you will not be heard. If you are not heard you will continue to be marginalized and not be taken seriously. Foucault (2001) speaks about these matters as *parrhesia*, a concept that communicates the need and responsibility of people to speak their truth as they see it.

Getting recognized

To set the scene, here is an example of this situation. Although it is about the teaching profession, its message is relevant for every workplace.

In the UK, and following the reforms of recent years, teachers are now recognized as the best judges of their own practice, and best placed to take main responsibility for the initial education of those entering the profession, as well as the ongoing professional education of those already in service. This new explicit recognition of the professional expertise of teachers has done much to enhance their status as professionals, and is manifested in a variety of ways, for example, in terms of the changed relationship between themselves and higher education institutions (HEIs). Whereas previously the work of HEIs was to pass on received wisdom about practice to teachers, teachers themselves are now seen as in charge of their own practice.

However, these changes are happening largely at the level of practice, and not so much at the level of theory. Although the professional competence of teachers is recognized, they still tend to be seen as competent practitioners, whose professional knowledge is about work in schools and classrooms. They are not widely recognized as competent theory generators, whose theoretical knowledge can inform policy. While these issues are aspects of debates about what should be the work of teachers and the extent of their capacity for influence, the issues are actually rooted in debates about what kind of knowledge should be seen as theory, and who should be regarded as a knower. Should practice be seen as a form of applied theory, or should it be seen as the grounds for theory generation? Should teachers be seen as appliers of other people's theory, such as academics in HEIs and business, or should teachers themselves be seen as practitioner-theorists?

These are core issues for all professions, because the directions the profession takes are decided mainly by policy. However, as noted earlier, policy formation and implementation tend to be informed not by research-based theory but by the values-based political commitments of politicians, who use research-based evidence selectively to support their politically motivated policies. Furthermore, the kind of research-based theory that politicians take seriously tends to be of the kind generated by professional elites, that is, academics in HEIs, business and think tanks, and also in the civil service and quangos, many of whom subscribe to neo-liberal and neo-conservative agendas (Furlong et al., 2000), and some of whom articulate a determination to keep practitioners out (Gorard, 2002; McIntyre, 1997). Teachers, so the story goes, may certainly be recognized as best placed to make professional judgements about practice, and to look after the internal affairs of the profession, but they should not aspire to be seen as theorists whose ideas will actually inform policy. Given the market orientation of many governments in the developed world to secure power and privilege for themselves, frequently driven by the values of self interest; and given the educational goals of many practitioners to work for social regeneration, frequently driven by the values of democratic ways of working, it is not surprising that the clashes of the underpinning values manifest as clashes of policy and political will. Consequently, and given that governments are kept in power by the publics who elect them, it then becomes a question both of whose ideas are more powerful and acceptable in public perceptions, and also of whose voices are most persuasive in making a case for their own positions.

The issue is highlighted again by John Furlong who, in his 2003 Presidential Address to the British Educational Research Association, made the point (returning to the example above) that teachers also still tend to regard their action research as a form of professional development that can lead to school improvement, and seldom make the link to the need to produce texts that will stand as quality theorizing (Furlong, 2004). He has also made the point that teachers do not yet take themselves seriously as practical theorists, which involves 'learning how to assess evidence, and address the values implicit in different courses of action; learning how to utilise such knowledge to inform practical judgements; fostering the abilities and dispositions to undertake practical theorising in relation to one's work' (Furlong, 2000: 13–14). These are core issues. Unless teachers and other practitioners are prepared to engage in these processes, their work will continue to be seen as a form of applied theory, and they will continue to be regarded as practitioners who are implementing other people's ideas rather than knowledge creators themselves.

So what does it take to turn your practice into a form of theorizing? It takes mainly two things:

- showing how you are learning to improve your practice;
- showing how your learning can stand as a contribution to new theory.

These issues are discussed in the following two chapters.

--- Summary ---

This chapter has addressed the question, 'Why do action research?' It has put forward two main reasons, to do with the importance of seeing yourself as both a competent practitioner and also a competent theorist. Currently, many practitioners still tend to see themselves as working in a practice context but not in a knowledge context, and action research tends to be seen as a form of professional development rather than a form of practical theorizing. In order to have your work taken seriously as a potential contribution to wider debates, including policy debates, you have to regard yourself as contributing to both practice and theory. These two issues are addressed in the following two chapters.

Further reading

Coghlan, D. and Brannick, T. (2009) *Doing Action Research in Your Own Organization* (third edition). London: Sage.
A useful text, this provides an accessible guide to action research in organizations.

Furlong, J., Barton, L., Miles, S., Whiting, C. and Whitty, G. (2000) *Teacher Education in Transition*. Buckingham: Open University Press.
This book is written from the perspective of improving teacher professional education, but its messages hold for any profession.

Sen, A. (1999) *Development as Freedom*. Oxford: Oxford University Press.
This is not an action research text, but is an excellent book for providing a key framework for doing action research, that is, freedom as a core criterion for creating one's identity and using one's voice.

Said, E. (1994) *Representations of the Intellectual: The 1993 Reith Lectures*. London: Vintage.
Also a key text for providing a rationale for doing action research, Said sets out his stall for intellectuals to appreciate the benefits and hazards involved in speaking for themselves.

Somekh, B. (2006) *Action Research: A methodology for Change and Development*. Maidenhead: Open University Press.
Bridget Somekh's work is highly respected, and this book sets out her vision of how action research can lead to change towards the good, and the conditions that nurture it.

SIX
Learning to Improve Practice

As a practitioner-researcher, your real work is to improve learning, both your own and that of others, in order to improve practice; and then to explain the process you have engaged in (see Chapter 7). Improvement is not something done by one person to another, but is a matter of the exercise of influence. You do not set out to impose change on people and their ways. Change imposed by an external agency does little for sustainable renewal. Change that comes from within, and in accordance with people's own wishes, does. Your work is to contribute to your own and other people's capacity to think independently and decide how you wish to live, recognizing that individuals are always in company with others. How do people learn to live responsibly? How do you influence their thinking about these things?

This chapter deals with these issues. It is in two sections.

1 Understanding influence
2 Exercising educational influence to improve practice

1 Understanding influence

People sometimes think influence is sinister and negative. This is not so. We are all influenced all the time, and we have the capacity to exercise influence. We learn how to think and act and make choices. This does not just happen. We learn from our books, families, friends and colleagues, according to the specific traditions of our particular culture. Some people choose not to be influenced by social norms, and do their own thing, but this choice is itself influenced by other voices. Our relationships of influence are multidimensional. They are horizontal across space and time, in terms of who we are currently interacting with, and vertical, existing through space and time. Most of us are influenced by what went before, and by visions of the future.

As well as being influenced by others, each person has the capacity to exercise influence. What we say and do potentially influences others, whether we realize it or not. This has enormous implications for you. How do you ensure that your influence contributes in a life-affirming way? How do you help yourself and others to grow? In which direction do you want to grow – towards critical self-reflection or towards reinforcing prejudices?

Visiting other theorists

Visits to the literature can help. Some theorists, such as Rousseau and Hume, believed that a child is born as a 'blank slate' or 'empty vessel' into which learning, usually information, is poured. They seemed to believe that people have to learn to become human. Conversely, Chomsky (1986) says that people have an infinite capacity for knowledge generation as part of their genetic make-up. On this view, we have unlimited potentials to learn an infinite amount of new knowledge. Polanyi (1958) says much the same, also maintaining that we know more than we can say. We know how things are, but cannot always explain why, and we know how to do some things without knowing the details of how we do it – riding a bike, for example. Polanyi calls this personal, or tacit, knowledge.

These ideas link well with an idea by Valéry, which is elaborated by Said (1997: 14). Like Polanyi and Chomsky, Said speaks about the idea that each individual is born with originality of mind, the capacity for independent, original thinking. They use this capacity to filter, or mediate, whatever they hear and experience. Consequently, when you say something to another person, that person does not necessarily immediately agree with everything you say, but filters it to decide which pieces to accept or reject. We all tend to do this (though perhaps not enough), when, say, we listen to a news broadcast and decide whether or not we agree with what is being said. This idea is important when it is a matter of understanding how learning happens (theories of learning).

Processes of coming to know (learning) are complex. One view is that we raise our deep tacit knowledge to an explicit level. This idea can be linked with Chomsky's (1965) and Goethe's (1988) ideas about generative transformational capacity, a developmental process that enables a present form to emerge as a new form.

Combining these ideas gives rise to a theory of learning that accepts the infinite capacity of humans to create an infinite number of new forms of knowledge, and to transform their existing knowledge into new improved forms. This means that each person should be recognized as having the capacity for creative choice and for making original contributions.

Now let us link this with an idea from Habermas (1975): in the processes of social evolution, he says, people are not capable of *not* learning, that is, we *must* learn as part of our genetic make-up. The question arises, how do people decide what to learn? This has implications for practitioners with agency. Do we exercise our influence in ways that respect each person's uniqueness of mind and unlimited capacity for unlimited acts of creation, or do we aim to influence so that we deny those opportunities? Do we give others the choice to exercise their capacity for choice?

Influence does not 'just happen', although it can appear to do so. Most of us are subject to persuasion and propaganda, as Marlin (2002) and Chomsky (1991) suggest. A vegetarian friend said that she bought a can of chicken sauce from watching a television advert. Accepting or rejecting influence is a matter of choice. We hear voices everywhere. Which ones we attend to is up to us. We are all able to exercise our originality of mind and critical judgement when deciding what to think and how to think. Having said this, it has to be recognized that some people choose not to think for themselves, and other people are persuaded to believe certain things. This is often a case of insidious influence.

It is a matter not only of you influencing others, but also of how you are influenced. What you do and how you do it is your choice. Choosing is one of your freedoms. While imprisoned in a concentration camp, Victor Frankl (1963) chose to adopt life-affirming attitudes, and Etty Hillesum (1983, quoted in Todorov, 1999) chose to forgive her persecutors. Most of us are able to choose, even though we may live in prisons of one kind or another. Retaining this capacity is sometimes impossible when a direct assault is made on controlling our minds.

Choices frequently involve tension, which can be both creative and obstructive. Try choosing between two equally attractive pairs of shoes. Choices are also not simply a matter of right and wrong, but often a question of choosing between competing rights. For example, members of a postal workers' trade union recently chose not to deliver what they saw as racially charged political leaflets. Their choice, as part of their contractual rights, not to deliver the post, denied their legal obligations and customers' rights to receive their post. Most moral debates are about choosing between rival claims to rights and knowledge. Often these cannot be settled, so unless we choose to resort to force, we have to learn how to negotiate a way through so that all can live as we wish in company with others who want to do the same.

2   Exercising educational influence to improve practice

You can show how you are improving practice by exercising your educational influence in your own and other people's learning. Does your account of practice show you thinking for yourself and encouraging others to think for themselves? Do you create the kinds of relationships that will encourage people to feel safe enough to critique? This means they can also critique you. How do you show that you are influencing in an educational way and not cleverly manipulating?

Sometimes these matters are too complex to resolve, and we have to go on trust. You can, however, do some things that will help people to trust you. If they have reason to trust you in some concrete things, they will be more likely to trust you in the intangibles.

Trust can be established when you show that:

- you are committed to your own knowledge; and
- you produce evidence to support what you are saying.

Making a commitment to your own knowledge

Polanyi (see above) says that any act of knowing involves commitment, a personal faith that the knowledge we create is potentially right. It can be difficult, he says, to make such a commitment while also accepting the possibility that one might be mistaken. Nevertheless, this should not prevent each one of us from making our claims to knowledge with universal intent (Polanyi, 1958: 327), that is, saying that we have learned something, with the intent of helping others to learn from our learning. We must also be open to ongoing critique, so that we can refine our learning in light of the critique.

There follows part of Peter Raymond's (2010) proposal to study for a PhD at York St John University through action research, which shows how he is prepared to do this.

Doctoral research proposal
Peter Raymond

Introduction

This proposal is for a PhD programme of study in which I hope to conduct an action enquiry into how I can exercise educational influence to promote creativity in education, as a Senior Lecturer in Initial Teacher Education (ITE) at York St John University (YSJU). Through the research, I will seek to describe, analyse and reflect upon my personal values and practice in order to gain a deeper understanding of my work and generate a personal living theory of practice (Whitehead, 1998 and 2008, McNiff, 2007 and Whitehead and McNiff, 2006). I will aim to make original contributions to knowledge in the fields of creativity in ITE and the primary curriculum and will demonstrate critical engagement with key theorists and my own values, beliefs and professional practice, encouraging other co-professionals and students to do the same.

Contexts of the research

Having been a primary school teacher/headteacher for 21 years, I have now taught for three years across undergraduate and postgraduate ITE.

My research is therefore located in a range of contexts:

- My teaching role with trainee teachers in ITE.
- My leadership and management roles as a multiple module director.
- My roles and relationships with existing and new school partnerships.

Aims

The primary aim of the research, which will act as the grounds for my original contribution to knowledge will be to theorise how I can best work with colleagues, students, schools and other education agencies in fostering creativity in teaching and learning in ITE and in primary schools. I will investigate the educational influence that I and other co-professionals exercise in the thinking and practice of those with whom we work. In doing so, I will investigate and reflect on how current and emerging practice in ITE and in schools can influence practice and how ITE and schools can exercise reciprocal influence to bring more creativity to learning and teaching. I will seek to identify and address the key tensions and dilemmas (Craft, 2005) in doing this and I will engage critically with the challenges to my beliefs, values and professional practice as they transform through studying my relationships and practices.

I believe that there is potential within this study to influence new thinking and practices in ITE and in primary schools at individual, institutional and systemic levels.

The evidence base of your claim to knowledge

The idea of evidence is crucial in all research, not only in action research. Research is a process of finding out in order to create new knowledge. If you say you now know something that you did not know before, you can be reasonably sure someone will say, 'Prove it.' While you cannot 'prove' it, nor should you even get into using such language, you can produce reasonable evidence to support your claim to knowledge.

At this point we want to return to the question of how you can demonstrate how you are exercising your influence to improve learning for improving practice.

When you produce your research report you will make the claim that you have improved your practice by improving your learning, and you have encouraged others to do the same. The others in question would be people such as your students, colleagues, peers and those in senior positions. Perhaps a significant triumph would be if you could say you had influenced policymakers to improve their learning about these things.

Your claim to improved learning would be supported by validated evidence (see Chapter 14 for advice on generating evidence). This can be problematic. It is straightforward enough to produce illustrative material to show people in action, but it is a far more rigorous process to produce evidence, which is about extracting from your data those instances that you believe are manifestations of your values in practice, which in turn have acted as your criteria. For you, your commitment to learning is a value that inspires your work. How to produce evidence of learning?

Producing evidence of your own learning is not difficult. You can, for example, show your learning journal, point to instances when you really did learn something new and were able to articulate what you had learned, and draw out the significance of that learning for you. You can produce memos and emails when you seemed to be saying new things, influenced by new learning. These also could stand as evidence of learning.

Producing evidence of other people's learning is more problematic, and means producing instances also of them saying and doing different things. You can surmise that they are doing this because of their learning, but your evidence would be much more robust if you could get their testimony that this actually was influenced by their learning. This means asking the people themselves to say what they have learned, and how their learning is significant for them. You would need to ask them, 'What were you thinking when you did this?' 'What had you learned?' Their accounts of what they were learning would stand as evidence of their learning, and could also supplement images and descriptions of them in action. In this way, it is possible to show how learning enters into action, so action is shown to be purposeful and committed and not just spur of the moment reaction (see the examples below).

A further step is needed, however, if you want to produce evidence of your influence in other people's learning. Again, this means asking them, using your own form of words, 'Have I influenced you? How?' The fact that they may learn to copy what you say, or use your language, is no evidence that they have learned to think for themselves. You can produce, say, video clips of people debating and using their capacity for creativity, but to claim that they are doing that because of your influence means getting their testimony that this is the case.

Producing evidence of your educational influence can be difficult, but it can be done. A main strategy is to find ways to structure your reflection on practice.

Structured reflection on practice

It is important to do some explicit reflection on your practice so that you can see the relationship between what you are doing and learning, and the significance of doing so; and how this then influences other people's learning. A useful exercise is to draw a chart labelled 'What did I do?', 'What did I learn?' and 'What is the importance of my learning?' (see Table 6.1 below). You can do this yourself, and you can also ask your participants to do so. Their responses would give you some indication about the extent to which they have been influenced by your own learning.

This is a common strategy used by us authors. We regularly write it into course materials.

Here are two examples from teachers involved in the Action Research for Teachers course that Jean was involved with in Qatar, October 2009–June 2010, provided by Tribal Education in collaboration with the Qatar Supreme Education Council. Part of this course was a master trainers course, from which the examples are taken. Because the idea of action research and reflection on action was new for the teachers, she focused a lot on helping the teachers regularly structure their reflections in their reflective journals using small exercises such as this (she also used artwork and visual metaphor as key strategies). The examples show the extended reflection of teachers on what they have learned about their practices and their appreciation of its significance. The exercise may be used by practitioners in all workplaces.

Table 6.1

What did I do?	What did I learn?	What is the importance of my learning?
I prepared a presentation of my research for an audience of peers	I learned that I have to spend time thinking about how I could communicate the key points of my research succinctly and in a way that did them justice	I had not realized how much I had done and learned through my research. It struck me that it was in fact useful and good quality.

The first example is from Azzam Abu Hannieh, Doha Independent Preparatory School for Boys, who reflects on his experience of a workshop that focused on developing the capacity for offering and receiving empathetic critique. He writes:

Prof McNiff, who was facilitating the workshop, shared her thoughts about different research activities. She did this without imposing her ideas, and people listened carefully. She asked all workshop participants to write a research question, to help the following discussions. This made the learning process easier for the teachers. She then invited teachers to present their ideas, and for others to ask critical questions, in a respectful manner, with consideration for the presenter's feelings.

Many of us teachers said that we really liked the action based, teacher-centred approach to learning. We asked a lot of feedback questions of the teachers who were presenting their work, taking care throughout to be polite and respectful.

After our discussions, we all agreed on the following:

- As teachers, we need to help our colleagues in school to appreciate the need for respectful relationships and communicate our own experiences to those colleagues.
- We agreed to take part in the action research forum at Qatar University in May 2010.
- The workshops were helpful and added a lot to our professional repertoires.

I really enjoyed these sessions. I liked the way our facilitators demonstrated thorough knowledge of the field and used an engaging way of interacting with participants.

I would like to sum up my experience by saying that I was really impressed by the workshops. The level of engagement and excitement of the participants was a surprise for me because action research is something new in our schools and is a new culture for our education community. I would feel a sense of achievement if I could see this same level of excitement in the coming months when the teachers I support in school begin to identify viable educational problems and develop a systematic approach to finding a solution that can help improve the situation in schools, and that works. I am hoping to help my colleagues to begin to identify an area of concern that they can realistically research, formulate a research question for their study, gather data and analyse it using qualitative and quantitative methods, and eventually make and justify a knowledge claim.

In this way I hope to enable them to find ways of improving teaching and learning processes in my school. (Pers. comm., 4 June 2010)

The second example is from Shaikha Hamad Al-Hajri. This is an abstract from her reflections on her Master Trainer course, and shows how she has developed her critical capacity in appreciating the significance of her work. At this point she was investigating ways of improving her presentation skills.

My critical reflection on the significance of my action research

I have learned much from doing my action research. My evidence tells me I am justified in claiming that I have improved my practice as a presenter. My peers corroborated this claim during a later presentation at the Master Trainer workshop. All agreed that I had improved my skills and knowledge. Here are the most important things I have learned.

I have learned the value of professional patience and courage. I call this 'long patience': it sustains you during processes of lifelong learning. Being a mother of four children and a working lady, I have learned another kind of patience – 'beautiful patience' – when you live with the hope that things will be better if you remain committed to what you believe in.

I have learned the importance of meeting the other person in their own space. I have to earn their trust for them to allow me to learn from them, and for me to be part of their learning, so that they may come to accept me as a resource for learning.

I have learned the importance of values, and not to underestimate the capabilities of others and myself. Julie [a colleague] wrote in her evaluation:

'I did at one stage feel totally involved and included within the session, even though it was being delivered in Arabic. Shaikha's gestures, nods, emphasis and drawings allowed me into her world and I understood what was being said and discussed. This is a special gift I feel.'

I wish to use this gift. I believe I am contributing to the creation of cultures of educational enquiry. There may still be far to go, but we are on the road together, each will help the other, and none will turn back.

(See also Tribal 2010: You can read the full text of Shaikha's report, and others, at http://www.jeanmcniff.com/userfiles/file/qatar/Qatar_Action_Research_booklet_email.pdf.)

Summary

This chapter has talked about improving your learning to improve practice. It has particularly looked at ideas to do with the nature of influence, and how you can exercise your own educational influence to improve practice. Doing action research emphasizes the need to exercise influence in a way that is educational.

This chapter has talked about improving learning. The next chapter deals with contributing to theory.

Further reading

Boyer, E. (1990) *Scholarship Reconsidered: Priorities of the Professoriate.* NJ: Carnegie Foundation for the Advancement of Teaching.
This seminal text is recognized as the first to articulate the need for a new scholarship, that is, to see practice (in this book, teaching) as the site for and focus of research.

Ghaye, A. and Ghaye, K. (1998) *Teaching and Learning through Critical Reflective Practice.* London: David Fulton.
A lovely book all about reflective practice. Written for the teaching profession, its messages are relevant across the professions. A really good read.

McNiff, J. and Whitehead, J. (2005) *Action Research for Teachers.* London: David Fulton/ Routledge.
A most accessible little book, this sets out the basic principles and practices of action research for teachers.

Said, E. (1997) *Beginnings: Intent and Method.* London: Granta.
Again not an action research text, this book provides the conceptual framing for understanding action research as transformational, and is relevant to many workplaces.

Stringer, E., Christensen, L. and Baldwin, S. (2010) *Integrating Teaching, Learning and Action Research.* Harlow: Pearson.
Written specifically for teachers, this book is a must for all readers.

SEVEN

Contributing to New Theory

While you remain a practitioner, your main concern is to improve practice. As soon as you become a researcher, your main concern is to generate new ideas, knowledge and theory. As a practitioner-researcher, your task is to show how you are connecting both your educational theorizing and your practice improvement. You theorize (describe and explain) the process of improving practice.

In Chapter 5 we began to make the case that practitioners need to become involved in theory generation. This present chapter develops ideas about why you should, and how you can do so.

The chapter is in two sections.

1 The need to contribute to new theory
2 How to contribute to new theory

1   The need to contribute to new theory

Most literatures on professional education tell you how to be good at your job. Important though this aspect is, being good at your job does not get you recognized as competent to make decisions about your job, or, further, about directions your profession should take and what to attend to as its matters of professional concern. Many books offer plentiful advice about how practitioners can develop your practice during their first few years of service, and go on to develop professional maturity. Some offer tips, and others offer advice about coping strategies, including strategies for surviving hostile environments. Not many, however, make the case that any practitioner in any specific profession should actually begin to investigate how they can develop the power to make decisions about the nature and purpose of that profession, and how this can contribute to wider debates about the nature and direction of the society we wish to live in. This idea seems not often to occur. We are told how to survive and hang on. By colluding in the oppression, however, by not seeing the need to challenge, or even entertain the idea that it is possible to challenge, practitioners agree to continue to be seen as worthy practitioners who can talk about practice, but not as highly competent theorists who can talk about the need to explain practice and specify what practice is for and whose interests it should serve. Nor does this process happen by accident. Practitioners are systematically persuaded to believe that they are not capable of thinking for themselves or contributing to theory.

This is how it works.

Manufacturing consent

Throughout his political writings, and especially in a wonderfully accessible little text called *Media Control: the Spectacular Achievements of Propaganda* (1991), Noam Chomsky explains that ordinary people are persuaded to believe that they are not capable of thinking for themselves. This is achieved via a sophisticated propaganda system. At the root of it all is the desire on the part of privileged minorities within the corporate business community to keep ordinary people from questioning the messages they are given, and not to aspire to get involved in debates about how countries should be run or what kinds of societies are worth living in.

Chomksy speaks of two models of democracy. The first is participative democracy, where people take an active part in running their own affairs. The second, which is the current orthodoxy, is what he calls spectator democracy, where people elect representatives to run their affairs for them, and then stand back and watch. Those who represent are seen as aristocrats, both by themselves and by the people who elect them. The rest are seen as serfs, whose job is to get the representatives into power and then let them get on with it without question. To keep ordinary people under control, the privileged elites use various strategies to frighten them. One such strategy is to produce bogeymen such as Saddam Hussein, Mahmoud Ahmadinejad or Jack the Ripper. Another is to persuade people of their own inadequacy in the shadow of more intelligent others, to instil the proper subservience.

This system works well, including in professional education. A key strategy is to present theory as an esoteric discipline that is conducted only by a privileged group with specialized skills, which it is not. Another is to persuade practitioners to see themselves as not capable, which they are. These mythologies are made real by aristocrats, and also practitioners themselves, who are persuaded to condone their own subjugation. Privileged persons in elite institutions produce authoritative books and papers that present theory as an abstract discipline (Pring, 2000). They also communicate messages that practitioners are not able to do research (McIntyre, 1997). Practitioners come to believe these messages, and so develop informal discourses, that enter into professional discourses, about how they are not interested in theory because it is irrelevant and above their heads. They say, 'Don't tell me about theory. Leave that for the specialists. I'm just a dentist/ teacher/social worker/you name it.' You can hear these discourses everywhere, and they are reinforced by the fact that most books on professional education simply do not mention the idea of theory generation, or that practitioners should get involved in it. The subject rarely arises as a matter for discussion. Which is where we came in.

We are saying in this book that you do need to get involved in it. You are not a spectator democrat who is content to have other people run your life for you, but an activist democrat who is prepared to take control of your own life and make statements about what your work is about and how it can best serve the interests of others. Foucault (2001) agrees. He says that it is a capacity, and a responsibility, to speak for oneself in the interests of a good social order. Your job is to generate your own educational theories of your own learning as a way of accounting to yourself and others for the life you are living in relation to your values.

Here is how you do it.

2   How to contribute to new theory

- First, consider what inspires your life. According to Fromm (1956), what gives our lives meaning is our ability to enjoy loving relationships and productive work. What are the values that give your life meaning? Articulating values can be difficult, but it is important to do so.
- Second, consider whether you are living in a way that is consistent with your values. If you are, how can you show it? If you are not, what can you do about it? Again, articulate this in some way so that people can access the descriptions you give for what is happening, and your explanations for why it is happening.
- Now show how you address this issue, again offering descriptions of what you are doing and explanations for why you are doing it. This will involve you in gathering data, and later generating evidence from the data to ground your claim that you have addressed the issue. You will also have to validate your evidence by testing it against other people's critical feedback.
- Finally, write a report of what you have done and give it to someone to read. Or produce a multimedia presentation and show it to colleagues in your workplace.

Although this process has been disciplined and systematic, it has been entirely achievable and not too difficult. It has in fact been a process of generating theory. Your descriptions and explanations of your learning as you work to improve your practice are your personal/collective theory of practice. There is nothing esoteric about this.

It is a systematic procedure for accounting for your practice, why you do what you do: you explicate (make explicit) the processes you have gone through. Furthermore it shows that you are not just doing it in a haphazard way, but you are thinking carefully and responsibly about your actions and their influence in other people's lives. (Further detailed advice is given in Part III, which takes you through action enquiry processes.)

Now let us tie this in with ideas about the need for you to believe in yourself, and not be persuaded that generating theory is difficult or that you are incapable of doing it.

- Be aware of what is going on. Be aware of the messages you are hearing. Which ones are true?
- Be aware that you are more likely to believe false messages and retain existing biases when you are on your own. Access some of the work already in existence and you will soon see that you are not alone and that other people also wish to overcome inappropriate biases and do not want to believe false messages. Plenty of practitioners are putting their theories of practice into the public domain, and other people are learning from them.
- Be aware that other people need to hear that they are not alone either, and should take courage, perhaps from accessing your work. You have something important to say.

So how are you contributing to new theory? You are contributing in the following ways.

- You are empowering yourself as a researcher. You are constantly generating valuable theories, and modifying them to keep up to date with your developing practice.
- You are reconceptualizing yourself as a researcher, not only as a shopkeeper, steel worker or secretary. Your practice is a form of research, and your research is a form of practice. Other people can learn from your example and empower themselves.
- You are refusing to be relegated as 'just a shopkeeper', 'just a steel worker', 'just a secretary'. You are creating a new professional identity as a practitioner-researcher, and you are developing new professional discourses with others who also regard themselves as practitioner-researchers.
- You are getting involved in debates about the nature of practice and its uses. You are not prepared to accept other messages that your work is to deliver a service, or a curriculum. Your work is to influence learning for improving practice.
- You are contributing to the wider body of knowledge, within a tradition called the new scholarship.

The new scholarship

This idea began within the field of education, specifically teaching and learning. In this book we are saying that the idea needs to be expanded to include all practitioners who are involved in development work, and should be redefined as a new scholarship of educational enquiry (Whitehead, 1999) for the advancement of practice. It is the task of all professions to promote the idea of the new scholarship in their own contexts. First, let us look at what the new scholarship involves.

In 1990, Ernest Boyer, then President of the Carnegie Foundation for the Advancement of Teaching, spoke about the need to develop a scholarship of teaching, that is, the systematic, high-level study of teaching practices. This would not simply be study of the actions of teaching, which could be understood by asking questions of the kind, 'What skills and techniques is the teacher demonstrating?', but study of practice from within the practice, that could be understood by asking questions of the kind, 'What am I doing to encourage learning?' 'How am I evaluating my work?' A scholarship of teaching in this sense would be undertaken by those who regarded themselves as research-active teachers as well as teaching-active researchers. Professional education would no longer be 'tips for teachers', offered on one-off in-service days and only in school settings, but an ongoing discussion across sectors, phases and disciplines about how practitioners can study and theorize their teaching and pedagogies.

This idea has profound implications for all practitioners, including teachers, in terms of how they understand their work and their professional identities, and what they see as the object of educational research. Like other practitioners, teachers in schools usually have no difficulty in seeing themselves as practitioners but are often reluctant to see themselves as scholars, whereas many higher education people tend to see themselves as scholars rather than practitioners. For all parties, the issue of what is studied is of key significance. Dominant traditions say that people should study their subject matter, rather than their practice (Lawlor, 1990). Boyer's (1990) idea of a scholarship of teaching was grounded in the idea that teaching (and by extension, practice) itself is a form of scholarship, whose findings need to be made public so that other people can learn from them. The findings that teachers generate from studying their practice can contribute to a knowledge base that is created by teachers for teachers, or, in the wider sense, by practitioners for practitioners in all workplaces.

It may be helpful briefly to outline how the new scholarship differs from traditional scholarship (see Box 7.1). (Some researchers refer to 'new paradigm' and 'old paradigm' research. Reason and Rowan's *Human Inquiry* 1981 is a classic that explains the origins of some of the different perspectives.)

Here is an example that shows new forms of scholarship in action. It is taken from the work of faculty at York St John University, where a core group of some 10 members of faculty have formed an action research group. We are aiming to build a knowledge base of what counts as action research in higher education, and how its quality should be judged. Some of us are pursuing these enquiries are part of our doctoral programmes, and all of us are writing and publishing our work. As part of our dissemination work, we try to present at all major international conferences. Here is an extract from the symposium we presented at the 2010 British Educational Research Association annual meeting. The presenters were Jenny Carpenter and Keither Parker, Clare McCluskey, Peter Raymond, Jill Munro Wickham and Jean McNiff.

Characteristics of traditional scholarship

In general terms, and regardless of subject matter, scholarship refers to a process of enquiry that involves study, generating evidence to support findings, and testing one's findings in the public domain. Traditional scholarship is a process of study of a particular subject matter. The usual aim is to support or refute a hypothesis, by conducting experiments, and manipulating variables to test the relationship between them. Knowledge tends to be regarded as an object, and findings are disseminated through written accounts. In professional learning contexts, the assumption is that theory can be applied to other people's practices.

Characteristic of the new scholarship

The new scholarship refers to newer holistic forms of enquiry, where a practitioner investigates their own work in order to generate theory from within the practice. Practice itself becomes the context for research, and contains its own theory. Knowledge is developed through the exercise of creative imagination and critical engagement. In professional learning contexts the assumption is that theory is always in process, and can contribute to new thinking about new forms of practice.

Pedagogical action research for improving teaching and learning in higher education
Overview

This interactive symposium offers an account of the pedagogical action research that we, a research group of academic practitioners at York St John University, are undertaking, out of a commitment to improve our understandings of how we can improve our teaching and learning. While there is a growing literature on the nature and uses of pedagogical research, little of this literature focuses on how pedagogical research is done by real-life practitioners, how it influences the learning of staff and students working together, and what its systemic potentials may be for institutional research. Our symposium explains how we engage in our action enquiries, offering our descriptions and explanations of practice in the form of our living educational theories (Whitehead, 1989), and how these form the focus of our doctoral programmes.

The symposium is innovative in the following ways:

- We are conscious of the need to demonstrate quality in our educational practices and research, and to produce authenticated evidence to test the validity of our claims to know our practices. Hence we produce multimedia evidence to show the realities of our collaborative learning together as well as with our students and colleagues. Our visual narratives show the manifestation of our relational pedagogies as we seek to exercise our educational influence in the learning of ourselves, our students and our colleagues.
- Further, we test the legitimacy of our knowledge claims by appeal to the audience at our symposium, and invite their critical feedback on our presentations, using

nominated criteria and standards by which we judge the validity of our knowledge claims. Thus the symposium itself becomes a site for the generation of educational knowledge by all participants.

By engaging in such practices in our efforts to demonstrate the truthfulness of our research-based practices, we aim to show how we hold ourselves accountable for our research and practices. We bring these understandings to our everyday work, and so contribute to what we believe is the development of a virtuous university (Nixon, 2008), that takes as inviolable the understanding that a university is about creating knowledge through and for morally-committed practices. We hold our work as contributing to new understandings of a curriculum for higher education, a profession of values that enable us to imagine what a decent society looks like and how we can contribute to its formation.

You can find the full text of the proposal at http://www.jeanmcniff.com/york-st-john-university.asp

---

You are contributing to a new scholarship of educational enquiry by showing how your practice stands as a process of rigorous theorizing. It simply does not matter that your context of practice is a shop or a factory or a university. You are potentially a valuable practitioner-researcher wherever you are. It is up to you to show it, and to stake your claim to your rightful place among the community of scholars.

Summary

This chapter has continued to emphasize the idea that you are a theorist as well as a practitioner, a knowledge creator in your own right. This involves challenging dominant messages that you should keep your station as a practitioner and not aspire to engage with theory. Advice has been given about how to contribute to new theory in terms of engaging with the new scholarship. The task now becomes how to show the value of what you are doing. This is the focus of the next chapter.

Further reading

Dick, B., Stringer, E. and Huxham, C. (eds) (2009) 'Theory in action research'. Special edition of *Action Research*, 7(1).

Elliott, J. (2007) *Reflecting Where the Action Is: The Selected Works of John Elliott*. London: Routledge.
One of the 'founding fathers' of 'post-Lewin second generation' action researchers, John Elliott presents some of the best of his papers in this edited collection, with a focus on

the relationship between research and theory. Well worth a read to get a good sense of where action research has come from and what key issues still remain.

Hymer, B., Whitehead, J. and Huxtable, M. (2008) *Gifted and Talented Education: A Living Theory Approach*. London: Wiley.
This text assumes that all children and adults have talents they can develop in the sharing of gifts. In a living theory approach, all are encouraged to share their gifts for the common good. The book has many practical examples to show how this can be done.

Scott, D. and Usher, R. (1996) *Understanding Educational Research*. London: Routledge. Written from a critical perspective, this book foregrounds the relationship between theory and practice.

EIGHT

Evaluating Your Research

Evaluation is about establishing the value or quality of something. The thing in question is the quality of your research, as this is communicated through your claim to knowledge (what you know) and your explication of how you have come to know it. The chapter focuses on the generic issues of what evaluation involves and how and why you should evaluate your own work. It is organized to address these two questions:

1 What does evaluation involve?
2 Evaluating your own work

1 What does evaluation involve?

We said earlier that when you make a claim to knowledge someone is bound to say, 'Prove it.' You cannot 'prove it'. The language of 'proof' is disappearing, as even the natural and physical sciences recognize that sustainable improvement in the natural world works not so much through cause and effect as through relationships and connections. This is the case in all contexts of sustainable improvement (as cited, for example, in the Department of Health, Social Services and Public Safety, 2006, http://www.dhsspsni.gov.uk/safety_first_-_a_framework_for_sustainable_improvement_on_the_hpss-2.pdf). We are only now emerging from the grip of a powerful empiricist tradition, and gradually developing a new language that includes the idea of reasonable evidence. This can be seen even in many legal systems.

Doing evaluation is never a neutral process. While evaluation is generally understood as establishing the value of something, different people prioritize different values, and use those values to inform their approaches to evaluation. Evaluation processes are always politically constituted and involve the exercise of power. Action research is about developing social justice, so evaluation in action research, like all its other processes, needs to demonstrate egalitarian values. This immediately raises questions:

- Who evaluates?
- What is evaluated?
- How is it evaluated?

Although the questions are discussed here as separate issues for analysis, they should be seen as interdependent with much overlap.

Who evaluates?

In the early 20th century, Frederick Taylor (1911) introduced the idea of scientific management, an idea that was going to be influential for the entire century. The idea was that people's work could be judged by a manager carrying a stopwatch. A worker could achieve so many units of work in so much time. The prevailing attitude was that people were automata, whose output could be judged in terms of designated targets. This idea has filtered into many social systems. Its influence is evident today, all over the technologized world, in fields like health care and education, and especially business, where people's capabilities and learning are judged in terms of how many targets they achieve in how much time. The quality of people's lives in many ways has become standardized. Apart from the obvious implications of deskilling and deprofessionalization, more insidious elements of centralized control are evident.

When this view enters evaluation, implications include the idea that an external evaluator makes judgements about other people's practices. In some places, the stopwatch has been exchanged for a checklist, but it is still visible in target setting practices, achievement tests and appraisal systems.

This inspection models permeates professional contexts. In many countries, hospitals, clinics, nursery schools and other institutions are regularly inspected, as are nurses, health care professionals, fire-fighters, veterinary assistants, teachers and many other practitioners. Most professions operate regulatory appraisal schemes, many of which take the form of inspection rather than consultation. In work that is submitted for higher degree accreditation, there is still a view that the examiner's decision is final and not open to question or negotiation.

New paradigm work has introduced new systems, which work from a different values base. Because of the underpinning values of justice and democracy, practitioners are able to exercise their own voices about who should evaluate, and on whose terms this should be done. This raises further questions about whether a practitioner is competent to judge their own work, how they will demonstrate its validity, and how they will assure the watching public that their findings are credible and trustworthy. These issues are especially important in current times of increasing calls for accountability and attempts to steer professional education processes through bureaucratic control to meet centralist political agendas.

Therefore if practitioners want to establish and retain the right to self-evaluate, they need to demonstrate publicly that they know what they are doing and that their judgement can be trusted. This means that they have to make their explanatory and evaluation processes visible, show that these are rigorous and robust, and produce strong evidence to show that they as practitioner-researchers are competent and capable.

What is evaluated?

So evaluation is not only about demonstrating the validity of the researcher's claims about the work, but also the validity of the researcher's claims that they are capable of doing the job. These shifts in evaluation practices have been emphasized in recent years. In his *Personalizing Evaluation*, Kushner (2000) explains how the emphasis has moved from programmes to people (see also Guba and Lincoln, 1989). Many problematics remain, however, especially in assumptions about how practitioners are viewed, and what is evaluated.

Practitioners still tend to be viewed as peripheral. This is demonstrated in books such as MacBeath (1999) and Cousins and Earl (1995), where arguments are made for including practitioners in evaluation processes. However, this works on the assumption that, although a professional evaluator seeks the practitioners' opinion, the evaluator is still in charge and the practitioners are subordinate. The view is reinforced by texts that espouse Wenger's (1998) ideas about 'communities of practice' yet distort the ideas to communicate hierarchies of voices, and, implicitly, hierarchies of knowers. There is nothing peripheral about practitioners. All practitioners are central. They are doing the work, no matter what form it takes, and they should be held accountable for the work; but this should be done first by themselves, in relation to their own work-based standards, not by external judges who operate from their own sets of standards that are often unrelated to the work in hand.

So the question remains: if personalizing evaluation means shifting from an emphasis on evaluating programmes, does this mean that it shifts to evaluating people? This returns us to the issue of who evaluates, how competent they are to make judgements, and whether this can be seen as a practice that realizes the values underpinning the celebration of human capabilities.

How is it evaluated?

Many contemporary evaluation practices work on an apprenticeship model. This calls into question what coaching or mentoring practices are used and what form a curriculum takes. The experience of many professionals is that they listen to an expert, take notes and write an essay (or do something equivalent), which is assessed by the expert in terms of what the expert expects to see, often a regurgitation and reinforcement of their own ideas. This can be seen as a closed shop mentality that perpetuates what Popper (1966) calls a closed society. To test out this perception, check with a workplace colleague or school student how many times they have been asked in their entire career what they know and what they think they should learn. Furthermore, coaching and pedagogical practices tend to be didactic, or at least delivery oriented. Many practitioners in organized education settings are heard to complain that they have to achieve the targets, cover the syllabus, finish the textbook or deliver the curriculum. The emphasis is on getting a functional job of work done, and delivering a product, rather than about working with people with real lives. Callahan's book *Education and the Cult of Efficiency* was written in 1962, but it represents the reality of practitioners' experiences in many quarters today.

Coaching and mentoring practices and pedagogies are rightly related to how curriculum is perceived. Bernstein (2000) speaks about how knowledge is pedagogized, that is, formed as specific pedagogic structures that often work as symbolic forms of the control of knowledge and identity. Technicist approaches view curriculum as an accumulation of information. The task of the educator is to get this information across to trainees. Pedagogies that emphasize delivery to the passive masses reinforce the perception of the differing status of experts and apprentices, them and us. Pedagogical practices control identities.

Action researchers see limitations in these technicist views. Like Habermas (1987), action researchers believe that all are participants in communicative action. Like Senge they believe that 'The organizations that will truly excel in the future will be the organizations that discover how to tap people's commitment and capacity to learn at *all* levels in an organization' (1990: 4, emphasis in the original). This means that all should be prepared to evaluate their own practice, in relation to what they are doing with other people, and test their findings against the critical scrutiny of the public world. This can be uncomfortable for those who like to be positioned as experts and managers. It can, however, be liberating for others who do not wish to be so positioned, and who wish to remove the constraining influences and be seen as a person doing a worthwhile job of work in company with others who are doing the same. To make this shift demonstrates considerable courage and vision, and frequently involves engaging with institutional politics, but it is essential if the values underpinning a view of human capabilities are to shift out of the rhetoric and become reality.

In 2005, Jean developed and negotiated to deliver a masters programme in Khayelitsha, a large township in South Africa. This was her initiative, not a requirement of any institution. However, she ran into fierce opposition from different groupings in South Africa and in the home university who would grant the award. A particular event stays in her mind. She mentioned the idea at a meeting with members of a South African university who had invited her to teach on their programmes. They became uncomfortable, and one commented: 'Why do you want to do that? They will not do the work. Even if they did, they would use the degree to work their way out of Khayelitsha.' Jean's response was, 'So what? What they do with their lives is their responsibility, not mine. It is our responsibility, as members of a university, to create opportunities for everyone who wishes to study and achieve.' The conversation stopped soon afterwards, and the topic of Jean's possible teaching was never again mentioned.

Jean continued with her plans and worked with those colleagues in her home university who supported the idea, and managed to get the masters programme established. There also she met with mixed reactions. Most colleagues were wholly supportive, and many members of staff covenanted money from their monthly salaries to pay for the South African teachers' course fees. Others, however, were not in favour and many obstacles were put in the way. Stories about these events appear variously in Jean's writings, available at http://www.jeanmcniff.com/writing.asp. You can also see Jean speaking about the project at http://www.youtube.com/watch?v=jsbelPVpUC8m where she pays tribute to Professor Pat Wade for her unflagging support of the project.

2 Evaluating your own work

If you want to be seen as sufficiently capable and competent to evaluate your own work (which you are), you have to fulfil certain conditions. Here is a summary of the conditions.

Explaining how you see your work as a rigorous research process, and what this implies

Let us recap. Research is a matter of identifying an issue of practice, formulating a research question, and then systematically engaging with that question by generating evidence from the data to ground your eventual claim to knowledge (see page 155). The question for most action researchers is, 'How do I improve my practice?'

Your claim will be that you have improved a specific area of your work with others, and you can articulate the significance of what you have learned from the research. These are your findings. You can explain how this area can inform other areas of your work, and how others can learn from what you are doing. You show how your work has improved through learning from your research, and you explain how other people's learning can be improved by accessing it. Be clear, however, that things seldom go according to plan and we sometimes make mistakes, so be honest when evaluating to say if things did not improve. But this would not stop you from producing a good quality action research report that shows how you have learnt from your mistakes.

Explaining that you are offering both descriptions of practice and also explanations for practice, and what this implies

Your accounts contain both descriptions of what you did, and also explanations for why you did it and what you hoped to achieve. This means articulating the values that inspired your work, and how you are hoping to realize those values in your practice. It also means engaging in some discussion around why you have identified those values and not others. It may involve explaining how your personal or work contexts promote or deny the realization of your values, and what you have done to celebrate or compensate.

Linking these ideas to the ontological values base of your work and what this implies in terms of your epistemological standards of judgement and their transformation into mentoring practices

- Think about the relationship between your different kinds of values.
- Your ontological values are what give your life meaning and purpose. These values are embodied: you live them through your being in the physical world. These transform into ...
- Your epistemological standards of judgement: these are the critical judgements you use to test the validity of a claim to knowledge. As you conduct your action enquiry, your embodied values become clear as they emerge through your enquiry: if you believe in justice, your embodied value of justice emerges into reality through the way you act. Your invisible embodied values become live, so now transform into your living epistemological standards of judgement. So when you say, 'I believe in justice, and I am trying to live in a way that is just,' you explain how you use justice as a standard by which you can judge your actions. Action researchers try to live their embodied values as fully as they can.
- You now transform your values and commitments into mentoring practices that show how you value the capacity of all to think for themselves, and how you ask critical questions to promote and sustain your own and others' critical thinking. You do not supply answers, but demand that people come up with their own answers, and are able to justify them. You also show how you test your own ideas against those of others, to ensure that you are not complacent or trying to justify your own prejudices.

Validating your claims to knowledge through the production of authenticated evidence: relating these to identified criteria and standards of judgement

You make clear how you have monitored practice, gathered data and generated evidence from the data. You relate your evidence to specific criteria, and use standards of judgement related to your values: for example, if your values include ideas about freedom and participation, you show how your evidence contains instances of practice where you encourage freedom and participation. You need to produce this evidence, and state why it should be seen as evidence and not simply illustration. This means articulating the standards you use, and saying why you are using these standards and not others.

Testing the validity of your claims by making them and your evidence archive available to public scrutiny

Producing authenticated evidence is still not enough to have your claims pronounced valid. You also have to subject your claims and their evidence base to the public scrutiny of others, such as your critical friends and your validation group. If these people say your claims are justified, you can proceed reasonably confidently to put your claims into the public domain for further testing (but see also next paragraph).

Being open to requests to modify claims if they are shown to be wanting by justified critique, or standing firm if the critique itself appears to be unjustified

Say that you know your claims are always provisional, and open to further testing, critique and modification. Do not present your claim as a final answer. It is always a temporary position, your present best thinking, that will probably change in light of further reflection, evaluation and feedback. In traditional scholarships, uncertainty tended to be taken as a sign of weakness. In new scholarships, it is a sign of strength, a statement that you are always open to learning and modification of your own ideas. Traditional scholarships aim for certainty and closure. New scholarships aim for creativity and transformation.

What happens if people's feedback tells you to rethink your position, when you believe your position is justified? In this case you go back and check. Check everything: the accuracy of your data; that you have produced authenticated evidence to support your claims to know; that you have tested your own stance. Are you reinforcing a prejudice? Is your thinking clear? If you feel that your position is justified, go ahead in spite of the feedback, but be aware of the critique, and take it as an indication that you need to be even more rigorous about demonstrating the validity of your position. Remember that in democratic evaluation it is possible for the majority to be mistaken, so be undaunted, but be cautious.

Self-evaluation is not a simple option. It is not a question only of reflecting on what you have done in practice and writing a report. It is an extremely rigorous and scholarly process. However, although it appears rather intimidating from what is written here, it is actually straightforward and achievable.

The potential rewards are high. By producing your own self-evaluation report you are contributing to a public body of knowledge on evaluation practices, and reinforcing the legitimacy of practitioners as capable and competent. Your hard work sets important precedents. The stronger the evidence base, the easier it will be for others to achieve what you have done, and public perceptions will be strengthened about the rightness of practitioners judging their own work.

Over the first year of the Masters programme in Khayelitsha, however, most of the teachers themselves worked against Jean: they were hostile to her personally, or did not want to study; and she often felt like giving up. She stayed with it, however, and, with hard work and goodwill,

---

relationships and attitudes changed. In 2009 ten teachers were awarded their masters degrees. This event fully vindicates and validates the original intent of creating opportunities for all practitioners. It also justifies the values base of the programme: Jean's sense of moral outrage that practitioners are denied access, which transformed, in this case, into a sense of validation that the original values of social and epistemological justice had been fulfilled. Today a strong evidence archive exists that shows the realisation of these values and the validity of Jean's claims that she has created opportunities for people and set important precedents in South Africa: see http://www.jeanmcniff.com/items.asp?id=1 and http://www.jeanmcniff.com/items.asp?id=16, and McNiff 2011b. See also the presentation of Jean's keynote address at the Nelson Mandela Metropolitan University, August 2010, available at http://www.jeanmcniff.com/items.asp?id=93).

During the writing of this book, Jean negotiated to supervise the first of the group of teachers for his doctorate from the University of Pretoria.

Summary

This chapter has set out the need for you to evaluate your own work. Self-evaluation raises political questions about who does evaluation, what is evaluated and how. Evaluating your own work is a rigorous process that involves the testing of any claims that you put into the public domain.

Now, in the next part, we deal with the practicalities of doing action research.

Further reading

Coghlan, D. (2001) 'Insider action research projects. Implications for practising managers', *Management Learning*, 21 (1): 49–60.
Another paper that engages with the problematics of assessing quality in action research.

Feldman, A. (2003) 'Validity and quality in self-study', *Educational Researcher*, 32 (3): 26–8.
Allan Feldman is one of a group of researchers to engage with issues of evaluating with integrity in self-study action research.

Denzin, N.K. and Lincoln, Y.S. (2000) 'Introduction: the discipline and practice of qualitative research', in N.K. Denzin and Y.S. Lincoln (eds) *Handbook of Qualitative Research* (second edition). London: Sage.
The Introduction to this book outlines some of the key issues in the field.

Lomax, P. (1994) 'Standards, criteria and the problematic of action research within an award bearing course', *Educational Action Research*, 1 (March): 113–26.
Pam Lomax was one of the first to support a living theory approach. Here is her take on some of the problematics of assessing quality in action research within an institutional context.

Scaife, J. (2004) 'Reliability, validity and credibility', in C. Opie (ed.) *Doing Educational Research: A Guide to First-time Researchers*. London: Sage. Chapter 4.
Not written from an action research perspective, this chapter is nevertheless a good guide to some of the issues involved in evaluating educational research.

PART III

How Do I Find Out?

This part considers the practicalities of doing action research. It contains the following chapters.

The chapters contain practical advice about how you can set about doing action research. They are meant not as definitive guides but as useful ideas that can get you started. At all times, you are encouraged to develop your own ways of doing things.

At this point in your enquiry into how and why to do action research you are asking, 'How do I address my concern?' In asking, 'How do I find out?' you signal your intent to take action by learning, and to use the learning to inform your practice.

NINE

Action Planning: Planning and Designing Your Action Research

Before launching into your research, draw up an action plan. This chapter offers advice on how to do this. You can easily adapt the advice to many other areas of your work. Chapter 12 extends the ideas into implementing your action plan.

This chapter is in five sections.

1 What does action planning involve?
2 Feasibility planning
3 Ethical issues
4 Drawing up your action plans
5 Examples of action plans

1   What does action planning involve?

Action planning involves planning and designing your action research. It acts as a plan to guide you through the process of engaging with the question, 'How do I improve what I am doing?' (Whitehead, 1989). You also explain why it is an important question, and why you should engage with it. Do not regard your initial plan as fixed: life seldom goes according to plan, so be prepared for the unexpected. Regard your action plan as a set of prompts rather than a fixed sequence of steps. Also remember that the word 'improve' does not mean something is wrong. It means that you want to evaluate your work at all points and check that it is up to standard. Any improvement is improvement, no matter how small.

The question 'How do I improve what I am doing?' often arises from a situation in which you experience yourself as a living contradiction; when your values are denied in your practice (Whitehead, 1989). As a clinical manager or educational leader, for example, you say you believe in democratic management and leadership but then find yourself behaving autocratically towards a particular colleague. As a parent you want to allow your children freedom of choice yet lay down the law about what kind of friends they can have. How do you resolve the tension? Should you try to do so? How do you justify your decisions?

Whitehead (1989, 2003) expresses these ideas as follows:

- I experience a concern when some of my educational values are denied in my practice.
- I imagine a solution to the concern.
- I act in the direction of the imagined solution.
- I evaluate the outcome of the solution.
- I modify my practice, plans and ideas in the light of the evaluation.

However, although the experience of yourself as a living contradiction may be a useful starting point for your action enquiry, you may also want to celebrate an existing situation. Whatever your starting point, you can develop an understanding of what action research involves as follows:

- We review our current practice,
- identify an aspect that we want to investigate,
- imagine a way forward,
- try it out, and
- take stock of what happens.
- We modify what we are doing in the light of what we have found, and continue working in this new way (try another option if the new way is not right),
- monitor what we do,
- review and evaluate the modified action,
- evaluate the validity of the claim(s) to knowledge, and
- develop new practices in light of the evaluation. (See also McNiff, 2010a; McNiff and Whitehead, 2010)

You can then transform these points into a series of questions that can act as your action plan.

- What is my concern?
- Why am I concerned?
- What kinds of data can I gather to show why I am concerned?
- What can I do about it? What will I do about it?
- What kinds of data will I gather to show the situation as it unfolds?
- How will I test the validity of my claim(s) to knowledge?
- How will I ensure that any conclusions I reach are reasonably fair and accurate?
- How will I modify my concerns, ideas and practice in light of my evaluation?

This is a generic action plan that can be modified to suit your own circumstances.

The dual nature of action research

In McNiff and Whitehead (2005), we introduced the idea that claims to knowledge constitute accounts of learning. This idea is now fully articulated as follows.
Action research involves two interrelated processes.

- You take action in the social world 'out there', by doing things differently in relation to the people you are working with.
- You think about what you are doing as you carry out the actions, and reflect on what you are learning. You learn *about* the action *through* the action.

The two sets of 'out there' and 'in here' actions go on during action research, and are both intertwined and of equal importance.

Most of the action research literature focuses more on social action 'out there' than on the learning 'in here', especially in terms of how learning arises from the action and feeds back into the action. The best action enquiries show the interrelated nature of learning and social action, and how one interrelates with the other.

2 Feasibility planning

Before embarking on your action research, think about whether it is actually feasible. This involves thinking about:

- possible opportunities and constraints; and
- what resources you may need.

Possible opportunities and constraints

Think about the following in relation to the questions in your action plan.

What is my concern?

In relation to your identified concern ask yourself about whether you can realistically do anything about it, and whether you will you be allowed to. What would happen if, say, you wanted to investigate how you could improve relationships among different religious groupings in your workplace or encourage greater staff participation in decision making? You would probably have to establish whether your workplace already encouraged good relationships, or experienced structural prejudice. Also be careful about upsetting some managers, who may try to block your enquiry. Will you be able to cope with the fallout? You cannot change wider systems immediately. What do you do?

What you do is keep the project small and manageable and focused on your own practice and learning. Do not worry about large organizational issues; rather focus on your relationships with only one or two persons. Keeping it small gives you a greater chance of having some influence, and also showing how organizational change works.

Why am I concerned?

Think about why your issue is a concern. Perhaps you are not living your values in practice, or are doing something contrary to what you believe in. Can you put it right, or would the cost be too high? Check this out by setting up a role-play and inviting someone to play you; or videotape yourself in action and see yourself as others see you. These and similar are risky strategies, and can be destabilizing, so be careful. They can however help you to see where you need to take action.

More often, however, institutional practices are the obstruction, when they engage with the rhetoric of participation but do their best to prevent participation. Take care if you decide to intervene: sad stories are told about whistle-blowers and broken lives (Alford, 2001). If there are dangers, focus on your own self-study, which no one can prevent you from doing.

What kinds of data will I gather to show why I am concerned?

You need to gather data and generate evidence from it to support (or refute) a claim that you have learned something new. This means observing yourself in relation with other people. Will you have access to the people you need and negotiate their help in your enquiry?

What can I do about it? What will I do about it?

Asking these questions means looking at your options and then deciding to take action. Check whether you need someone's approval, or have to go through a permissions process. Will you meet with opposition? Geoff Suderman's classroom research was blocked by a university's ethics committee, an experience that has been shared by others. He found other ways through without compromising the original research intent, and studied his own learning in the process of getting ethical approval (Suderman-Gladwell, 2001).

Also consider whether you will have the stamina, time and resources needed, and the support of family and friends. What will you give up in order to find time for your research? Will you maintain your moral convictions when you have to miss the match on Saturday to go to a validation meeting?

What kinds of data will I gather to show the situation as it unfolds?

This means gathering more data to show how people are learning in response to your influence. Think whether you will be able to gather data on this ongoing basis, and have enough time and equipment. Sometimes people think that you are researching them instead of yourself – how will you cope with this? Key participants leave, or withdraw from the research, parents refuse to sign permissions slips and managers want evidence of progress. Sometimes principals want you to show how your research is changing students' attitudes and behaviours, which is often impossible. You will need to persuade them that learning can take time, and not to expect concrete results too soon, if at all.

How will I test the validity of my claim(s) to knowledge?

How will you test the validity of your claim that you are influencing someone's learning? You can influence your own learning by deciding to question and change your own assumptions. You can influence the learning of others you work with, and you can influence the learning of social formations, groups of people who share the same practices. How will you gather data and generate evidence about these things?

How will I ensure that my conclusions are reasonably fair and accurate?

You will need to find critical friends and convene a dedicated validation group who are prepared to offer you constructive critique about your evidence and claims to knowledge. Will you find a group, and will they be willing to meet with you regularly? Organizing meetings takes enormous amounts of time and energy. Are you up for it? How will you deal with any adverse critique? Will you have the courage to rethink your position and challenge your own prejudices in light of their feedback?

How will I modify my concerns, ideas and practice in the light of my evaluations?

Be prepared to be open to new learning according to what the data reveal. Sometimes data show us disconfirming data, things we would rather not see, which will mean changing practices.

So far – the perils and pitfalls of action research. However, while you need to be aware of potential difficulties, do not be deterred. Your new insights are essential to helping others learn. You develop those insights by studying your practice and improving your capacity to learn.

Thinking about resources

Resources can be understood as time, equipment and people.

Time

Doing your project will take time. Some organizations, such as higher education and business, encourage practitioners to do action research and make time for it within the working day, and some, but not all, allocate research time. Doing your project will probably take more time than you are granted in reading and reflecting, meeting with people to negotiate access, gathering data, testing the validity of the evidence, producing progress reports and writing the final report. Putting your research into your life means taking something out. Do you need to negotiate this with family, friends and colleagues? What is negotiable in your life and what is non-negotiable? Remember, however, that it will be most worthwhile. Sometimes people become obsessed with their research, but try to avoid this. Time out for recreation and relaxation is essential, and you must prioritize family and friends. Whatever you decide, be prepared to dip into your private time, and do not complain later.

Equipment

Equipment means money, so check beforehand whether you can use your organization's equipment or must buy it yourself. What data gathering equipment will you need: stationery, camera, video? You will definitely need a computer. Will you use the organization's, or your own? What about reprographics and photocopying? Draw up a list of what you may need and check availability in advance. Also remember that you can access online resources, and many research journals are available electronically. A search on the Internet for the topic of your enquiry is a good way to see what others are thinking about it.

You will need four or five key books, perhaps more, depending on how deeply you want to develop the scholarly aspects of your work. Be prepared to buy these yourself, unless your organization has a policy of supporting professional learning. Suggest to a manager to develop a staff library – or develop one yourself, if you are the one with the money – to include subscriptions to journals such as *Educational Action Research* and *Reflective Practice*.

People

Although the focus of your research is you as you investigate your individual 'I', you are never alone. You are always in company with others who are also studying their individual 'I's'.

The people you need to involve are participants, critical friends and validators, and interested observers.

Participants – Remember that your research participants have the same status in your research as you. They are not objects to be investigated, or somehow subordinate: they are equals. Your research is about studying you, not them, to see if you are influencing their learning and your own, so check how they are responding to you as you interact with them. You ask, 'What am I learning with and from you? What are you learning with and from me?' Your participants mirror yourself back.

Critical friends and *validators* – The aim of your research is to make a claim to knowledge, specifically, that you have learned how to improve practice. This claim has to be justified, otherwise it could be seen as your opinion. If you say, 'I have influenced the quality of relationships in my business', you need to produce evidence to show that this really is the case and you are not making it up. This public testing is especially important in educational action research, where claims to knowledge are grounded in subjective experience. Aim to submit your data and findings to rigorous critique at all stages.

One way to do this is to ask critical friends to give you feedback on your data and ideas. These persons can include other colleagues, parents, clients, students or anyone else who is going to give you a sympathetic but critical hearing. You may have one or several critical friends, depending on your needs.

Validation groups – You will also form a validation group for the duration of your project. This group will number about 3–10, depending on your circumstances. Their job is to meet at crucial stages of your project, especially at the reporting stage, to scrutinize your evidence and listen to your claims to knowledge. They will agree or not whether your claims and evidence are coherent and believable. You should be prepared for people to raise questions about taken for granted aspects, which means going back and thinking again.

Validation groups meet with you of their own free will, so never abuse their commitment. Thank them properly, and acknowledge them in your report.

Interested observers – These are people who are interested in your work, but not directly involved, such as your manager or the parents of students who are your research participants. Treat them with consideration. Again, they do not have to put their time and energy into your research, so thank them properly and let them know they are valued.

3   Thinking about ethical issues

Involving other people in research demands ethical awareness. In the current climate of sensitivity to abuse, this is not just of a matter of courtesy but also of the law. Involving children and vulnerable people requires special attention. If you involve them in your research without prior permission or clearance, it could cost you dearly.

Ethical considerations involve three aspects:

- negotiating and securing access;
- protecting your participants;
- assuring good faith.

Negotiating and securing access

You must negotiate and get formal permission, in writing, to do your research before you begin. Organize letters for all participants. For those persons who cannot read, still give them a letter and read it through with them. In the case of children or vulnerable people, seek and get permission from parents or legal caregivers, as well as from the child or vulnerable person themselves. Keep letters requesting and granting permission for reference. Place a copy of letters to participants as an appendix in your report, and have your original letters available if readers want to see them. This is a matter of sensible negotiation in research projects that deal with sensitive issues, where you may decide on limited disclosure. To repeat, this is not just about courtesy but about avoiding potential litigation.

An example of a letter requesting permission is on page 97. You can modify this for your own purposes.

Protecting your participants

Do not name or otherwise identify your participants, unless they wish to be identified. Many participants in action enquiries wish to be named and often to contribute their own accounts of their learning. When participants do not wish to be identified, give them numbers or initials such as 'Student 3' or 'Colleague M'. This is important when using video data, when people are easily identifiable. Difficulties can be avoided by being open about what you are doing from the start, and seeking and obtaining permission. You should also be clear throughout that you are researching your own practice and not theirs. Also be careful about naming your location. Check with your manager or principal about this. Often people are only too glad to be identified and to celebrate their work. In this case, go ahead and identify them, but make sure you have their written permission before you do.

Assure your participants that you will put their interests first, and will maintain confidentiality at all times for those who wish it. Never break this promise. It could be expensive if you do. Also promise that participants may withdraw from the research at any time and that you will destroy all data about them.

Let your participants know you are to be trusted. Draw up and give an ethics statement to every person involved. Include a tear-off slip for their signature to show they have received it, and keep these carefully (see the example on pages 97 and 98).

Assuring good faith

Always do what you say you are going to do. This means maintaining good faith at all times. Create a reputation for integrity, and protect it. People are more willing to work with someone they trust.

Having observed all ethical aspects, you can now exercise your duty to yourself, and go ahead and do your project. Ensure that you protect and exercise your own academic freedom, to speak from your perspective as a person claiming originality of mind and telling your truth with universal intent (Polanyi, 1958). Your work is important, and you have a duty of care to others to publish your findings so they can learn with you and from you, with the intent that they should do the same for others.

A letter requesting permission

Your institutional address
Date
Name of recipient
Address of recipient

Dear [Name]

I am hoping to undertake an action research study into how I can improve lines of communication in my department. I would be grateful if you would grant permission for my research to proceed.

Two copies of this letter are enclosed. Please sign and date both. Keep one copy for your files and return one copy to me.

With thanks.

Your name .... Date ....
....
....

I hereby give permission for [your name] to undertake her/his research in [name of organization].

Signed .... Date ....

An ethics statement

To whom it may concern (or Dear colleague, or Dear [Name])

I am undertaking an action enquiry into how I can improve lines of communication in the department, and am asking you to be a participant in my research.

I will give priority to your interests at all times. I promise the following.

Your identity will be protected at all times unless you give me specific permission to name you.

You are free at all times to withdraw from the research, whereupon I will destroy all data relating to you.

I will check all data relating to you before I make it public.

I will make a copy of my research report available to you prior to its publication.

Two copies of this statement are enclosed. Please sign and date both. Keep one copy for your files and return one copy to me.

Your name .... Date ....

I have received an ethics statement from [your name].

Signed .... Date ....

---

4   Drawing up your action plans

Here are some ideas about how you can draw up your own action plans. It can be helpful to write ideas down in note form, so here are some ideas about how to do so. You can use columns, straight text, spider diagrams, and pictures and cartoons. You can also produce computer-generated visuals. After each set of ideas here, do a similar task for yourself and draw up your own worksheets. Remember that your action plan is not a fixed schedule, but a guide to your thinking and action. Any action plan you draw up is notional only, and subject to change at all times. Be as creative and original as you wish.

Here is the action plan in detail.

What is my concern?

Identify what you want to research, keeping your issue small, focused and manageable. For example, you may want to find ways of managing your time more successfully, how to improve the quality of your educational leadership or how to encourage good staff relations.

Turn your research issue into an action research question, beginning with 'How do I ...?'

Research issue

- Improving my time management.
- Improving the quality of my educational leadership.
- Encouraging good staff relations.

'How do I ...?' action research questions

- How do I manage my time better?
- How do I improve the quality of my educational leadership?
- How do I encourage good staff relations?

Task

Write down your research issue and turn it into a research question. This is especially helpful for letting you see the immediate transformation of an issue into a question. Your eventual claim to knowledge is directly linked with your research issue and your research question. You ask, 'How do I manage my time better?' and you claim, 'I have learned how to manage my time better'. Your data and evidence show the processes involved in moving from question to claim.

Why am I concerned?

Say why this is an issue for you. Perhaps it is simply bothering you, or has implications for your work. Perhaps it is something related to your values, but you are not realizing them. Write down what value underpins your practice, and say whether you are or are not living towards it. Give some examples of situations to show whether or not this is the case. For example:

Table 9.1

Value	Participation
Am I living towards it?	Yes
How can I see that?	Everyone participates in meetings
Value	Freedom
Am I living towards it?	No
How can I see that?	People are not able to express what they think in meetings
Value	Empathy
Am I living towards it?	No
How can I see that?	People do not relate well to one another

Or you could write:

Value	**Am I living towards it?**	**How?**	**How not?**
Participation	Yes	Everyone participates in meetings	

Task

Write down the key value in your situation, say whether or not you are living towards it, and how this can be seen.

What kinds of experience can I describe to show why I am concerned?

How will you gather data and generate evidence to show the situation as it is? On page 150 we explain the differences between data and evidence. Briefly, 'data' refs to all the information you gather about a particular issue. 'Evidence' are those special pieces of data that show the issue in action. Evidence is therefore embedded in artefacts such as books, emails, memos, transcripts, computer files, videos, pictures, text messages and so on. Imagine where you could find evidence, that is, in what sources of data you would find instances of what you are looking for. In your notes, write down the value at the heart of your research, and then think about where you would look to find it being shown in action.

For example, if you were looking for the exercise of kindness, think where you might find it in action. You could write:

Table 9.2

Kindness	Yes, apparent in a text message from a friend saying she is experiencing understanding from her colleagues following an illness
	No, not apparent in the minutes of a staff meeting when one colleague asks when Ms X is going to resume normal duties
Good relationships	Yes, apparent in a photograph of colleagues laughing together at a party
	No, not apparent in an email to all staff sending New Year good wishes from the manager via their secretary
Justice	Yes, apparent in field notes from your conversation with a colleague where they say they have negotiated a good pension plan
	No, not apparent in a memo from a colleague saying he is being bullied.

Or write it like this if it is easier.

Value

Kindness: is kindness evident in your situation?

Artefact/source of data

Letter from friend saying she is experiencing understanding from colleagues following an illness.

Minutes from staff meeting asking when Ms X will resume normal duties.

Task

Using whatever kind of notes suits you, write down the value that is (or is not) being shown in practice; what kind of evidence you could find to show the situation as it is; and which artefacts you could look at for data that show the value in action. If the value is not evident in action, you could say that the value is being denied.

What can I do about it?

Think about what you could do to improve the situation. You are not going to force a decision on anyone. You are going to try to exercise your influence so that they will re-think and perhaps do things differently. In your notes, write down what you might do. For example you might write the following.

Issue 1

My concern

My colleague has written me a letter saying that she is not experiencing understanding from others following her illness. This denies my values of care and compassion. What can I do?

My options

I can do the following:

- Explain her situation to management and encourage their understanding.
- Encourage her to approach peers and senior colleagues and explain her position.
- Tell her to buck up.
- Encourage peers to be more understanding.

Issue 2

My concern

I see a photograph of colleagues laughing together at a party. I wonder what I can do to maintain good relationships.

My options

I could:

- actively think about ways of maintaining staff relationships;
- produce reports to say why staff relationships are so good;
- organize a small social committee.

Issue 3

My concern

I receive a memo from a colleague saying he is being bullied. This causes me deep concern and denies my values of justice and kindness.

My options

I could:

- talk with my colleague and find out more;
- encourage him to stand up for himself;
- arrange a meeting between him and the bullies with me as mediator to talk it through.

Task

In your own way – making notes or drawing a graphic – write down how you might deal with the situation.

What will I do about it?

Now think of a possible way forward. Choose one option only and follow it through. Keep track of what happens. If it seems to be working, continue. If it is not working, try another option. Using the same examples as above, you could write:

Issue 1

Chosen option

I will encourage peers to be more understanding of M.

Follow-up plan

I will speak with individuals and small groups, suggesting how they can be more supportive of M, and arrange for someone to sit with her at coffee breaks. I will arrange for the office to send her a bouquet and a good wishes card.

Issue 2

Chosen option

I will find ways of encouraging staff to maintain their good relationships.

Follow-up plan

I will invite three members of staff to form a social events committee. I will find some money to pay for a group dinner. I will initiate a task group on how to maintain good relationships.

Issue 3

Chosen option

I will encourage my colleague to stand up for himself.

Follow-up plan

I will invite him to imagine what he can do for himself. I will urge him to have confidence. I will role-play a situation with him to let him imagine other options.

Task

Using a framework like this, map out a possible course of action.

What kinds of data will I gather to show the situation as it unfolds?

How will you influence other people's learning? Will they come to think and act differently? What do you think will happen?

You are now into your second round of data gathering. What kinds of data will you gather to show the evidence of your influence in other people's thinking and action? Will you use the same data gathering techniques as before, or different ones? What kind of artefacts, such as journals, emails and memos, will you expect to find the data in? Here are some ideas.

Table 9.3

Artefact/data source	Evidence of my influence
e-mail	E-mail from a colleague saying you have helped them to rethink their position and act differently
Photograph	Photograph of colleagues enjoying a joke together, when before they wouldn't speak. Note on the back of the photograph saying thank you for bringing them together
Examinations result	Results of so-called 'learning disabled' student you especially encouraged and who has now passed an exam.
	Letter from student saying it was because of your influence that they passed

Task

Say where to find evidence to show your influence. Your sources may be the same as or different from your previous set of data gathering.

How will I test the validity of my claim(s) to knowledge?

How do you make judgements about your influence, and whether you are achieving what you hoped to achieve? Write down the original value that inspired your work, and say whether you feel you are living towards it, at least in some instances. Where could you find examples of this realization of your value?

For example:

My value	Fairness
Where would I look for evidence?	I would look in assignments I have returned to my students. My comments to them would probably show me offering fair critique. My comments would be written in pencil, which is less violent than traditional red pen
My value	Freedom
Where would I look for evidence?	I would look at the minutes of staff meetings, and search for instances that show me encouraging others to speak their minds, and to challenge my own ideas

My value	Inclusiveness
Where would I look for evidence?	I would look in the records of the peace talks to find instances of me honouring others' rights to live according to their own traditions

Task

Write down your value and what kind of evidence you would aim to produce to show you living in the direction of your value.

How will I ensure that any conclusions I reach are reasonably fair and accurate?

How will you ensure that people will see your claim as unprejudiced, authentic and not simply your opinion or wishful thinking? Throughout, aim to involve critical friends and validation groups to endorse, or refute, your claims to knowledge by scrutinizing your evidence and agreeing, or not, that your case will withstand rigorous critique. Make sure you are confident about the differences between data and evidence, and between criteria and standards of judgement (Chapter 14). Write down what you are hoping to claim and what you hope your validation group will see as your evidence. For example:

Table 9.4

My anticipated claim	What I hope my validation group will see
I hope to claim that I have improved the smooth running of my firm	I hope they will see my well-kept records and strategic action plans. I hope they will see an improvement of productivity and income this year
I hope to claim that I have encouraged students to be more responsive	I hope they will see videos of my students taking an active part in lessons. I hope they will see students taking a teaching role
I hope to claim that I have exercised my academic leadership	I hope they will see more faculty enrolling for academic study. I hope they will see a greater publications output

Task

Write down what you are hoping to claim through your research, and what kind of evidence will help your validation group and critical friends to make judgements about what you have done.

How will I modify my concerns, ideas and practice in light of my evaluations?

What do you think you may do differently in light of what you will learn? You cannot plan for this at this stage because you will not know until you get there.

However, the fact that you are prepared to ask these kinds of critical questions is an indication that you are determined not to take no for an answer, and keep raising new problematics to ensure that your value of non-complacent participation is always held as a guiding principle to action.

5 Drawing up your own action plans

Now, draw up some action plans of your own. You may stay with the notional action plan above or modify it for your purposes. The following boxes present some examples.

Box 9.1

How do I encourage greater environmental awareness among staff in a turbine manufacturing unit?

My context: What is my concern?

I am the newly appointed director of a small turbine manufacturing unit, which so far has been run in a fairly autocratic way. I believe that sustainable organisational growth comes from participative working towards democratically negotiated goals. I am also aware of the pressure on industry for greater environmental awareness, which happens to be a passion of mine too. I was appointed partly on the basis that I could exercise my influence to encourage a culture of environmental awareness, but this would mean first encouraging new attitudes and practices towards new organisational practices. So my project becomes twofold: (1) encouraging democratic participation in order to (2) encourage more environmentally-friendly practices. How do I do this?

Why am I concerned?

I am concerned because I hold values around democratic ways of working that expect all to participate in decision-making processes. I believe that all colleagues are able to speak for themselves, but they do not do so because of the previous regime's norms. The situation denies my values of social justice and the exercise of individual accountability. I also want to encourage greater participation to develop imaginative recycling initiatives for the reduction of emissions in new products, but I cannot hope for this when the staff do not feel engaged so may not commit to my proposals.

What kinds of data do I gather to show the situation as it is?

I will gather data to show the realities of a non-participating staff and the possible influence on the business culture. I would like to videotape a whole staff meeting but

(Continued)

---

this would possibly be too threatening at this stage of my enquiry. I can instead interview some key members of staff, such as heads of department, and two junior members of staff. I can also interview four or five trainees. This means that I need to draw up my ethics statements, and my letters requesting permission to do my research, which need to be given to those I would like to invite as research participants. I also need to explain my plan at the next staff meeting, and to the board of management, and get permission. I need to reassure people that I am investigating how we develop our work together, and not necessarily inspecting theirs.

What can I do?

As noted, I could ask some key members of staff if they will act as my research participants. I could invite other senior management colleagues to act as critical friends throughout. I could conduct short interviews with the identified members of staff to check whether they share my educational goals of maximum participation for improving environmental awareness. Should I involve administrative staff at this stage too?

What will I do?

I will do all the above but I will not invite administrative staff yet. First I have to encourage greater confidence in participation from staff on the shop floor. Over time I hope to build stronger relationships between the manufacturing staff and the administrative staff. I will also share the data I gather with my senior management critical colleagues, and invite their feedback on whether I am achieving my goals of encouraging staff or simply putting pressure on them.

How will I gather data to show the situation as it unfolds?

I will continue to gather data with my research participants. I will especially ask them if they feel more involved, and whether there is an atmosphere of more positive attitudes and openness to ideas about environmental awareness. I will invite them to develop with me a new approach to staff meetings that will involve greater participation, and ask them to think about how these may be discussed with the full staff. These reports, and the minutes of staff meetings, will stand as important data. We will also need to work out strategies for checking how well we are doing in developing new recycling practices, and try to establish a relationship between more democratic working practices and the greening of our organization.

How will I evaluate my potential influence?

I will outline the standards of judgement I will use to judge whether or not I can claim to be realizing my goals in my practice. These goals can be understood in terms of my values of social justice and personal environmental accountability. Do these values come to life in my own and others' practices? Are people participating more? Are they beginning to show awareness of the need for green practices? Can I show how my values act as my living standards of practice and judgement?

How will I ensure that any conclusions I reach are reasonably fair and accurate?

I will invite my senior management critical colleagues to meet with me and look at the initial and subsequent data. This will help me establish whether the initial data show a situation in which there was (1) minimal participation by the staff, to a situation where there is more participation; and (2) minimal consideration for recycling to a situation where we have a full recycling programme in operation. We probably still have a long way to go, but even the smallest amount of improvement is still improvement. I will ask them whether I am justified in claiming that people are listening to me, or whether these things are simply an outcome of the departure of the old regime. Perhaps they will not be able to say, and we will need more time for things to become clear. I also recognize that this is a sensitive situation, and that we all have to tread with care. I hope they will give me feedback that confirms my intuitions, but you never know.

How will I test the validity of my claim to knowledge?

Doing this will help me to test the validity of my claim to knowledge, which will be to do with whether I am encouraging greater organisational participation in order to encourage more environmentally friendly practices. In presenting my account of learning to my critical friends and validation groups, I will draw their attention to my focus on methodological rigour, including my articulated criteria and standards of judgement, and I will ask them to focus on the explanations I give for my learning as well as my conclusions. I will note carefully what they say in my constant attempts to demonstrate the methodological rigour of my claim to knowledge.

How will I modify my concerns, ideas and practice in the light of my evaluation?

I will develop my action enquiry into a new cycle that focuses on involving the more junior members of staff and helping them to build their confidence to become active participants. My overall plan is to work with people individually and in small groups, and so build up local relationships that may influence the formation of wider relationships. Ultimately I hope our organisation will be seen as committed to democratic working practices and an environmentally-aware unit that contributes to world stability.

Box 9.2

How do I enable visually impaired students to gain easier access to continuing education?

My context

I am a learning support tutor for visually impaired students who wish to access continuing learning opportunities in further education. I want to find ways of helping them gain easier access.

What is my concern?

My concern is that the students I teach, who are all visually impaired, are not getting the opportunities they should to go on to further education. Although legally they have right of access, practically they are disadvantaged in that they don't know systems and find it difficult to negotiate information.

(Continued)

(Continued)

Why am I concerned?

I have strong values around the worth of each individual person, and that no one should be disadvantaged because of physical, mental, or emotional impairment. I do what I can to ensure that all have equal opportunity of access and outcome. I am not sure, however, whether my students are being disadvantaged at a systemic level because of their visual impairment.

What experiences can I describe to show the situation as it is?

I can produce statistical analysis of fully sighted students who do gain access to further education, and compare it with an analysis of the rate of access of visually impaired students. If both sets of statistics appear commensurable, I do not have grounds for concern. However, from conversations with visually impaired students, I know how much of a struggle it is for them to gain access. I can make some tape recordings of their stories to show that there are grounds for concern. I will ask two students to become research participants, so that I can see whether listening to the tapes does help them gain confidence around knowing what to do.

What can I do about it?

I can make greater use of resources that appeal to their fully operational senses, in this case, audiotapes. I aim to make audiotapes of the information they need to gain access to further education, as well as the stories of students who have already successfully enrolled and are pursuing their studies. I am hoping that my current students will gain confidence and inspiration from listening to the stories of successful students. I will give my students my letters asking their permission to be research participants. Because they cannot see well, I will ask a trusted colleague to act on their behalf and sign. I will also conduct audio-taped conversations with them, explaining my request for their permission, and getting their agreement on tape. One copy of the tape stays with them and one with me.

What will I do about it?

I will ask my principal for funding so that I can make these tape recordings. I will contact a local drama group to get speakers with clear speaking voices. I will ask them to read the college prospectus, and explain to listeners what they have to do. I could turn these into audiobooks. I will invite three students in particular to give me regular feedback on how they respond to these initiatives.

How will I gather data to show the situation as it unfolds?

I will gather responses from the three students, and any others who wish to be involved, to see whether they feel they have the information they need, and what further resources may be useful. I will ask them to tape record their experiences as they go for interviews or fill out forms. I will later incorporate these ideas into a handbook for wider college use. I could arrange for the production of the handbook as an audiobook for use by prospective visually-impaired candidates.

How will I evaluate my potential influence in learning?

I will take my values as my living standards of judgement. Are the audiotapes enabling greater ease of access to further education? Have I learned how to counter-balance disadvantage by introducing new systems?

How will I ensure that any conclusions are reasonably fair and accurate?

I will present my provisional findings to critical friends and a small validation group, and I will think carefully and act on their feedback. I will later present my findings to a staff seminar. When I produce the handbook I will create it as a living document which regularly incorporates feedback and good ideas.

How will I evaluate the validity of my claim to knowledge?

I will ask my critical friends and validation groups to focus on the explanations I offer for my learning. I will ask them to comment on whether I explain how I make my own validation processes clear so that readers can see how I am aiming for transparency in my attempt to establish the validity of my account.

How will I modify my concerns, ideas and practice in the light of my evaluation?

Provided the initial feedback is reasonably positive, I will continue to develop audiotapes as resources. Perhaps I will build up a resource bank. I will definitely let people in other colleges know what I am doing, and perhaps write a paper for wider dissemination. It would be helpful if I could liaise with other colleagues in similar situations to find new ideas and test existing strategies.

Summary

This chapter has given practical advice about the feasibility and planning and design of an action enquiry. It has considered what action planning involves, and set out the details of what you need to think about at each point. It has set out different ways in which you may implement an action plan. Examples of action plans have been given to help you see what planning and designing involves and how it can be done.

The next chapter gives advice on how to implement your action plans.

Further reading

Arhar, M.L. and Kasten, W.C. (2008) *Action Research for Teachers: Travelling the Yellow Brick Road* (third edition). Upper Saddle River, NJ: Prentice Hall.
A delightfully accessible and attractively presented text with clear guidelines on how to conduct an action enquiry.

Bell, J. (2005) *Doing Your Research Project: A Guide for First-time Researchers in Education, Health and Social Science* (fourth edition). Maidenhead: Open University Press.
One of the most popular books in educational research, this has a place on your bookshelf.

Davies, M.B. (2007) *Doing a Successful Research Project: Using Qualitative or Quantitative Methods*. Basingstoke: Palgrave Macmillan.
A useful guide to methods in educational research.

Morton-Cooper. A. (2000) *Action Research in Health Care*. Oxford: Blackwell.
A useful guide to methods in action research in health care.

Wilkinson, D. (ed.) (2000) *The Researcher's Toolkit: The Complete Guide to Practitioner Research*. London: RoutledgeFalmer.
Much as the idea of a 'toolkit' is to be treated with reservations, this book nevertheless offers lots of ideas about how to do practice-based research.

TEN

Engaging with the Literatures

Designing and doing your action research project involves engaging with the literatures. This means finding out what other people have already said about any particular areas or contexts you are studying, and its possible relevance to your enquiry. It also means being aware of how to engage with the ideas of others and reference them, and ensure that your work is seen as making its original contribution to those same literatures. The chapter helps you do this. It is organized into three sections, which discuss these questions.

1 Why engage with the literatures?
2 What literatures to engage with?
3 How to engage?

1   Why engage with the literatures?

There are several reasons why you should engage with the literatures:

- To find out what other people have already said about your topic.
- To test your findings against the views of key authors.
- To demonstrate critical engagement in research and scholarship.
- To develop your conceptual frameworks.
- To demonstrate originality of your contributions to knowledge of the field, and their significance.

Finding out what other people have already said about your topic

The aim of your action research is to generate a claim to knowledge about how you have improved your practice in a particular area or context. Remember that making a claim to knowledge does not mean simply stating your opinion about something, but showing that what you are claiming is grounded in validated evidence, and tested against the critical scrutiny of your peers. Your peers will wish to see, therefore, that you have made efforts to find out what other people have said. This means reading as widely as possible about your topic, in a focused manner. This is usually referred to as doing a literature search.

Sati is the manager of a cosmetics retail business, and is presenting her work-based report as part of her modular masters degree in business administration. She wants to introduce new organic lines into her range, so needs to find out how other managers have done so in retail cosmetics as well as other areas. She also wants to try out new adventurous marketing practices, such as displaying her goods at local retail fairs and developing a dedicated website for her products.

Doing a literature search does not mean reading everything ever written about the topic. It means reading as much as you can about relevant issues, within reason. Your peers and other critical readers know what your study programme involves, so will make judgements about the quality of your work accordingly. They would expect to see perhaps 10 references in a work-based report, whereas in a doctoral thesis they would expect 100.

Sati reads as much as she can about current trends in organic cosmetics use and production as well as how to implement innovation in a retail business and judge its effectiveness. She identifies ten key texts about fashion trends in cosmetics and ten in business management for her study module. These form the nexus of her literatures.

Testing your findings against the views of key authors

Your claim is your original claim. No one has made it before. However, other authors have had ideas about it and you need to show familiarity with them. You can also use the ideas of others to justify and support your own claim (but not to reinforce prejudices – see below). You are now demonstrating your capacity for scholarship (focus on existing knowledge in the literatures) as well as research (focus on generating new knowledge).

Sati hopes to show through her module assignment that she has successfully introduced new ranges in organic cosmetics, and has increased sales through her innovative marketing techniques. She draws on the literatures to show that she has learned from other key authors: on contemporary literatures to show that she is up to date, and earlier literatures to show that she appreciates the need for a firm grounding from past experience.

Demonstrating critical engagement in research and scholarship

However, do not use others' ideas to reinforce your own prejudices. The quality of your work, and the report you write, is judged largely in terms of (1) whether you have made a contribution to knowledge of your field and (2) whether you demonstrate critical engagement. Exercising critical engagement means you can agree or critique what you read, and consider whether ideas are justified and believable. You also engage critically with your own thinking and reflect on whether you are justified in taking a particular stance or whether you may be mistaken.

Sati reads about current trends in cosmetics. The latest trend for bright colour-ways appeals to her, but she is not keen on heavily chemical-based products. She feels that women would resist anything that will potentially cause allergic reactions in sensitive skin. To support these views, she draws on the feminist literatures about the power of women's voice and personal identity-formation, as well as health and physical and emotional well-being. However, she recognizes that her views are influenced by her cultural experiences and that they may be inappropriate for other cultures.

Developing your conceptual/theoretical frameworks

Broadly speaking, a concept is an idea, and a theory is an explanation for that idea. A conceptual or theoretical framework is a set of ideas within which you locate your thinking and writing. Examples of conceptual or theoretical frameworks are freedom, gender, colonization, liberation theory and the need for people to speak and act for themselves. These concepts are also values, the same ones that guide your thinking, research and scholarship. As you read you will consider how those values inform the writing of other authors. Your values therefore transform into living frames of reference and you draw on ideas in the literatures to fill them out.

Sati sees that her values of women's voice and identity formation are echoed by writers such as Butler (1999) and Morrison (1999). She locates her writing within these values-based frameworks.

Demonstrating the originality of your contributions to knowledge of the field and its significance

Knowledge can be discovered and also created. Through discovering and engaging with the ideas of others you show how you reconfigure and recreate them as new ideas. You make those reconfigurations your own and make them public, so other people can learn from you and reconfigure your ideas in turn. Thus knowledge is both recycled and also transforms into new forms. Be aware of how you are reconfiguring ideas and how this sparks off new ideas, and the significance of doing this. It means you are contributing to an ever-growing body of knowledge about a particular field. Also, the field will never be bounded, since new people are always contributing to its knowledge base. Knowledge itself, and knowledge creation, are ongoing unbounded transformational processes.

Sati can say that she has made significant contributions to knowledge of the field of women's rights and human well-being, and also to business knowledge. She has demonstrated critical engagement throughout.

---

2   What literatures to engage with?

Your action plan begins with the following questions.

- What is my concern?
- Why am I concerned?

Asking these questions means you identify your research issue and say why it is an issue and needs investigating. In saying why you wish to investigate it further, you outline your research contexts, and each context has accompanying literatures. Here are the most common contexts.

Personal

Tell your reader anything they need to know about you and link it to the literatures. If you are Irish and writing about the changing face of Ireland within the new economy, drawn on literatures such as Kuhling and Keohane (2007). If you are deaf and still wish to take an active role in politics, draw on Jack Ashley's (1994) work.

Professional

Explain what is going on in your professional context. Draw on the literatures of, say, animal welfare, if you are a vet, or issues of environmental enrichment if you are a landscape gardener. Aim to locate your work within a broader context so your reader can see that you are up to date with wider issues.

Policy

Your research may be located within policy debates about your profession. As a member of a university staff anywhere in the world, you will need to know about international debates about the purposes of universities (Nixon, 2008; Rowland, 2000); and as a member of a local council in an underprivileged area you will need to know about new trends in management research (Alvesson and Deetz, 2000).

Methodological

In any kind of research it is important to justify your research methodology. There is a now a vast body of literature on action research, which is often compared with other kinds of research. You should engage with some key texts that will enable you to justify and defend your choice of methodology: for example, Cohen et al. (2007) and Whitehead and McNiff (2006), as well as this book you are reading.

Theoretical

Similarly, you need to show that you are fully conversant with key theoretical approaches in the literatures, and can critique them as appropriate. You may or may not agree with particular approaches to leadership and management, as communicated in Cockerell (2008), but you must show that you are familiar with the debates in order to critique them and justify taking your own stand.

Context-specific

Your reader needs to know anything special about your context. If you work as a swimming instructor, outline the main literatures appropriate to your profession, as well as draw on more philosophical texts such as respect for life or the need for attending to the other's well-being.

Other …

You may need to draw on literatures from other fields. Use your common sense and be guided by the idea that what your reader knows about you is what they read on the page. Give them as much information as you think they may need about what is happening in wider contexts. It is your responsibility to help them understand what you are saying, not their responsibility to fill in the gaps. The more you help them, the more sympathetic they will be to you and your work.

3   How to engage?

You engage with the literatures when you (1) read them and (2) write about them.

When you read the literatures

Here are some ideas about reading. We are using a traditional heuristic device by asking 'Wh–?' questions.

What do you do when you read?

Think about the ideas you are reading. Read with critical appreciation and judgement, and decide for yourself whether you agree or not with what the author is saying. Keep a record of what you read on your computer or on index cards or in a special notebook.

When do you read?

Aim to read about key issues prior to doing your research, but keep at it all the time. Ideas may change, so your reading will change with them. Make time for reading, and do at least a little each day to keep in touch with your thinking. Negotiate with family and friends for time out to read. Reading is an invaluable investment so do not skip it.

Where do you read?

Use every opportunity to read – on the bus, waiting for the kettle to boil. Use library resources to find books and journals. Use your own computer to access websites and Internet forums. Exchange text messages about key books and articles. Set up discussion seminars with critical friends using one of the many online communication fora.

Who do you read?

Everyone has their favourite authors. Find yours, and treat them as good friends. Try communicating with them if they are alive and available, perhaps through email. Write out relevant quotations ('quotations', please, not 'quotes') in your quotations book and use them, but always reference them properly (see below). Also read other authors, including the ones you disagree with. You need them, too, to justify your own opinions (though you may come to see that they were right).

Which works do you read?

Common sense says you read relevant literatures, but anything that takes your interest can be useful for your study. Books on architecture or landscape gardening can be relevant to organizational studies, by explaining how to organize and structure aspects of social living.

How do you read?

Everyone has their own answer to this, and whatever works for you is right. Commonsense advice is to focus on what you are reading so you read actively and with engagement.

Why do you read?

You read for the reasons outlined above, and also, hopefully, for sheer enjoyment. Any source of writing can be worthwhile: newspapers, advertising copy, film and television, social networking: all these sources can be referenced and used in your study. Some of the greatest authors began their careers as part-time writers on the local paper.

When you write

Again, the criteria for judging good writing include demonstration of the capacity to make original contributions to knowledge of the field, which means writing for your context, and critical engagement, which means engaging. This has special relevance for the following.

Writing a literature review

In an action research account, you do not have to write a literature review but you must show that you have reviewed and engaged with the literature. You can write a review if you wish: Bernie Sullivan (2006) wrote a special chapter about Traveller education in Ireland as this was a key topic (see http://www.jeanmcniff.com/items.asp?id=47) and Chris Glavey (2008) wrote a special chapter on forms of leadership (see http://www.jeanmcniff.com/items.asp?id=44). It is a requirement of social science reports that they should contain a chapter or section called 'literature review' but not for action research, where your review runs right through the text.

A review is not a list of books. Too often people write lists of who wrote what, with annotations about the key features of the text. This will not get you any credit. You have to show that you have engaged with what you are reading and give some kind of informed commentary about it.

Name dropping

Similarly, do not drop names – 'Many writers comment on the need for fairness in football refereeing (Beckham, 2010; Cappello, 2007; Ferdinand, 2009).' You should at least summarize the views of the key authors. Michael Bassey (1999) calls such practices 'kingmaking' and 'sandbagging', by which he means that the writer is trying to overwhelm the reader with the brilliance of their knowledge about football but the brilliance is not substantiated. Readers (especially examiners) are experienced and will see through it immediately.

Do not plagiarize – learn to reference properly

Plagiarism is one of the most serious and prominent issues of contemporary academic writing. It is easy to plagiarize without it being seen as plagiarism in legal terms. You take an author's ideas or words and move them around slightly, so it does not count officially as plagiarism. It is, however, still dishonest. Bear in mind that someone may do the same to you one day so do not do it first. Always reference ideas and words you get from other people meticulously. It will be honourable for you, and respectful to them. Besides, plagiarism is illegal, and, for some, including higher education personnel, it can mean dismissal and a ruined career.

Do not make sweeping statements. Do not say what is not the case

Avoid sweeping, unfounded or absolutist statements, such as 'Research shows that ...' or 'It is always the case that ...' You may find that it is not always the case, and unless you back up your 'Research shows that ...' with concrete references to the research in question, people will not take you seriously.

Use 'I'

It would be possible to write hundreds of 'dos' and don'ts' for showing how you engage with the literatures but perhaps the main 'do' is to write in the first person; to use 'I' with conviction and celebrate your capacity to write high quality texts that will withstand the most rigorous critique. Previously, the use of 'I' was avoided; today, in action research and most case study research, the use of 'I' is expected. This is your research, and your original claim to knowledge, so go ahead and celebrate it with honour and panache.

A note on keeping references

Aim to compile a systematic record of references. Whenever you read a book, have your 'References' workbook with you. Keep a record of what you have read. Write it like this:

> Author's family name, initial (date of publication), title. Town of publication, publisher.

This gives you:

> Jones, B. (1996) *Working with Data*. London: Sage.

If you read a particular phrase or sentence that you like, write it down accurately, word for word, and *note the page number*. When you use quotations in your reports, you must give a page reference. Do not ignore this advice. It can take hours to track down a missing page reference, and it is virtually impossible if the book is back in the library. Do not forget to record the page numbers of the chapter in your references if you are quoting from a book or a journal article: for example:

> McNiff, J. (2007) 'My story is my living educational theory', in D.J. Clandinin (ed.) *A Handbook of Narrative Inquiry: Mapping a Methodology*. Thousand Oaks: Sage. 308–29.

Also, when you put a reference to a journal article into your references list, you must record the pages of the article: for example:

Whitehead, J. (1989) 'Creating a living educational theory from questions of the kind, "How do I improve my practice?"', *Cambridge Journal of Education*, 19 (1): 137–52.

It may not be necessary to quote lengthy passages from the literature, but you must show that you have read key authors and know how to reference them. This is part of good quality scholarly practice.

Summary

This chapter has been about engaging with the literatures, when you read them and when you write about them. Advice about how and why to engage has been given, as well as about which literatures to engage with. Showing that you have engaged with the literatures to help you ground your research and develop strong conceptual frameworks is a requirement of higher degree study, and enables you to explain the original nature of your claim to knowledge.

Further reading

Easterby-Smith, M., Thorpe, R. and Jackson, P. (2008) *Management Research* (third edition). London: Sage.
Chapter 3, Doing a Literature Review, is a good chapter for outlining how to engage with the literatures and do a literature review.

Bell, J. (2005) *Doing Your Research Project* (fourth edition). Maidenhead: Open University Press.
See Chapter 4 on reading, referencing and the management of information; and Chapter 5 on literature searching; Chapter 6 on reviewing the literatures. Very useful ideas.

Grix, J. (2004) *The Foundations of Research*. Basingstoke: Palgrave Macmillan.
A useful book that explains different processes involved in carrying out research.

Koshy, V. (2005) *Action Research for Improving Practice*. London: Paul Chapman.
Good sections on reviewing and engaging with the literatures.

ELEVEN

Doing Action Research: Carrying Out Your Action Plan

Now you are ready to begin doing your action research. Here are some ideas about how you can carry out your action plan, in relation both to social action and to learning. The chapter sets out the different questions in your action plan, and offers ideas about each one.

Here is your action plan again. Remember that you can change these questions to suit your own circumstances. It is important, however, that you do ask questions.

1 What is my concern?
2 Why am I concerned?
3 What kinds of data will I gather to show why I am concerned?
4 What can I do about it?
5 What will I do about it?
6 What kind of data will I gather to show the situation as it unfolds?
7 How will I test the validity of my claim(s) to knowledge?
8 How will I ensure that any conclusions I reach are reasonably fair and accurate?
9 How will I modify my concerns, ideas and practice in light of my evaluations?

Now, here is your action plan in action.

1 What is my concern?

Go back to the issue you identified in your action plan, or identify another issue that has arisen in the meantime. Make sure it is something you can do something about. You cannot change the organizational system you work in, but you can change your immediate work situation. You cannot change the policy around inclusion of patients in hospital decision-making practices, but you can include them in your enquiry.

Keep the bigger picture in sight as a goal to be worked towards, and walk backwards to basics and ask what you can do to address the issue in your immediate practice context.

Having identified your research issue, turn it into a 'How do I ...?' action research question. Here are some examples.

Research issue	'How do I ...?' action research question
I need to manage my time better	How do I manage my time better?
I want to negotiate a more productive relationship with colleague M	How do I negotiate a more productive relationship with colleague M?
I want to find ways of supporting my mature students more effectively	How do I support my mature students more effectively?

Your question may change over time, and so may your issue. This happens in action research, because it is a developmental process where nothing stands still. Your question, 'How do I manage my time better?' may transform into 'How do I find protected time for my research?'; and 'How do I support my mature students more effectively?' may transform into 'How do I ensure that my mature students have access to distance learning facilities?' Parlett and Hamilton (1977) describe these kinds of processes as progressive focusing.

Now, relate your issue and your question to a value. Here are some examples.

Table 11.1

Research issue	I need to manage my time better
Research question	How do I manage my time better?
Underpinning value	Integrity in professional practice; responsible practice
Research issue	I want to negotiate a more productive relationship with colleague M
Research question	How do I negotiate a more productive relationship with colleague M?
Underpinning value	Respect as the basis of quality relationships; inclusion and collaboration

You could set this out as follows:

Table 11.2

Research issue	Research question	Values
I need to manage my time better	How do I manage my time better	Integrity in professional practice; responsible practice

Doing this gives you your explanatory framework, which shows the overall scope of your project, its direction and purpose. You can show clearly why you are doing your research and what you hope to achieve, in relation to your values.

Focus on your social action 'out there', and on your learning 'in here'. The best projects show both. An initial focus on learning may also transform into a later focus on action, informed by the learning, and which informs future learning. These two foci may give rise to different action–reflection cycles. Here are some different examples that show this possible transformation.

Example 1

First research cycle, with a focus on learning

Research issue	I want to find ways of ensuring equal access to continuing day care provision for people with dementia, within a system that make access difficult. Am I right in doing this?
Research question	How do I check that I am thinking for myself, and not giving in to bureaucracy?
Value	Integrity of self; shaping one's own identity; honesty

Second research cycle, with a focus on action informed by the learning

Research issue	I want to ensure continuing day care provision for people with dementia. I am concerned that the current system is denying them access.
Research question	How do I ensure access to continuing day care provision for people with dementia?
Value	Personal and social justice; entitlement; democratic forms of living

Example 2

First research cycle, with a focus on learning

Research issue	I want to understand the power relationships in my workplace, so I'd like to learn more about the ideas of Foucault. I am working in a context where power relationships are getting in the way of participative working.
Research question	How do I learn more about the ideas of Foucault?
Underpinning value	Freedom; personal and social integrity; need not to be colonized by dominant discourses

Second research cycle, with a focus on action informed by the learning

Research issue	We need to develop a coherent staff development plan, to encourage new thinking about participative working.
Research question	How do we develop a coherent staff development plan?
Underpinning value	Relational and empathetic ways of working; morally committed and socially oriented planning as the basis for action

Example 3

First research cycle, with a focus on learning

Research issue	Why am I speaking to voters in this way? I want to ensure that I am presenting issues fairly and not communicating my own prejudices as truth.
Research question	How do I evaluate my speech-making and my influence?
Underpinning value	Honesty; personal and social integrity; social justice

Second research cycle, with a focus on action informed by the learning

Research issue	We need to evaluate our political influence.
Research question	How do we evaluate our political influence?
Underpinning value	Personal and social accountability; integrity; truth, justice and honesty

2   Why am I concerned?

Setting out your research issues, questions and underpinning values like this can help you to see your work as attempting to realize your values in your practice. Now think about how your 'How do I ...?' question can transform into the articulation of your research purpose. So when you come to make a claim to knowledge, you can show how you transformed your practice so that you were living out your values, and how you transformed your question into a claim to knowledge.

Remember that practices are informed by values. Actions are not necessarily practices. Smiling or tripping over are actions but not practices. Practices are purposeful, value laden and socially oriented. Aim to show that your practice is more than action: it is praxis, that is, considered, committed and morally oriented.

Write down the values that inspire your work, and show the relationship between your values and other aspects of your research and ultimately your claim to knowledge. You may identify several values. Here are some ideas.

Doing this will help you justify your work by showing how your values came to act both as the living standards that guided your practice and as the living standards by which you made judgements about your work.

Table 11.3

Research issue	Research question	Values	Anticipated claim to knowledge
Improving the quality of my relationship with colleague M	How do I improve the quality of my relationship with colleague M?	Relational and empathetic relationships; recognizing the other	I have improved the quality of my relationship with colleague M for the purposes of better working practices

(Continued)

Table 11.3 (Continued)

Research issue	Research question	Values	Anticipated claim to knowledge
Encouraging students' interest in history	How do I encourage my students' interest in history?	Importance of understanding the basis of social actions; need to transform the past into a better present	I have encouraged my students' interest in history for the creation of a more sustainable world
We need to create a resources centre that will benefit our community	How do we create a resources centre that will benefit our community?	Need for knowledge; learning; access to information; sustainability of community	We have created a resources centre that is benefiting our community

3   What kinds of data will I gather to show why I am concerned?

Aim to gather data throughout your project to show the reasons for your concern, using any of the techniques described in this chapter, with an eye to your research question. If you ask, 'How do I stop the bullying?' look out for data that show bullying in action, or possibly what could be the reasons for the bullying. Watch out for key pieces that may get turned into evidence. In your enquiry about how you can improve the quality of relationships in your organization, you may receive a text or email from a colleague, which shows how caring relationships are not prioritized. You could highlight an entry from your personal log, saying that you needed to take action in relation to the bullying or developing better relationships. You should gather data that are representative both of the social situation and also of how you responded to the situation. You are hoping to understand better, as the basis of action aimed at improvement. Here are some examples of how you can do this.

Reason for my concern	Bullying of one colleague by another
What evidence can I produce?	Email from victim to you, asking for help. How do I help?
Reason for my concern	Need to maintain caring relationships
What evidence can I produce?	Videotape of staff party showing some people not talking with one another. How do I intervene?
Reason for my concern	Need to maintain full participation in staff meetings
What evidence can I produce?	Minutes of staff meeting recording affirming comments. How do we keep it this way?

Store your data carefully. Check out ideas about your data with your critical friends, and keep records of these meetings, perhaps by audio or videotape recording. This recording can itself stand as evidence when you come to write your report. Note especially whether you are beginning to question your own assumptions about how you are interpreting data. How did you react when you got the message from your colleague? What did you think when you saw the video of the staff party?

4 What can I do about it?

What are your options? What can you do in relation to others? What do you need to learn? How are you going to find out?

Now is a good time to consult with others who may or may not be involved in your research. Get insiders' perspectives, and also get more distanced opinions. Getting others' reactions helps you check out your perceptions and possible prejudices. Are the difficult relationships real or do you perceive them as such because you are personally feeling under pressure? Is dealing with the bullying more a matter of firm encouragement? Getting others' opinions on possible courses of action can help you avoid inappropriate action. Here are some examples of how this can be done.

What do I need to find out?	Who do I consult?
What can I do to stop the bullying?	Trusted colleague who has also experienced bullying
How do I improve/maintain good staff relationships?	Small group of experienced staff who could later form an anti-bullying taskforce.
How do I keep staff meetings enjoyable?	All staff at staff meeting, requesting feedback about possible strategies

5 What will I do about it?

Having considered your options, try one out. If that one does not seem to work, try something else. Do not get discouraged if things do not go as you wish, or if you make mistakes. Mistakes can be valuable sources of learning. You may develop a new project from how you learned from mistakes.

This can, however, be uncomfortable. It is easier to stay as we are and not try something new, but if the way we are is not right, we have to do something about it. No one else will. It is our responsibility.

Keep careful records as you go. Keep records of action in your research diary, and records of learning in your reflective journal. These can be different journals or the same. For example you could write in one column of your journal, 'What did I do?', and in a second column, 'What did I learn?' Leave a space after entries, or a blank third column, so that later you can ask, 'What is the significance of my action and my learning?' Here is an example.

Table 11.4

What did I do?	What did I learn?	What is the significance of my learning?
I spoke to the bully. She told me to mind my own business.	Perhaps I should have concentrated on encouraging the victim.	Externally imposed solutions do not always work. Solutions developed by those involved lead to more sustainable scenarios.
I asked a small group of experienced staff to help.	They were pleased at my approach.	Relationships are in people's practices. People themselves need to decide how to manage their own affairs.
I consulted with all staff and requested feedback.	They appreciated being involved and gave me positive feedback on my actions.	Good leadership involves enabling other people to take control.

6   What kinds of data will I gather to show the situation as it unfolds?

Throughout aim to gather data at intervals the frequency of which you decide. If you are doing a three-week project you may need to gather data every two or three days. If it is a three-month project, every week will do. When you gather data, make sure they are relevant to your research question. Asking 'How do I encourage participation?' means you will gather data to show aspects of participation (or non-participation, as the case may be).

Remember that you are not trying to change something in the sense of directly impacting on someone. Change can work like this, when one person gets someone else to do something, or does something to them, like wash their face or cut their hair. The values underpinning control are usually to do with self-interest, aimed at domination. You are aiming not for control but for sustainable change, rooted in the values of empathy and relationship, and intended to encourage negotiated forms of living.

So instead of thinking about changing things, think about exercising your influence. How do you exercise your influence? Do you keep in mind that people can think for themselves, and they decide whether to be influenced or not? Many people are told that they cannot think for themselves, and have to think in a certain way, and they come to believe this. Do you think people should internalize what you think, or come to think for themselves? How do you do this? How do you find ways of freeing your own thinking as well as helping others to come to think for themselves?

Maintain careful records of what you are doing in relation to your social action and your learning. You can use the same data gathering methods throughout, or you can vary them. Be imaginative. Do not instantly opt for a questionnaire. Think creatively. Go for an interview, artwork or videoconferencing. Keep your ethical considerations in mind, and get permission from the author for any piece of work they produce that you would like to use as data. If you are using other people's work, ask them to sign and date the piece of work, and sign and date it yourself. This is an important form of authentication.

Sort your data regularly and consolidate them at intervals. Bear in mind that you are showing development, where people, including yourself, came to do things differently. You need to show how processes unfolded, and what influences were at work. In your report you will comment explicitly on these processes.

Here are some ideas about which data sources may possibly contain evidence of your influence.

Table 11.5

Where will I find evidence?	What kind of evidence might I find?
A participant's research diary	Diary entry saying she found your support invaluable for helping her settle in at work
Transcript of a tape-recorded conversation with a colleague	Extract from conversation in which colleague says that you have helped her become more confident
Video of workshop you have run to improve self-assertion	Clip of shy person holding her own in a problematic conversation with others

7 How do I test the validity of my claim(s) to knowledge?

Remember that the centre of your enquiry is you. You are monitoring your actions and learning, as you try to influence further learning, in relation with other people. How do you make judgements about whether or not you are contributing to improved learning?

Go back to your values. Are you living them out? Are you working in ways that are just, truthful and free, both in your social contexts and in your own thinking? If you claim that you are, your claim must be backed up by authenticated evidence. Your claim should show your values in practice, so these values come to be recognized as your standards of practice and judgement.

Remember that you are not evaluating other people's practices. They can do that for themselves. You are evaluating your practice: you are saying whether or not you feel you are justified in maintaining that you are achieving your own high standards.

Here are some examples of claims to knowledge you could make, and the standards you could use to make judgements about those claims.

Table 11.6

My claim	My standards of judgement
I claim that I have encouraged good working relationships	My data archive contains instances of people being courteous and considerate to others. Previously these kinds of relationships were not so much in evidence.

(Continued)

Table 11.6 (Continued)

My claim	My standards of judgement
	My values of care and participative working are being realized as my living standards of judgement
I claim that I have influenced the quality of communication in our department	I can produce instances of practice, such as e-mails and text messages, to show that colleagues are communicating well and pleasantly. My values of relationship and empathy are being realized as my living standards of judgement
I claim that I have encouraged my occupational therapy trainees to think for themselves	Professional portfolios and assignments show the exercise of original thinking and critical judgement. My values of freedom in thinking and the exercise of critical judgement are being realized as my living standards of judgement

8 How will I ensure that any conclusions I reach are reasonably fair and accurate?

You need to test your claims against the critical judgement of others. You do this at validation meetings and in informal chats with critical friends. They may comment on the quality of your methodology, whether you are observing good ethical practice, whether your data appear to be authentic, whether you have generated valid evidence in relation to clearly articulated standards of judgement, and whether the conduct of the whole research gives people reason to believe you. This process of public critique is essential to all forms of research, and especially in action research where claims to knowledge are rooted in subjective experience. Specifically, the task of critical friends and validation groups is to see whether you are offering explanations as well as descriptions, and to check the rigour of your methodology. Be prepared for feedback that may tell you what you do not want to know, for example, that things are not going as you think they are. This is called disconfirming data. It can help as a valuable steer to your project and prevent you from making unjustified claims. It is up to you whether or not you act on the advice of critical colleagues, but be prepared to defend your decisions and future actions if you don't.

9 How will I modify my concerns, ideas and practice in the light of my evaluations?

How do you change your ideas and practices in light of what you are finding out? It takes courage and commitment to let go of old ways and head for the future.

If you feel your new way of working is reasonably satisfactory, you will probably continue working like this for as long as it remains satisfactory. This may not be for long, however, because people change all the time and their social situations change with them. This is one of the delights of working in an action research way, because you can see how one research question can transform into another, and also how one issue can act as the grounds for new issues to emerge. Nothing is ever static. We are constantly changing ourselves and our contexts.

This kind of transformation can help you organize your ideas and practices as ongoing cycles of action and reflection. Focusing on one issue can lead to new learning. This learning can feed back into action, and the action can act as the grounds for new learning. It is an ongoing spiral of spirals that helps us to realize our potentials for unlimited new ideas and boundless forms of new practices. We create our futures as we live our presents.

Here are some ideas about how you could organize your evolving research questions into cycles, and how the research questions change their focus.

Example 1

Research question in first cycle

- How do I manage my timekeeping?

Emerging research questions in subsequent cycles

1 How do I protect research time?
2 How do I negotiate with others about my work schedule?
3 How do I manage the process of writing reports?

Example 2

Research question in first cycle

- How do I persuade others to be cooperative?

Emerging research questions in subsequent cycles

1 How do I understand cooperative practices?
2 How do I encourage others to speak for themselves?
3 How do I educate for freedom?

Example 3

Research question in first cycle

- How do I exercise my educational influence?

Emerging research questions in subsequent cycles

1 How do I exercise my influence for good relationships?
2 How do I contribute to the education of social formations?
3 How do I work with others for sustainable good social orders?

This returns us to the idea of why we should hold ourselves accountable for what we do. By using our research projects to evaluate our work, we show how we are ensuring that today is the best we can do, and this gives us hope that tomorrow will be even better.

Summary

This chapter has taken you through an action research plan, step-by-step, with ideas and examples of how you can do this for yourself. Remember to adapt the suggested questions into questions that suit your own circumstances. Use your imagination about how you do your research.

We now move to Part IV, which deals with issues about demonstrating validity in action research.

Further reading

Hopkins, D. (2008) *A Teacher's Guide to Classroom Research* (fourth edition). Maidenhead: Open University Press.
Written for teachers, this has become a classic, a must-read.

McNiff, J. and Whitehead, J. (2010) *You and Your Action Research Project* (third edition). Abingdon: Routledge.
An A to Z guide to planning, designing and doing an action research project, this also is a must for your library.

Stringer, E. (2007) *Action Research in Education*. Upper Saddle River, NJ: Pearson Prentice Hall.
This text is for teachers, leaders, families and community members, especially for those who ground their enquiries within community.

PART IV

How Do I Generate Evidence to Support My Claim to Knowledge?

All research, including action research, aims to make a claim to knowledge. In action research, you aim to explain that you now know something that you did not know before. This is often about how you have learned about your practice by studying it, and you are able to describe and explain what you are doing.

Claims to knowledge need to be supported by validated evidence, so that the claim does not appear as opinion or supposition. Evidence is generated from data, so this means gathering quality data from which you will select pieces to stand as evidence.

This part contains the following chapters.

Each chapter offers practical advice about what you need to do to generate evidence.

In terms of your own action enquiry into understanding the nature and uses of action research, you are asking, 'How do I generate evidence to support any claim to knowledge I hope to make?'

TWELVE

Monitoring Practice and Looking for Data

This chapter is about what you need to do and think about in order to gather useful data, and not waste time gathering irrelevant data that you will probably discard later. At this point you need to decide what you are looking for and where and how you might find it. This will involve decisions about how you are going to monitor what you are doing in order to track developments over time.

In your action research you are looking primarily for two things:

1 Episodes of practice that show the developing educational influence of your own learning
2 Episodes of practice that show your educational influence in the learning of others

The chapter is organized as two sections to address these questions.

1 Episodes of practice that show the developing educational influence of your own learning

Three main questions emerge.

- What data am I looking for?
- Where will I look for the data?
- How will I monitor my practice over time?

What data am I looking for?

To decide what you are looking for, remind yourself what your research is about and specifically what your research question is. Whatever you look for will be in relation to your research question.

Asking action research questions can be rather complex. First, action research questions involve the generic question, 'How do I improve my work?' Perhaps your specific question uses a different form of words, such as 'How do I help ...?' or 'How do I find ways of ...?' Whatever form of words they use, action research questions are always linked with the idea of improvement. Second, improvement happens over time, so you will look for episodes of practice that show the development of your own practice over time. Third, practice does not just happen. Actions can 'just happen', such as laughing, but these are actions and not practices. Practices are always informed and intentional. They are informed by learning; their intent is improvement. So when you look at your practice you are really looking at the influence of your learning. What you are looking for, therefore, when looking for data, are episodes that show initial contexts, when perhaps you did not know something so well, and later episodes when you knew it better, that show the influence of your own learning.

For example, imagine your research question is, 'How do I help my trainee managers to improve their writing skills?' Underlying this question is the deeper question, 'How do I learn how to help my trainee managers to learn to write better?' This means that you will look for episodes of practice that turn the question into reality. Bearing in mind that improvement happens over time, you will look for episodes when you did not know so well how to help your trainees to improve their writing skills, and for later episodes when you began to help them more successfully. Bearing in mind also that practice is informed by learning, you will look for episodes when you began to learn about these things and how your learning developed as you tried things out in practice.

Classroom management as creating communities of practice

Hessa Al-Shammari

Hessa Al-Shammari has been working as a newly qualified science teacher for two years in Al Nahdah Primary Independent Girls' School in Qatar. She has high hopes for the achievement levels of her Grade 6 (11–12-year-old) girls, but initially they were not focused and found it hard to settle in lessons. Hessa undertook her action enquiry into how she could encourage the children to exercise self-discipline. Because she was new to teaching, she appreciated that she had much to learn.

She first had to understand what the situation was like, and why it was like this, so she gathered data using the following range of techniques:

- she issued a questionnaire to the students using an online surveying tool, to find out their attitudes to her pedagogical style;
- she videoed students' interactions during lessons;
- she kept a reflective journal.

Through scrutinizing the data she concluded that she needed to maintain students' attention and interest. She implemented a range of strategies to do so. She gathered further data to see whether her strategies were influencing students' behaviours, using different data gathering techniques, including the following:

- she set up a school blog, so students could exchange ideas and say how they were getting on;
- developed a newsletter to record achievements in sport and other fields;
- set up an electronic guestbook for parents.

Using strategies like this, she was able to check whether the students felt that her interventions were influencing their own behaviours.

This project was part of the Tribal Action Research for Teachers course in Qatar. You can read Hessa's work at http://www.jeanmcniff.com/userfiles/file/qatar/Qatar_Action_Research_booklet_email.pdf

---

Where will I look for the data?

Here is an example. It is deliberately exaggerated to show how 'ordinary' artefacts can be rich sources of data.

Think about experiences when episodes of learning occurred. Perhaps the time when you began to understand that your students needed help was when two of them were marked down in examinations because of their poor spelling. You were shocked to receive notification of the exam results (source of data). You made a note of this in your record book (source of data). You noted in your journal (source of data) that you would do something about it. You consulted with colleagues through email (source of data) about what you could do, and read books (source of data) about possible strategies. You decided to try some new 'look and say' spelling strategies, and began to keep detailed records (source of data) of what you were learning as you tried them out. You also kept detailed field notes (source of data) about how your students were responding, and you invited them to keep their own journals (source of data) about what they were learning (see also Section below).

Over time your strategies seemed to be working. You could show examples of poor spelling from the students' written exercises and notebooks (source of data), and how they worked with the exercises you gave them (source of data). You could show how their spelling improved over time from later written exercises (source of data). Finally, you could show how the two students passed their resit exams, and produce notification of results as a possible source of data.

Some points to note:

1 It is unlikely that you would use all the possible sources of data in your account. You would use your own common sense about what was sufficient to make your point.
2 When you are monitoring practice it is vital to monitor the learning that informs the practice. This is essential for when you come to explain the significance of your research (see Chapter 22). Then you will say that you have contributed to new practices – you have found ways of helping students to improve their spelling – and

---

you will also say that you have contributed to new ideas and new knowledge – you know what you did and why you did it, in relation to learning how to help students to develop their own capability.

3 It is also important to remember that you are not claiming to have caused the students to spell better, or even that you were the only influence in their learning. However you can hope to claim that you had an influence somewhere, but this claim would have to be supported by your students' testimony (see Section 2).

How will I monitor my practice over time?

You need to decide the following.

- How are you going to monitor practice? This will involve choosing data gathering techniques that are appropriate for what you want to find out. Chapter 14 gives advice about what techniques are available and what they are appropriate for.
- How often are you going to gather data? You need to make some commonsense decisions about frequency of data gathering. The longer the project, the more you can space out your data gathering.
- Which data gathering techniques will you use? You can use the same techniques throughout your project, or mix and match them. You may use field notes throughout, but use memos, text messages and email correspondence as they occur. There are no general guidelines except to remind you that you will be producing a report in which you present your data as evidence, and you need to keep your audience in mind. What will they be able to attend to at any one time? Too many data will confuse. Too few will weaken. Use your judgement to get a balance.

2   Episodes of practice that show your educational influence in the learning of others

This section asks the same questions as before, but with a different focus.

- What data am I looking for?
- Where will I look for the data?
- How will I monitor my practice over time?

What data am I looking for?

You are now looking for data that show how your practice (informed by your learning) is influencing the learning of others (as manifested in their practice).

Let us take another example. Imagine you are a project manager for a new construction operation. You know that quality work comes from good relationships, so you ask, 'How do I help the engineers and the construction workers to develop good relationships?' You are of course asking, 'How do I learn to help them learn how to develop good relationships?' Asking the question signals your intent to learn.

As in Section 1, you look for episodes of practice that show how your learning is influencing your practice, and you resolve to gather the data in recordable form. You also need to show how your learning is influencing the learning of others, otherwise your later claim that you have improved your practice will not make sense. You can do this in different ways:

- You can produce the testimonies of others who say they have learned because of your influence.
- You can produce examples of people acting in new ways, which you claim have developed through your influence.

The kind of testimonies you are looking for are when people say things such as, 'You have helped me to learn' or 'I feel much more confident now, thanks to you'. The kinds of actions you are looking for are those about which critical friends and validation groups say things such as, 'That is evidence of lively enquiring minds' or 'You have clearly enabled them to think for themselves'.

Remember that you must get permission from your participants to involve them and to use their words. We said earlier that you do not need permission to undertake your own self-study, but you must have permission from those your self-study involves.

Where will I look for the data?

As above, look for episodes that occur over time and that show the development of your participants' learning in relation to your own. Here is another example, again exaggerated to show potential sources of data.

Box 12.1

Sources of data

You decide to put in place a staff development programme. Because you do not think you have the right facilitation skills, you engage the services of a professional facilitator (letter to facilitator is a source of data). You arrange a series of staff development days (the firm agrees to support this), and send out a memo (source of data) inviting all to attend, on a non-compulsory basis. Most do, including a loudly spoken colleague and two new colleagues. You also become a participant.

Over the series of meetings the facilitator introduces different strategies that help people see how they influence others and how they might modify their practice. With

(Continued)

---

the written permission of all, she makes video recordings (source of data) and invites people to comment on what they see (field notes and personal jottings are sources of data of their learning). She makes her own records and personal evaluations available to you (source of data of her learning). She insists that everyone keeps a reflective journal (source of data of their learning), which they may let others see if they wish.

The videos come to be a visual narrative (source of data) that shows the transformation of attitudes and behaviours. Gradually the loud colleague comes to cease forcing her opinion on others. One video (source of data of her learning) shows her listening carefully. The two newcomers begin to speak up. After the series of seminars one of them writes you a thank you note, saying that he has learned much from the experience (source of data of his learning).

Six months later, when the programme has ended, at a staff meeting you ask people's opinions about the seminars. Most say it has been useful for helping to bond the staff. This is recorded in the minutes (source of data). You put out a questionnaire (source of data), the results of which make you feel optimistic. You later receive a written request (source of data) to support the development of a staff social committee.

This story is primarily in relation to your own learning, but contains episodes of other people's learning. It may be that other people also began to regard their participation as a research project, and your words and actions became sources of data for them. You could have developed the initiative into a collaborative action research project, where everyone monitored what they were doing in relation to others.

Bear in mind also that examples like this are fairy stories, and things often do not go so well or so smoothly. The story is presented to give ideas about where you can look for data. However, most real-life stories contain episodes of forward and backward movement. It is important to record them all, so as not to give the impression that it was an easy ride or a victory story (Lather, 1994, cited in MacClure 1996). It is important also to show times when your values were denied in your practice, so that you can show the transformation that you can claim to be a living out of your values.

How will I monitor my practice over time?

Again, remember to look for episodes of learning, such as recordings in journals or statements by people that perhaps they never thought of that, as well as episodes of action that appear to be manifestations of critical learning. Critical episodes of underlying learning are those that show new, clearly changed attitudes and behaviours, such as when a colleague listens carefully for the first time, or an indoor decorator learns how to prepare woodwork for painting. Perhaps if you interviewed them (a transcript or notes from the conversation would be sources of data), you would hear them say that they had thought carefully about the influence they were exercising on others. Instances such as these can be elusive, but they definitely occur. Also remember that your job is not to get people to confess to their shortcomings, but to encourage them to think and learn for themselves. When you come to generate evidence these episodes will be key pieces of data.

Aim to build up your data archive to show the unfolding of the learning and action over time. It is important to label your data and date them, so that you can show the sequencing. Make sure you store and sort your data (Chapter 13) so you can show the relationship between your own action and learning, between the action and learning of others, and the relationship between the action and learning of all participants. This will also help you see practice and learning as a web of interconnected relationships and practices. The best action research reports show this complexity, yet present the complexity in such a way that their reader can appreciate how the actions they see represent deeper meanings related to learning.

Summary

This chapter has discussed issues of monitoring practice and gathering data. The main point is to know what kind of data you are looking for and where to look for them.

You are looking for data from which you will be able to extract evidence that shows your educational influence at work, so you will look for episodes of practice that show these elements.

The next chapter deals with how to gather, sort and store data.

Further reading

Henon, A. (ed.) (2010) Creativity/WORKS. Radstock, North East Somerset Arts. Retrieved 1 August 2010 from http://www.actionresearch.net/writings/henon/creativityworkslowah.pdf
An imaginative and captivating text, this shows different approaches for looking for data by a socially engaged artist. It extends ideas about the forms of representation used in research accounts for monitoring practice.

McKernan, J. (1996) *Curriculum Action Research* (second edition). London: Kogan Page.
A good guide to data analysis and interpretation.

Norton, L. (2009) *Action Research in Teaching and Learning*. London: Routledge.
Although written for a higher education context, this book is useful for other sectors too.

Robson, C. (2002) *Real World Research* (second edition). Oxford: Blackwell.
A comprehensive guide to doing practice-based research, this book gives advice for how to gather data, where to look for it, and how to analyse and interpret it.

THIRTEEN

Gathering, Sorting and Storing Data

This chapter deals with gathering, sorting and storing data. It contains the following sections.

1 Gathering data
2 Sorting and storing the data

1 Gathering data

Gathering data involves several processes: knowing where and when to look for data; observing what is going on; recording, storing and sorting the data; and knowing how to retrieve the data later. Many of these processes overlap, so take the following advice as a guide to help you get to grips with the task, not to be interpreted in a linear way.

This section deals with the questions:

- How do I gather data? Which observation and data gathering techniques are available?
- Where do I gather data? When do I look for data?

How do I gather data? Which observation and data gathering techniques are available?

At this point you are observing what is going on and finding ways to record it. Remember that you are not simply looking at action, but trying to see and record how learning enters into action. Many techniques are available, some of which are appropriate for monitoring actions and how these may be indicative of learning, and others that aim to focus on what kind of learning is going on.

Observation and data-gathering techniques to observe and record the action

You can use the following techniques to observe and record your own action as well as other people's actions. These are perhaps the most commonly used data-gathering techniques, but they are just a selection from a vast array.

Field notes

You make notes as you observe actions or listen to interactions. You can write them into a special notebook, or on the back of your hand, in which case you would write them up later. You can write in straight notes, or try mind maps, spider diagrams and pictures.

Notes from a clinical supervision session

N (trainee) was unhappy today. Said she wasn't managing her practicum. Long conversation. Offered more intensive email support. Said she would keep trying.

Notes from the shop floor

Sales of toys going well. 'Magic mouse' seems slow. Wrong location? Better lighting? Talk to display team.

Figure 13.1 shows an example of a mind map. You can produce many different forms of mind map: the right form is whatever works for you.

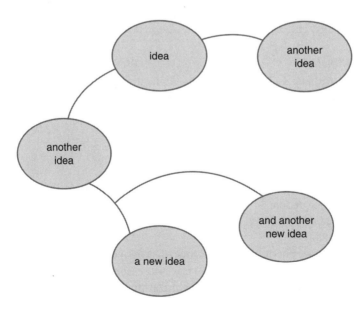

Figure 13.1   An example of a mind map

Record sheets and observation schedules
These are the different sheets you produce to gather data and maintain records, such as observation schedules, analyses of actions and pictorial representations of action. The best are the ones you devise yourself, but here are some ideas to get you started. Note that the tally marks refer to the number of interactions. Also note the use of the 'five-bar gate' to count in multiples of five.

Table 13.1
Record sheet to show number of interactions between nurse and patient

Minutes	1	2	3	4
Interactions between nurse and patient	Ⅼ卅 卅 Ⅱ	Ⅲ	卅 卅 Ⅱ	卅 卅 Ⅰ

Record sheet to record number of times participants speak at a business meeting

Participant	Number of contributions
Mr Green	卅 卅 Ⅱ
Ms Black	Ⅱ
Mrs White	卅 卅 卅 Ⅱ
Mr Grey	卅 Ⅱ
Ms Pink	卅 卅 卅 卅 Ⅰ

Sociometric analysis
Figure 13.2 on page 143 shows an analysis in graphic form of the interactions among members of a meeting. Note how many times each person talks, and who they talk with.

Observation and data-gathering techniques to observe and record learning

You can use the following techniques to observe and record your own learning as well that of other people.

Written accounts
You can use prose, poetic or other forms to show your own and other people's experience and learning. Here is an extract from the PhD thesis of Paul Roberts (2003), a management educator and organizational change consultant. You can download this from http://actionresearch.net/living/roberts.shtml.

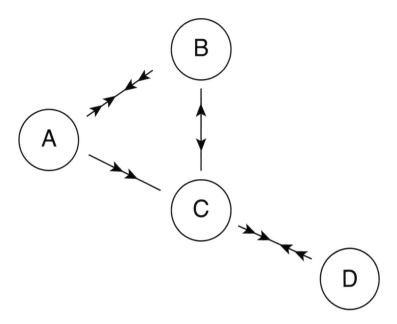

Figure 13.2 An example of sociometric analysis

A learning journal
Paul Roberts

When I began the CARPP [Centre for Action Research in Professional Practice] programme at the University of Bath, my interest was in attaining a PhD in order to pursue an in-depth programme of study in a number of areas that interested me. I wanted further to develop my professional practice to encompass these areas in a way that gave greater satisfaction and purpose to my working life.

After attending the initial workshop on the programme in February 1997, I wrote the following passage as part of the first entry in the learning journal I was to keep for the next three years.

What came across to me most strongly from the first CARPP event in February was the importance of choosing research that is significant and central to my life. I would like the research to provide a focus to draw together the different strands that I am interested in.

These strands are:

- complexity theory
- archetypal psychology
- organizations as religion – this could be a further image of organizations to be added to Gareth Morgan's (1997) list of metaphors, which would help locate this idea in an attractive and rigorous theoretical framework.

At the end of this first entry, I also wrote the lines:

This question of practice is extremely important, not just for the research but for my working life, as I want the research to help lead me in a direction which can reorient my work.
   At the moment I identify with the lines of Dante's (1949) poem:

In the middle of the road of my life
I awoke in a dark wood
where the true way was wholly lost.

I don't know if it is too much of an extravagance to hope that the research will enable the 'true way' to be rediscovered.

Personal logs and diaries

These are the records you keep of personal action, reflection on the action and the learning arising from it. It does not matter whether you call them logs, diaries or journals, whether you keep a research diary and a reflective diary or use the same journal for both purposes. It can be helpful to differentiate episodes of action from episodes of learning, for example, by using different fonts or colours. For example:

Mr K came to the obesity clinic today. He has still not managed to lose as much weight as he ought.

How do I persuade him to take more exercise?

Text messages and emails

Social networking can be a rich source of data. Keep a record of a particular thread of an e-seminar or different contributions on social networking sites. The problem with these kinds of data is that they can be difficult to track, so make sure you keep on top of things and store them in easily accessible ways.

Questionnaires

Do not rush into questionnaires. They may seem an easy way to collect data and there are many texts explaining how to construct them. If you do use them, use them to get a sense of trends and directions. Also pilot them many times to make sure they are providing the kind of information you need to move your enquiry forward. This advice also applies to the next item about surveys and interviews.

Surveys and interviews

You can conduct closed, semi-structured and open surveys and interviews. Closed questions that look for 'yes/no' answers are easier to analyse, but do not give much information. More open questions that allow personal responses are more difficult to analyse, but provide rich information and insights.

A closed response question

Are you married?   Yes ☐   No ☐

An open response question

Question: What do you think of banning women's face veils and burkas in public?

Answer: ....

Table 13.3   A Likert-type scale

	Strongly agree	Agree	Don't know	Disagree	Strongly disagree
Women should not wear face veils or burkas in public					

Where do I gather data? When do I look for data?

Places for gathering data

The kind of data you are looking for are to be found in the textual accounts of people's practices, both documented and living, real and virtual. The practices in question can be current or historical.

Documented practices

Documents are both private and public and record both current and past practices. Diaries, autobiographical narratives and personal letters are examples of private records. You can also look at public records such as institutional archives, agendas and minutes of meetings, and policy statements. These records will contain information about what people were thinking and doing at a particular time and place. They can be invaluable for helping you address your questions, 'What is my concern?', 'Why am I concerned?' and 'How can I produce evidence to show my concern?', because they may show whether the values that guide your own work also guided the practices in earlier situations. Accessing and looking at records such as these is often called 'desk research' or 'library research'.

Living practices

You would gather most of your data within your research site, where you and your participants meet together. You would gather data about the current action.

In some cases you would also be able to gather data about your learning as it happens, but this may not always be the case, because sometimes it is important to step back from the action in order to make sense of it. Schön (1983) talks about this as reflective practice that involves both 'reflection in action' and 'reflection on action'. In order to make practical decisions about the next move, we have to reflect in action, but often it is not until later in a quiet space that we reflect on action. This reflection on action involves learning, which is still a form of action and needs to be recorded. Remember that you are monitoring your learning as well as your social actions.

You can also set up situations so that people can explore their learning and find ways of articulating it. Some examples of how you can do this are as follows.

Virtual worlds
Many organizations use virtual learning environments (VLEs) and virtual worlds such as Second Life, where real-time individuals create avatars that represent themselves. Although these strategies have come in for a lot of criticism, many people see benefits in them, especially in cost and time. You can convene a meeting of international delegates in Second Life with no cost implications.

Role-play and performance
You can set up role-play and performance situations in which participants take the part of others and then offer feedback on the experience. It is important for them and you to keep records of their experience and learning from these episodes.

For example, Jack Whitehead (2004b) includes a performance text in his enquiry into 'How valid are multimedia communications of my embodied values in living theories and standards of educational judgement and practice?' To communicate the meanings of his embodied values of academic freedom and social justice, Whitehead reconstructs his response to a Senate Working Party on a matter of academic freedom in a performance text that includes a videotaped extract in the visual narrative.

Artworks
You can encourage participants to produce their original visual representations in the form of artwork. You would ask the participants themselves to give their own interpretations of how their artworks represented their experience and learning. You would keep records of these interpretations.

Have a look at the prologue of the PhD submission of Eleanor Lohr at http://www. actionresearch.net/living/lohr.shtml (Lohr, 2004). See how she uses artwork and video as an integral aspect of her evidence. Or look at Section Three of Eden Charles' (2007) doctorate, 'How can I bring Ubuntu as a living standard of judgment into the academy? Moving beyond decolonization through societal reidentification and guiltless recognition' at http://www.actionresearch.net/living/edenphd/section3.pdf. Ubuntu has its genesis in an African Way of Being and its influence is spreading with the recognition of the importance of relational and inclusive ways of being. Section Three of Eden's thesis is focused on the 'Influence of an African Cosmology with Ubuntu' and on pages 103–107 he explains the humanizing influence of his art in his 'Living and Learning My Values in Africa'.

Video and multimedia recordings

Video enables you to move beyond written accounts and show the actions as they happen. This can be especially powerful when you come to generate evidence in support of a claim to knowledge. When you say, 'I am claiming that I have influenced the quality of relationships in my workplace', you can produce videotaped material that shows people's visual expressions and bodily language to communicate how they are feeling. The development of multimedia narratives is important. Universities everywhere are now accepting multimedia accounts as part of masters and doctoral theses; you can produce your professional portfolio using video as a main form of representation; and many electronic journals such as *Electronic Journal of Living Theories* (http://ejolts.net/) publish videoed work as normal practice: see also *Turkish Online Journal of Qualitative Inquiry* at http://www.tojqi.net where you can read a multimedia account of Jean's work (see McNiff (2010b) http://www.tojqi.net/articles/TOJQI_1_1/TOJQI_1_1_Article_1.pdf).

When do I gather my data?

A certain amount of entrepreneurialism is needed in data collection. As well as planning to gather the data, you also have to be on the lookout for opportunities. The most obvious place to gather data is in your direct research practice, when you email participants or conduct an observation. Many opportunities arise, however, out of hours and also off-site, while walking the corridors or in a park, which are good opportunities for relaxed conversations.

Also aim to gather data formally on an ongoing basis. Do not avoid data gathering or put it off, especially in the early stages. If you are wondering where to start, tape- or video-record a conversation with a trusted colleague about why you are doing your job and what keeps you doing it. This should help you (and the colleague) to clarify and articulate the values that inform your work. Keep the recording and transcript safely, and refer back to it when you are making a claim to knowledge to remind yourself of your core values and how these enter into practice.

You can record data about your reflections anywhere you have a quiet space. You can reflect on the bus, in the shower or while watching television. Have a notebook (paper or computer) handy for recording thoughts immediately: this is common practice for journalists. Do this systematically. An idea that seems obvious in the middle of the night can flit away at daybreak. Keep your rough field notes, ideas and reflections in this workbook and sort them and write them up later. Ideas about your research may occur to you during other work activities.

2   Sorting and storing the data

Remember that you gather data to generate evidence. Generating evidence involves analysing data, and analysis is made easier if you know what you are looking for and where to find it. The more systematic you are about storing your

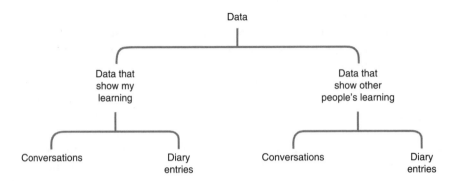

Figure 13.4 Organization of data into categories

data, the easier it will be when you come to select those pieces that you want to stand as evidence.

Your accumulated data are called your data archive. You may store a lot of data on your computer. You can store physical artefacts in a box or in your bag. It is not a good idea to put material into a box any old how. Aim to sort it regularly into categories.

When you begin gathering data, do so with a few broad categories in mind, such as:

- data that show my learning;
- data that show other people's learning.

Put the different data into their own files, and then sort the data into more refined categories, such as:

- File 1: data that show my learning

  conversations
  diary entries

- File 2: data that show other people's learning

  conversations
  diary entries

You could regard the job of organizing your data archive something along the lines of Figure 13.4.

Organize your data into as many categories as you need, and put them into different files or containers (modified cereal boxes are good). Colour coding your files can be helpful. If you are storing data on your computer, work out a similar coding system. As your research progresses, the number of categories will probably increase, along with the increasing depth of analysis. 'Conversations' may turn into 'conversations with participants' or 'conversations with critical friends'.

'Diary entries' may become 'diary entries about reflection' or 'diary entries on the research experience'. Keep on top of your data. Examine the data regularly and frequently. Sort them into new categories and new files, and keep your filing system on the move. This does take time, and also space if you are saving the data in physical files, all of which has to be negotiated with colleagues in your workplace or with family members if you keep them at home.

Finally, you have a data archive to be proud of. Now comes the task of analysing it and turning it into evidence. This is the focus of Chapter 15.

Summary

This chapter has offered advice about gathering, sorting and storing data. It has talked about different data-gathering techniques and which ones may be appropriate for different purposes, whether recording the action or recording learning. It has also talked about putting together a data archive in a coherent way.

The next chapter gets to the heart of the matter by discussing how you can select key pieces of data and turn them into evidence in support of your claim to knowledge.

Further reading

Campbell, A., McNamara, O. and Gilroy, P. (2004) *Practitioner Research and Professional Development in Education*. London: Paul Chapman.
The book has good sections on data gathering and analysis.

Davies, M.B. (2007) *Doing a Successful Research Project*. Basingstoke: Palgrave Macmillan.
A straightforward and accessible guide to designing and doing research.

Miles, M.B. and Huberman, M. (1994) *Qualitative Data Analysis: An Expanded Sourcebook* (second edition). Thousand Oaks, CA: Sage.
Still one of the best books on data gathering and analysis.

Tidwell, D.L., Heston, L. and Fitzgerald, M.L. (2009) *Research Methods for the Self-Study of Practice*. Dortrecht: Springer.
This is an excellent text on the different methods for gathering, sorting and storing data and self-study and action research enquiries.

FOURTEEN

Turning the Data into Evidence

You now have substantial amounts of data. You need to turn the data into evidence to support your claim to knowledge. Producing evidence is part of the process of establishing the validity, or truthfulness, of a claim. For example, if you say, 'This way of working is better than previous ways', you need to support that claim with evidence, otherwise what you say could be construed as your opinion.

Evidence is not the same as data. 'Data' refers to the pieces of information you gather about what you and others are doing and learning. All these data are in your data archive. Your task is to turn some of these pieces of data into evidence. These will be those special pieces of data that you identify specifically in relation to your research issue and your claim to knowledge. The pieces of data do not change their form, but they do change their status. A comment remains a comment and a picture a picture, but it now comes out of the larger body of data to stand as evidence. Think about when you drag and drop an icon on your computer. You drag the item out of the data archive and drop it into your evidence archive. The piece of data no longer officially keeps company with other data; it now keeps company with a claim to knowledge.

Remember also that evidence is more than illustration. Illustration is used when you organize your data to show a point in action. You could, for example, produce documentation around a new work schedule or a videorecording to show you mentoring a colleague. These uses of data remain illustrative, because you do not make a value judgement about whether they show improvement in a previous practice, or offer an explanation for why they are better.

Generating evidence is a rigorous process, and part of the larger process of testing the validity of a claim to knowledge. It involves:

1 Stating what the claim to knowledge is
2 Establishing criteria and standards of judgement
3 Selecting data
4 Generating evidence

This chapter is organized as four sections to address these issues.

1 Stating what the claim to knowledge is

The aim of a piece of research is to make a claim to knowledge. When you write your report, you state what your claim to knowledge is. You say, 'My claim is that I have contributed to knowledge of my field of nursing/dentistry/teaching/ management'. Making a claim to knowledge means that you know something now that was not known before. This knowledge is being put into the public domain for the first time and is adding to the public body of knowledge. The knowledge may be about a substantive issue, such as a new clinical nursing practice, or it may be about the process of creating new ideas and explanations. If it is about substantive issues, the knowledge is usually about practice. If it is about making sense of things, it is usually about theory. Knowledge generated through action research is about both practice and theory. You offer descriptions of what you did and explanations for why you did it. Your descriptions and explanations together become your theory, your living theory of practice.

Your claim to know in relation to practice would be something of the kind:

- I have developed a new work schedule.
- I have improved my mentoring practice.
- We have created better communications in our office.

Your claim to know in relation to theory would be something of the kind:

- I have developed my understanding of the need for a good work schedule.
- I have created my theory of mentoring practices.
- We know how and why to communicate better in our office.

Both kinds of claims are related. One cannot stand without the other. Your theory of practice (explanation for practice) has been created from within the practice. You can describe and explain your improved mentoring practice because you have studied your mentoring practice and worked systematically to improve it. You know what you have done and how and why you have done it.

We have said throughout that the need to show how you are contributing to theory and not only practice is important in all action research, and especially in reports that are submitted for accreditation. The criteria for accreditation usually state that a candidate has to show that they are making a claim to knowledge of their field (see Chapter 20). If the report shows that the candidate is making a contribution only to practice, the report could well be rejected.

2 Establishing criteria and standards of judgement

Making a judgement about something involves using criteria and standards of judgement. Criteria and standards of judgement are different though intimately related. Criteria tell you in advance what is expected in a thing or action; standards of judgement tell you how well or to what extent the criterion is being achieved. The criteria for safe driving, for example, would involve observing traffic flows and driving within speed limits. A driving instructor would probably bring a checklist of criteria to a driving test and tick them off when the learner driver did these things. Whether or not the driver passed the test, however, would depend on how well the instructor judged the driver to have done them. How did the driver negotiate the traffic flows? Did they drive responsibly within designated speed limits? The instructor uses these values of safe and responsible driving as their standards of judgement. When you make judgements about your practice it is not enough simply to work to criteria in the form of achieving targets, such as 'I took the patient's temperature' or 'I completed my work on time', although these are initial elements. You also have to explain the nature of what you did and why you believe it should be perceived as good.

When we make a judgement about something, we do so in relation to specific standards. Having standards is important to ensure that our work is good quality. However, questions need to be asked about which standards are appropriate, who sets the standards and who says who should make decisions about these things.

Which standards? Whose standards?

Many debates about quality argue that practices should be judged in terms of practitioners' performance, in relation to specific skills and competencies, which often appear as targets. In many technologized societies, ambulance drivers and ·fire crews have to reach their destination in a specific amount of time, and hospitals must achieve a designated turnaround of patients. The emphasis on quantity can, however, jeopardize quality. Stories are sometimes told of patients not receiving quality care because doctors have to achieve their quotas of patient appointments. This approach to target setting and performance is part of the current managerialist and consumerist culture.

Professionals use different kinds of standards to judge the quality of their work, related to the values that inspire the work. A business manager may judge their leadership by how well they encourage motivation and purpose among employees. A foster-parent may judge their success in fostering by their capacity to demonstrate love in times of trial. Professional values are to do with care, compassion and respect for the other. Most action researchers try to find ways of living these values. The manager judges their work in relation to employees' increasing motivation and purpose. The foster-parent judges their work in relation to the foster-child's capacity to develop independence through loving relationships with the new family.

As a practitioner-researcher, your job is to set your own standards of practice and judgement, and show how you are fulfilling them. In relation to practice, do you live out your values of love, compassion and purpose? In relation to judgement, do you use these values as your standards? Furthermore, do you articulate these standards and communicate them to others, so that others can see how you judge your practice and negotiate your judgement with you? If you are submitting your work for higher degree accreditation, the validating institution will have its own criteria and standards of judgement. You have to show how you fulfil these, as well as any that you set yourself.

Mary Hartog (2004) submitted her PhD thesis to the University of Bath, to be judged according to the university's criteria, which were:

- that the thesis demonstrates originality of mind and critical judgement;
- that the extent and merit of the work are appropriate;
- that the thesis contains matter worthy of publication.

As well as observing and fulfilling the official criteria, Mary asked her examiners to consider the standards of judgement she had chosen for herself. In her opening pages she writes as follows.

Standards of judgement

If this PhD is differentiated or distinguished as a research process, it is because its methodology is underpinned by the values I as a researcher bring to my practice. It is with this in mind that I ask you to bring your eye as examiners to bear on the following questions, asking yourself as you read this thesis whether these questions are addressed sufficiently for you to say, 'Yes, these standards of judgment have been met':

Are the values of my practice clearly articulated and is there evidence of a commitment toward living them in my practice?
Does my inquiry account lead you to recognize how my understanding and practice has changed over time?
Is the evidence provided of life-affirming action in my teaching and learning relationships?
Does this thesis evidence an ethic of care in the teaching and learning relationship?
Are you satisfied that I as a researcher have shown commitment to a continuous process of practice improvement?
Does this thesis show originality of mind and critical thinking?

Your judgment may be supported by applying the social standards of Habermas's 'truth claims':

- Is this account comprehensible?
- Does it represent a truthful and sincere account?
- Is it appropriate – has it been crafted with due professional and ethical consideration?

Mary's examiners made their professional judgements about the quality of the work in relation both to the university's established criteria and also to Mary's personally selected standards of judgement, and she was awarded her doctoral degree (see http://www.bath.ac.uk/~edsajw/hartog.shtml).

---

3   Selecting data

Having established your criteria and standards of judgement, you now need to search your data archive and find instances of values in action. The hospital manager (see the example on page 155) may select the minutes of a meeting in which she urged people to have faith in themselves, promising that she would support them. She also selects an email sent to her by a colleague to say that they were organizing a staff get-together. The foster-parent may produce a card from a previously fostered child, now an adult, expressing their thanks to the parent for helping them get through a difficult adolescence. These physical artefacts may be seen as containing participants' testimonies to practitioners' capacity to live their values in practice.

Triangulation

A key strategy in establishing validity is triangulation. It involves three processes:

- demonstrating the authenticity of the data;
- negotiating the authenticity of the data; which then transforms into
- negotiating the validity of the evidence.

Demonstrating the authenticity of the data

You need to show your readers that your data is authentic, that is, you have not fabricated it. For example, you would have printed the time and date on a photograph, or email or text message; you would ask the sender to sign and date a written note; you would state the time and date at the beginning of a audio recording. You would keep systematic records of meetings, conversations or virtual learning experiences: how you do this is up to you, but you do need to keep your data under control. It is of course possible to fudge the data, but this is so in all kinds of research and is part of wider debates about ensuring quality in research (think of the stories of different people who have claimed to have cloned human beings).

Negotiating the authenticity of the data

Now you need to show your data to your critical friends and reviewers. They have to agree with you (or not) that your data is authentic. They would look for the signs that show authentication – signatures, times and dates, and so on. Triangulation refers to the process of showing your data, and later your evidence, originating from at least three different sources. The more sources you can show, the greater the robustness of the evidence and your claim.

Negotiating the validity of the evidence

In the next section we explain how to generate evidence from the data. Again this has to be negotiated, but now the discourse moves into a higher league: you no longer speak about authenticity, but now about validity. You move from the technicalities of authentication to the moralities of claiming and demonstrating that you are telling the truth.

4   Generating evidence

When you produce evidence to support your claim that you have improved your work, you search the archive and find artefacts that contain data, such as audio-recorded comments, pictures, field notes, email exchanges and minutes of meetings. You take out of these data those specific instances that you feel show your values in action, such as a special comment, a picture or an email. You use those data in your research report, but now you explain how they represent both your capacity to realize your values in practice, and also your capacity to articulate and communicate your specific standards of judgement.

Your explanation is key. In your report you specifically articulate the fact that you are producing evidence in relation to your articulated standards of judgement: this explains why you have selected those data and not others. You say you know what you are doing and why you are doing it. You explain that the values and principles that underpin your work (your ontological commitments) have now emerged as living standards of practice, and you are articulating and communicating them to others as the living standards by which you judge your claim (your epistemological standards of judgement) and the validity of your contribution to new knowledge. You also need to ensure that any evidence you select can be shown as authentic or genuine. For example, an email would carry the date and time of sending; a letter would carry the signature of the sender. This is part of demonstrating your methodological rigour.

Here are two examples to show this transformation of ontological values into epistemological standards of judgement. The first example is fictitious. The second is an extract from a validated PhD study (Punia, 2004). These examples show how people specifically articulated their standards of judgement as part of their process of testing the validity of their claim to knowledge.

The hospital manager's story

I work in a large regional hospital, which is also a teaching hospital. I understand that quality on-the-job learning by nurses can be influenced by the quality of teaching of mentoring nursing staff. In order to teach in a way that inspires enthusiasm and a sense of purpose among students, mentors themselves have to have a sense of purpose. How do I inspire them to develop that sense of purpose?

I take as one of my guiding principles the idea of commitment to work-based learning. As I constantly evaluate my practice I note how I try to communicate my own commitment to learning to all staff, so that they also develop a sense of purpose about their work as mentors and coaches, which in turn they communicate to their trainees.

As I monitor my work I gather data around my research issue. I conduct surveys, make audiotapes and videotapes of myself in interaction with staff, and of their interactions with trainees and one another, to see whether a development of that commitment is evident. I store my data in colour-coded files on my computer.

I take the idea of a commitment to learning as the core value that inspires this aspect of my work. As I sort through my data I note specific instances where I see demonstrations of this commitment. I see nursing coach M working in a way that enthuses his trainees to learn more. I receive email requests from two trainee nurses asking for time to go to the library for independent study. I see myself listening carefully to mentoring and trainee nurses and suggesting ways in which they could do things differently, with the urge to try them out and see. I see these actions as instances of the demonstration of my value of commitment to learning in action.

I think of how I am going to generate evidence. I first need to establish criteria. My criteria are around commitment to learning and whether others and I demonstrate it. I observe from the data that this is the case, so I can say that my criteria are being met in my own and other people's practices. I can say that my standards of practice are being fulfilled. What about standards of judgement?

I begin to think about turning the data into evidence. Now I need to take those special pieces of data out of my archive, and place them in relation to what I say I believe is happening, that is, what I now know (because it seems to be happening) that I didn't know before (because it wasn't happening). I look at the survey results, the audio- and video-recorded data, and I say to my critical friends: 'Look. Here are examples of how I believe my value of a commitment to learn is being demonstrated in practice. Here are data to show the realization of that value.' In articulating this, I am showing how I am using specific standards of judgement to judge practice. The main standard of judgement I use is related to my original value of a commitment to learn.

I am actually doing more now than just making explicit my standards of practice and judgement, and showing their significance for my own and other people's learning. Because I explain to my critical friends that I know what I am doing and why I am doing it, I can now claim that I am developing my own living theory of practice. My living theory of practice is my theory, not anyone else's, and can therefore be seen as my original contribution to knowledge.

My CV is my curriculum: the making of an international educator with spiritual values

Ram Punia

This autobiographical self-study presents my living educational theory of lifelong learning as an international educator with spiritual values including belief in cosmic unity, and continuous professional development for personal and social development of life in general. The landscape of knowledge includes India, the UK, Singapore, Hong Kong, Fiji, Samoa and Mauritius in several roles including a lecturer, teacher trainer, change agent in curriculum, staff, school development, a training technologist in corporate learning and a student in the University of Bath.

A living educational theory approach begins by asking questions of the kind: How do I improve my work? Practitioners produce accounts of their learning. A living educational theory is living in two ways: people and their theory change as a result of learning and they are living what they learn. New knowledge emerges in the process. A useful epistemology of lifelong learning of an international educator has emerged from this inquiry. Taking responsibility for my roles and contextualizing problems and solutions to problems to match the contexts were the essential dimensions of my lifelong experiential learning. These dimensions originated from my spiritual belief in cosmic unity of life and ethical aims of education.

The originality of my contribution to the knowledge base in the living educational theory approach to action research is how I integrated my spiritual and ethical values with technical knowledge to enhance the quality of my professional development and the development of technical and vocational education in the international context.

You can access Ram Punia's doctoral thesis on the University of Bath's website (http://www.actionresearch.net/living/punia.shtml). You can access other masters and doctoral abstracts in the 'Living theory' section of http://www.actionresearch.net

Summary

This chapter has taken you through the different stages of generating evidence. These stages are:

- deciding on what you are going to claim;
- establishing criteria and standards of judgement;
- selecting data;
- generating evidence in relation to your criteria and standards of judgement.

You have worked through the procedures of generating evidence, but you now have to test its validity. This involves processes of private and public testing, which are dealt with in the next part.

Further reading

Cohen, L., Manion, L. and Morrison, K. (2007) *Research Methods in Education* (sixth edition). Abingdon: Routledge.
Everyone knows this book, and so should you. It covers virtually everything there is to know about research methods, and is especially strong on gathering, interpreting and analysing data.

Whitehead, J. and McNiff, J. (2006) *Action Research: Living Theory*. London: Sage.
An in-depth discussion of the philosophical aspects of action research, with a focus on assessing quality in action research.

Whitehead, J. (2004) 'What counts as evidence in self-studies of teacher education practices?', in J.J. Loughran, M.L. Hamilton, V.K. LaBoskey and T. Russell (eds) *The International Handbook of Self-Study of Teaching Practice.* Dordrecht: Kluwer.
Perhaps the most insightful guide for explaining what data is in action research, where to look for it, and how to transform it into evidence in relation to values that act as criteria and standards of judgement.

PART V

How Do I Test and Critique My Knowledge?

This part deals with testing the validity and legitimacy of your claim to knowledge. Validity is concerned with establishing the trustworthiness of a claim, which is largely a matter of methodological procedure. Legitimacy is concerned with getting the claim accepted in the public domain. This is largely a matter of power and politics, because people have different opinions about who is entitled to speak and whose voices should be heard. At a deeper level, this means that people have different opinions about which kind of knowledge is valuable and who should be accepted as a knower.

The part contains these chapters.

In terms of your own action enquiry into the nature and uses of action research, you are now at the stage of evaluating the quality of your understanding, and you are asking: How do I validate my knowledge? How do I show that any conclusions I have come to are reasonably fair and accurate?

FIFTEEN

Testing the Validity of Your Claims to Knowledge

Having generated your evidence, you now have to show its authenticity. Furthermore, you have to seek validity for your knowledge claims, and legitimacy for the account. Authenticity, validity and legitimacy are different things. Authenticity refers to the genuineness of something, such as a piece of evidence or a person. Validity refers to testing and establishing the truth-value of a claim, or its trust-worthiness. This is a matter of rigorous methodological procedure. Legitimacy refers to getting the account accepted in the public domain, by getting people to listen to you and take your work seriously, in the hope that they may be open to learning from it or trying out something similar for themselves. Establishing legitimacy is a matter of power and politics, because people may or may not want to listen, in spite of your having demonstrated the validity of your work.

The previous chapter dealt with establishing authenticity and genuineness, as part of the process of testing validity. This chapter deals with issues of validity proper. The next chapter deals with legitimacy. All aspects are inseparable. We are setting these issues out as separate for purposes of analysis, but they are intertwined in the real-life contexts of getting people to listen to you and see the importance of your work.

The chapter is organized as two sections.

1 Validating your claim to knowledge
2 Examples of validation procedures

1 Validating your claim to knowledge

By producing validated evidence, you have satisfactorily demonstrated to yourself the internal validity of your claim to knowledge. You now need to get other people to agree that your claim to validity is credible, that is, establish its external validity. If you want to engage in public debates; it is no use talking only to yourself. You have to talk with other people and get them to engage. This means you have to put your claim into the public arena with an explicit articulation of your procedures to demonstrate its methodological rigour, so that its validity can be tested against other people's critical assessment. Once they agree with you, you can regard your claim as valid (but see next paragraph), and proceed with greater confidence. It may be of course that in the process of public testing, they may not agree with you, so you may have to go back and think again. This can be difficult for several reasons, including the common reaction that people tend to see critique as critique of themselves and not of their ideas. Critique is, however, an essential part of scholarship (and of many other human practices), so do not avoid it. Go for it with vigour, and show that you do have something important to say, and make sure that you are listened to.

As noted earlier, bear in mind that in some situations, such as in the case of Galileo, when people in authority judge you to be mistaken, you may in fact be correct. Although having your claim judged democratically goes a long way towards testing its validity, this does not necessarily establish the validity of your claims. You may in fact be right when others are mistaken. If you are convinced that you are right, and can justify your stance to yourself, you have good reason to stand firm. This is, however, a risky business and you need to be aware of the risks involved.

[Note: the people in the following example are fictitious]

'Velda McPhee's story' – see following pages

My name is Velda McPhee and I am a health visitor in Mpumalanga, South Africa. I counsel local people on sexual health in the wider effort to stop the spread of HIV and AIDS. I believe I am making progress in some places, in that a lot of village women now practise safe sex, and insist that their husbands and partners do so as well, but this can be difficult in the face of strong traditions. These include the ideas that women should not avoid contraception but agree to the practice of producing babies. They also include the idea that it is 'manly' for a husband or partner to have many relationships outside marriage; and women – even educated women – go along with these traditions and so sustain them.

Different approaches to testing validity

We explained earlier that researchers such as Furlong and Oancea (2005) called for a uniform response by the practitioner-research community about what kinds of criteria and standards should be used when making judgements about the quality of practice-based research. Their contribution was one among many; researchers had for years been arguing for new ways of testing validity, that would replace the traditional criteria of positivist forms of research (mainly generalizability and replicability). Many had come up with new ideas about new forms of validity. Familiarity with these concepts will help you decide whether or not to use them in your own research.

Here are some of the most common.

Catalytic validity – This term, coined by Patti Lather in 1991, expresses the idea that the experience of a study would enable people to move to new, more productive positions.

Construct validity – Refers to the idea that a researcher already has ideas and models (constructs) about the topic they are researching. It is therefore important to use multiple ways of establishing that what they are investigating really is going on, and is not just them imposing their existing constructs on the reality they are observing.

Face validity – An issue appears as basic common sense; you recognize its truthfulness at face value.

Ironic validity – The researcher does not take things simply at face value but interrogates underlying assumptions.

Rhizomatic validity – Another term coined by Lather that refers to the interconnected nature of human enquiry and the power of a study to have influence in multiple directions.

Additionally, prominent researchers such as Bullough and Pinnegar (2001, 2004) and Feldman (2003) focus on demonstrating quality in self-study action research. Agreeing with ideas from Whitehead (1989), Bullough and Pinnegar make the point that establishing quality and demonstrating validity are grounded in a researcher's ontological values; and Feldman also argues that validity has to be linked with one's moral purposes in the world.

These and others are useful ideas for helping you appreciate the need to establish the validity of your claims to knowledge. The key fact remains, however, that you yourself need to be open to critique and to seek it actively in testing the validity of your knowledge claims. Here are some ideas about how you can do this.

Arranging for critique

If you are on a professional development or award-bearing programme, you may be assigned a supervisor to offer you guidance and critique. Do not expect your supervisor to tell you that your work is good when it is not. Their job is to guide you and invite you to question your own assumptions, so do not get hostile when they ask problematizing questions about your work rather than give you immediate affirmation. Their job is to encourage you to extend your thinking. You can see some good examples of one-to-one critical supervision at http://www.action research.net/multimedia/jimenomov/JIMEW98.html in the multimedia account: 'How valid are multimedia communications of my embodied values in living theories and standards of educational judgement and practice?' (Whitehead 2004b).

You should also seek out critique from groupings of critical friends. The kind of constructive, unsentimental feedback you are looking for will probably come from people who are sympathetic to what you are doing but are also aware of the need to challenge your thinking, especially in relation to your own assumptions and established ways of thinking. They will probably be drawn from your circle of colleagues, peers, students, parents, friends or interested observers. There are no rules about who to invite.

Having identified these people, you now need to invite them to act as critical friends and companions. Explain carefully in advance what this will involve. They will have to meet with you throughout your research, listen to you explain what the research is about, look at your data, and consider contextual aspects and the internal coherence of the research. Above all they have to be prepared to offer critical feedback, to enable you to see things you have perhaps missed, or to find new directions. It is their job to help you to see whether you are extending your thinking and developing new insights, or whether you are doing your research to justify and continue your existing assumptions.

I regularly invite women from the villages to work with me in establishing the validity of my findings, and my thinking, about how best to proceed. Sometimes they agree that we are making progress through the counselling and workshops that I provide. Sometimes they feel that we could do more by working together more coherently. They offer advice about what seems to be working and what could be better.

Critical friends

Ideally your critical friends will agree to stay with you for the life of your research, but this is often not possible. Some may drop out, others in. You do need one or two people, however, who are going to stay the course, so that they can give feed-back about how original issues have developed, especially in terms of your own learning. While ideal, this may also not be possible, and it emphasizes the idea of getting baseline data in the form of, say, a critical conversation with a colleague to say why you are doing the research and what you hope to achieve.

You may meet with your critical friends singly or in groups, depending on your needs and their availability. Treat them carefully. They are valuable people, essential to your research and you need to maintain their goodwill. Write to them about meetings and give them plenty of advance notice. Write a thank you note after your meetings. Never abuse their kindness. They are giving their time and energy for free and this needs to be acknowledged gracefully.

After each meeting with a critical friend, write a brief record of the event and sign and date it. Give two copies to your friend and ask them to countersign and date them. One copy is for their files and one for you. This copy can stand as a powerful piece of evidence when you come to show the integrity of the procedural aspects of your research.

A core group of five women and I have built close working relationships. I have given them extra training in prevention measures, so they can take over my work when I am

---

away visiting other villages. I have also given them books and other resources to develop their subject knowledge. They maintain records of our meetings together, so that they can learn from our developing insights together. They in turn act as critical friends to one another. When I return, we hold validation groups together, so we can all evaluate our individual and collective work and improve it where necessary. Therefore, as well as acting as critical friends to me and one another, the group of women have formed themselves into a task group whose job is to clear their village of disease.`

Validation groups

Your validation group will consist of 3 to 10 people, depending on the size of your project. You may invite any or all of your critical friends to join this group, and you can also recruit new people. Again, they should be drawn from your professional circle, but this time you should aim to include people who are not directly involved in your research or associated with you, such as the head of another department or an interested outside observer, or perhaps someone from the business community. As before, they should be competent to offer you educated feedback, not be unnecessarily picky, but be seen as capable of offering an informed and reasonably unbiased opinion.

The job of your validation group is different from that of your critical friends. They have to meet with you at regular intervals to listen to your research account. Accept that not all members of the group may be available on all occasions, but try to ensure continuity. The job of your validation group is to listen to you, scrutinize your data and evidence, consider your claims to knowledge and offer critical feedback. Validation meetings are seldom cosy or comfortable experiences for researchers, because the rationale is to raise questions and to critique, and not to approve anything without solid evidence that shows its internal validity. This means that you have to articulate the standards of judgement you have used and show that you are aware of the problematics of generating evidence. Your validation group would also expect you to be able to articulate the potential significance of your work and to indicate some of its implications.

Validation groups can convene to consider work in progress and also final submissions. Meetings to consider work in progress act as formative evaluation meetings, while those that consider final submissions act as summative evaluation meetings. For your formative evaluation meetings, you should prepare and provide a progress report that outlines the research design, work done so far, any preliminary findings, provisional conclusions on those findings and comments on whether the research is proceeding satisfactorily or any suggestions for possible new directions. Summative evaluation reports, that is, final reports, should set out from the start what your claim to knowledge is (you may make several claims), and how you feel you are justified in making the claim. This will involve an explication of methodological issues, such as research design and processes, and also explain how evidence has been generated from the data in support of your claim. It will also contain epistemological issues of why you feel you are justified in claiming that you have developed your own theory of practice. This means that you are able to describe what you did and how you did it, and also to explain why you did it and what you believe you have achieved in terms of your educational and social goals. You are able to articulate the standards of judgement you have used in making your claim to knowledge, and explain their part in the development of your theory of practice. Showing how your work can constitute a theory of practice is essential if you wish it to be seen as a potential contribution to educational theory.

As with critical friends, do not take your validation group for granted. Let them know that their help is appreciated. Give them advance notice of proposed meetings and enquire about their availability. People have busy diaries and need time. Try to negotiate travel expenses for those at a distance. If this is not possible, say so, and thank them for their effort and commitment.

> I believe that the work the women and I are doing is having an influence on the health practices of the women in the village, and a drop in the incidence of HIV and AIDS. A key feature of its success is the involvement of the five local women. They have been able to work with their neighbours and develop the kinds of intimate relationships that I cannot. I would like to write up and disseminate the work, emphasizing the centrality of collaborative working in any community effort. So I have secured the encouragement and enthusiasm of our district health visitor as well as from the regional university to help me establish the credibility of the work. They have agreed to visit with me twice a year, to listen to our research, scrutinize our evidence, and offer advice about how the work may be developed further and how it may be written up and disseminated in the wider public domain.

In advance of the meeting, send a briefing sheet to each member of the group (see the example on page 167). After each meeting, write up a record of what was said, sign and date it, and send two copies to each member of the group. Ask them to countersign and date these, keep one copy for their files and return one to you. Keep this safely. Produce it in your final report as evidence both of what was said in response to your claim to knowledge and also of the meticulous care you paid to the methodological aspects of your research.

It can help to secure the services of one of the group as a minuting secretary. They do not need to keep detailed minutes, or notes of individual speakers' comments, but they do need to keep a reasonably accurate record of what points were made and what actions recommended. If no one volunteers, you will have to keep minutes yourself. This can be difficult because you will be focusing on responding to questions, so try to get someone else to keep records for you. Give them an exemplar sheet, such as the one below to help them.

Remember in validation meetings that you have little control over what happens and what people will think and say. This is one of the reasons why careful preparation is important. You have to prepare a case for why others should believe you and acknowledge your credibility and the legitimacy of your research.

2   Examples of validation procedures

Here are some ideas about how to draw up a briefing sheet for a validation meeting and how a validation meeting might be conducted.

Validation meeting briefing sheet

If you are presenting your work, please check:

1   Have you said at the beginning what you are claiming to have achieved through the research?
2   Have you made clear …

- your research question?
- your reasons for doing the research?
- the conceptual frameworks you have used?
- your research aims and intentions?
- your research design?
- an awareness of ethical considerations?
- the methodology you chose and why?
- how you monitored practice?
- how you gathered data, interpreted the data and generated evidence?
- the criteria and standards of judgement you used?
- how you came to some provisional conclusions?

3   Are you explaining that you are now testing your claims to knowledge? Are you inviting critical evaluation of the claims?
4   Do you show how doing the research has led you to develop new forms of practice and new learning?
5   Do you show the significance of your work in terms of your possible contributions to new practices and new theory?

If you are listening to a presentation of research, please check:

1   Does the researcher make an original contribution to knowledge? In what way?
2   Does the researcher demonstrate critical engagement throughout? In what way?
3   Does the researcher demonstrate an awareness of ethical considerations?
4   Does the researcher make clear the standards of judgement used to test claims?
5   Does the research contribute to new educational practices and new educational thinking? In what way?
6   Does the researcher present the work in a way that clarifies its significance and future potentials?
7   Does the researcher show a critical engagement with the ideas of others?

Minutes of a peer validation group meeting, 20 November 2010, Carnegie Bridge, Mpumalanga

Present

Velda McPhee (presenting)

Margaret M. (town resident, deputy health counsellor)
Maria G. (town resident, deputy health counsellor)
Alice M. (town resident, deputy health counsellor)
Fia X. (town resident, deputy health counsellor)
Carrie M. (town resident, deputy health counsellor)
Jean-Philipe Latour (hospital representative)
Tamana Terre-Blanche (university representative)
Robert Maidment (publisher)

Velda McPhee presented her research account to the validation group covering all aspects of the briefing sheet supplied. She was closely questioned about the validity of her claim to knowledge and critical issues were raised about:

- The justification of her standards of judgement – some members of the group requested further evidence to be supplied at the next meeting in relation to Velda's claim that she was encouraging the growth of new knowledge and new health practices through the involvement of a women's group in the village.
- Her claim to be developing a new approach to dealing with HIV and AIDS – further evidence was requested.

Recommendations of the validation group

Velda should continue her work and her research in its present form, but attend to the issues raised by the validation group. Further evidence to be supplied at the next validation group meeting on 9 March 2011.

Velda should work closely with Robert Maidment (publisher) on preparing her work for further dissemination.

She should also work closely with Tamana Terre-Blanche in preparing to give a series of talks to health workers at the regional teaching university.

A real-life example of a validation meeting in an education context

One of the best examples of a validation group meeting is in the MA dissertation of Martin Forrest (1983). As a professional educator, Martin's concern was to investigate the quality of his educational influence in the professional learning of the teachers he supported. To judge the quality of his work, he posed two questions:

1 How can we know that an improvement has taken place in the school classroom? What criteria do we use to judge whether an innovation has led to an improvement in the quality of learning?
2 In the context of my work as an in-service tutor, how effective am I in my role as a disseminator and supporter of innovation? What evidence is there to support my claim to be helping teachers to improve the quality of their children's learning?

He decided to investigate his practice especially in relation to how he supported two primary teachers, who were themselves interested in evaluating their use of historical artefacts in the classroom. One of the teachers, Sue Kilminster, took as her standards of judgement the then current Aims of School Education (DES, 1981), which included:

- to help pupils to develop lively, enquiring minds, the ability to question and argue rationally and to apply themselves to tasks and physical skills;
- to help pupils acquire knowledge and skills relevant to adult life and employment in a fast-changing world.

In an attempt to encourage these capacities in her pupils, Sue developed the idea of a 'feely box', which was a closed cardboard box into which artefacts were placed, and the children were invited to 'feel' the objects through a hole in the side of the box and guess their identity. The event was videoed. The children were invited to discuss their ideas as they explored, and at the end of the lesson, when the objects were revealed, their group discussion was also recorded.

At a validation group meeting, Sue said, 'I was amazed at the quality of the questions being asked by the children, because they were actually thinking about the time of the object and asking questions about that time.'

Members of the validation group were given Martin's two questions (see above) as the basis on which to make their judgements. Comments from the validation group included the following:

'The thing that impressed me most was the way, somehow, these children came to their conclusions through dialogue and discussion themselves.'

'I just wanted to say that I was very impressed by the evidence of lively enquiring minds.'

'"It couldn't be a library book because you couldn't keep a book out of the library for as long as that." Obviously they've got some concept of time, haven't they?'

During subsequent validation meetings, Martin was questioned closely about his role, and required to produce documentary evidence to support his claim that he had exercised his educational influence in the learning of the teachers he was supporting.

--------- Summary ---------

This chapter has set out ideas about establishing the validity of a claim to knowledge, that is, showing its truthfulness or trustworthiness.

This is done primarily by arranging for critique. This may come from critical friends or validation groups. The chapter has also given examples of documents used in validation procedures. The next chapter deals with establishing the legitimacy of your claims to knowledge.

Further reading

The idea of assessing quality in action research and testing the validity of claims to knowledge remains a sticking point in some quarters. These texts engage with the issues.

Bullough, R. and Pinnegar, S. (2001) 'Guidelines for quality in autobiographical forms of self-study research', *Educational Researcher*, 30 (3): 13–21.
The authors offer guidelines for assessing quality – a valuable contribution.

Habermas (1987) *The Theory of Communicative Action Volume Two: The Critique of Functionalist Reason.* Oxford: Polity.
Throughout his work, Habermas has emphasized the need to articulate criteria and standards that will enable researchers to make judgements about the quality of their own work in relation to their communicative and social interests.

Kok, P. (1991) 'The art of an educational inquirer'. MA dissertation, University of Bath. Retrieved 1 August 2010 from http://www.actionresearch.net/living/peggy.shtml
Kok's dissertation shows how Richard Winter's six criteria for judging the quality of action research may be used to enhance the rigour of an action research account.

Lather, P. (1991) *Getting Smart: Feminism Research and Pedagogy With/in the Postmodern.* London: Routledge.
Lather, P. (1994) 'Textuality as praxis'. A paper presented at the American Educational Research Association annual meeting, New Orleans, April.
Two important texts from Lather's postmodern critical perspective that offer new criteria and standards for judging quality in research.

Winter, R. (1989) *Learning from Experience.* London: Falmer.
Winter's six criteria for assessing quality in action research remain relevant and timeless.

SIXTEEN

Establishing the Legitimacy of Your Claims to Knowledge

If validity is about establishing the truth value of a claim, legitimacy is about establishing its acceptance in the public sphere. Both processes involve getting the agreement of others that what you have to say should be believed and incorporated into public thinking. While you have some control over validation processes, by showing the internal coherence and methodological rigour of your claim, you have less control over legitimation processes, because you are presenting your claim within the socio-political context of other people's interests, including their personal and professional ambitions. This can be tricky, because those people may or may not agree that your work is valuable depending on how its suits their purposes.

In other writings, including McNiff and Whitehead (2010), we have cited the examples of Galileo and Bruno, who were made to suffer for their work. In both cases the validity of their ideas was clearly demonstrated, yet they were silenced (Bruno was burned alive) when the dominant institution, which at the time was the Church, mobilized its resources of power against them. The same has happened to people throughout history. Jesus and Socrates are outstanding examples. People in power have silenced others who have something useful to say, yet which seems to threaten the authority and stability of their own power base. This has also happened to action researchers, for example when they encounter the procedures for gaining ethical approval for their enquiries (see the case of Geoff Suderman-Gladwell (2001), referred to on page 92, on *The Ethics of Personal Subjective Narrative Research* at http://www.actionresearch.net/writings/values/gsgma.pdf). How do you prevent it happening to you? How do you show both the validity and the legitimacy of your research in a way that engages the attention of all and ensures its acceptance in the public domain? Unfortunately, in some cases this is not possible, and you have to find new strategies for dealing with the situation (see Chapter 17).

This chapter gives advice on how you can show the value of your research so that it stands a good chance of getting accepted by different audiences. One of your greatest strengths is that you are both a practitioner and a researcher. In both contexts you will be recognized as a member of that particular community of practice, and can speak to other people's experience. However, we have made the point throughout that, while you are likely to be recognized readily by the community of practitioners as capable of making valuable contributions to practice, there may be some resistance to recognizing you as a member of the community of researchers, when you maintain that you are advancing knowledge.

Here are some ideas about how you can deal with the situation. The chapter is organized as two sections.

1 Getting recognized by the community of practitioners
2 Getting recognized by the community of researchers

1   Getting recognized by the community of practitioners

Getting recognized involves being able to articulate the significance of what you have done, so that people can see that there is something in it for them. If you are convinced that you have done something worthwhile, and can explain why, people will be more likely to listen to you, including your peer community of practitioners.

Articulating the significance of your practice

Practitioners will be interested if they can see that your work is relevant to them and how your ideas can enrich their lives. This is good news for you because you can immediately show what others can learn from what you have done. It can also be problematic, because often people say, 'Tell me what you did. Tell me how I can do the same.' There is often an expectation that you should give them ready-made answers, which they can apply to their own practice. Action research does not work like this. People have to do it for themselves. This is also why it is important that you do not present your work as a finished product, which you now expect others to apply to their practice. In your report you explain how you have learned from the experience and what they could also learn by doing something similar in their own context. You are showing the significance of your learning, and inviting others to learn with and from you.

You can do this in relation to several learning contexts.

Your own learning

By producing your account of what you have done, you show how you have learned to do things differently and better. Your new learning has fed back into new action, which has in turn generated new learning. This is an ongoing process and has become a way of life that will continue into the future.

In Chapter 8 we told the story of Jean's work in the township of Khayelitsha. She worked with 10 teachers to help them get their masters degrees. Each of the teachers is able to say how they have engaged in their own learning, so that the learning has led to new attitudes and insights, and, ultimately, has improved the quality of their teaching and the learning of their students.

Here we take the example of Luvuyo Ngumbe, a history teacher (Ngumbe, 2008). The account is slightly edited from his original, which was an assignment for a module on his masters programme.

I was born, and started my schooling in the Eastern Cape in Port Elizabeth, under the apartheid system of education, within a context of laws that enforced racial segregation. ... We were taught in a teaching style where teachers were regarded as owners of knowledge and masters of the teaching matter. We were also taught to be obedient, hardworking, submissive and acceptant of normative hierarchies of power in preparation for a capitalistic world. ... I brought these understandings into my own later practices as a history teacher. This attitude reflected in my students' responses to the subject matter. They were passive and showed no insight when dealing with questions of history or any sense of being critical. This situation was contradictory to my values of interest and personal engagement in learning, so I decided to do something about the situation. I distributed a questionnaire to my students, the results of which told me that my teaching did not inspire them. My teaching style, grounded in a separation between myself as an educator and them as learners, had built a wall between myself and my learners, which made it difficult for them to acquire any educational knowledge that would help them become responsible adults. The question of the wall reminds me of Maxine Greene's ideas: 'The wall has to be viewed as a personal challenge, as an obstacle, but it becomes such only to those risking free choice' (Greene 1988: 6). I began to appreciate the deep divisions between us, and what this was doing to the learners, so I decided to change my practices. I put the learners into small groups, and each person had their own responsibility, such as lead, scribe and encourager. Over time they came to appreciate their capacity for learning, and quickly began to ask questions and engage in debates. I reflected that the improved performance of my learners indicated an improvement of my own teaching practice. This reminded me of Foucault's words, that 'The main interest in life and work is to become someone else you were not in the beginning' (Foucault 1971: 1). (Ngumbe, 2008: 6–7)

The learning of others in your workplace

By accessing your account, other people in your workplace and professional contexts can see how they can do something similar in their contexts. They will not necessarily do the same as you, because you have not presented your account as a model. You have learned by doing, about what worked and what did not, so next time you do it you may do things differently. Your story shows how you constantly tried to live in the manner of what you believed in and how you transformed your present context into a new one in which all were benefiting from working together.

Luvuyo continues his story, about how he began to get his colleagues interested in action research. Again the account is slightly edited.

Through studying my practice both as a teacher and as a departmental manager, I became aware that I had to move away from traditional hierarchical styles of interaction and develop more dialogical approaches, with an acceptance of mutual power and influence. I then began to experience cooperation and teamwork from colleagues in my department, to the extent that they became interested in undertaking their own action enquiries. I have come to appreciate that progressive cultures of teaching and learning in classrooms cannot be realized without cooperation and teamwork among educators in an institution. Colleagues and I are working collaboratively to find ways of developing a research-based institutional culture that is grounded in the values of care for others and love of learning. (Ngumbe, 2008: 4)

On 19 September 2009, Luvuyo was awarded his masters degree by the University of Surrey.

The education of social formations

Jack Whitehead (2003, 2004a) speaks about 'the education of social formations', that is, helping others everywhere to understand how they can work together in a way that will help them to improve their social contexts. This is especially important for understanding how practitioners can act as agents. A social context is not an abstract entity, but comprises people who make decisions about how they should think and act. Sometimes these decisions become solidified into accepted rules and structures, and sometimes the rules and structures take on a life of their own to rise above the heads of the people who made them in the first place (Habermas, 1987). People come to serve the rules, rather than have the rules serve them, and to see the rules no longer as temporary answers, which were appropriate for a particular situation at a particular time, but as fixed norms. They also often do not see that it is in their power to change the rules, even when the rules are out of date. Your strength as a practitioner-researcher lies in how you can show that you have changed the rules of your context by changing your practice. You have deconstructed old ways and have established new ones that are recognized by others as an improvement. By accessing your account, other people can see that they can do this too. When they see that you have done it, they will understand what it takes for them to do the same.

Many accounts show how this can be done. Ivan O'Callaghan (1997) showed how he reconceptualized his work as a principal to develop new forms of participatory working. Jackie Delong and Heather Knill-Griesser (2002) show how they integrate issues of power and ethics in valid explanations of their educative influence as a teacher-consultant and a superintendent (see also higher degree accounts in the same publication). Dave Abbey (2002) explains how he develops his teacher-consultant's role in developing and facilitating an interdisciplinary studies course. Melanie Rivers (2003) shows how she created an inclusive atmosphere to support an autistic student in her classroom. These stories of scholarly practice are in the public domain and accessible to all. (For workplace accounts see http:// schools.gedsb.net/ar/passion/index.html; for higher degree accounts see http:// schools.gedsb.net/ar/theses/index.html.

New work is happening in Khayelitsha. Jean is continuing her involvement with the teachers, but now helping them to develop their capacities as professional mentors and coaches. Because they achieved their masters degrees, some have been promoted as principals and deputy principals, or to positions in local education authorities; so they now have the power to sustain such developments. Together, Jean and some of her colleagues hope to develop professional education programmes in schools and also further a field. The story of the original project is told in McNiff (2011b) and also at the following websites (http://www.jeanmcniff.com/items.asp?id=23 and http://www. jeanmcniff.com/items.asp?id=1). The kinds of accounts being produced have the potential to influence the education of the teaching profession, both in South Africa, and in other contexts around the world. One member of the group is now studying with Jean for his doctorate.

By producing your account of practice you are not only helping other practitioners to see how they can help themselves but also contributing to the public evidence base of practice, and to the public knowledge base of theory (see Section 2 of this chapter).

Strengthening the evidence base of practice

Getting recognized also involves both methodological and political and economic aspects. All are equally important.

Methodological aspects

First, it is vital to show the methodological rigour of your evidence base for your claims of the kind, 'I have improved my practice.' You show how you have collected data to support your claim to knowledge, which you have authenticated and subjected to the critical judgement of others, so that you can now claim it as evidence. The claim appears robust.

Political and economic aspects

Your account now goes into the public domain and joins many others already there. The mass of public accounts comes to form a large body of knowledge, itself an evidence base that supports the idea of practitioner research. This body of knowledge comprises accounts of the personal theories of practitioners as they give explanations for what they are doing and why they are doing it. Further, the accounts show how practitioners have learned from one another, and how this process has influenced their future lives and learning. The following example is from Eleanor Lohr (2004).

Having just submitted my PhD thesis I am thinking, 'Ah well, so that's over. Now I can get on with the rest of my life!' But that's not possible. In wanting to hold to what I have learned in writing my thesis, I find that I must continue to write, to reflect, to act, to inquire. And by returning, by reworking, by thinking through my action research journey within a community of others on similar expeditions, I hope to continue to reform myself and thus improve what I do with others on similar expeditions. (Posted 1 December 2004, retrieved 2 December 2004 from the 'discuss the article' section of http://www. arexpeditions.montana.edu/articleviewer.php?AID=80 [no longer active])

Politically, you are showing that you are not alone. Your voice is one among many, all of whom are doing similar things to yourself. Voices in community usually have a much stronger influence than lone voices. Here is an example that shows how political-economic influences can be a major conceptual framework for an enquiry. Graham van Tuyl (2009) has included these influences in the generation of his living theory of his life as a change agent in the oil industry, in his doctoral thesis.

From engineer to co-creative catalyst; an inclusional and transformational journey. An inquiry into the epistemology of how traditional management 'tools and theory' can be used and evolved in enhancing organizational effectiveness in an industrial setting, and how to value and evaluate change. (See the abstract to his thesis on page 244; available also at http://www.actionresearch.net/living/gvt.shtml.)

---

2   Getting recognized by the community of researchers

Getting recognized by the community of researchers can be far trickier, because practitioners have not traditionally been perceived as thinkers. Their job has been to do, rather than think, and now here you are claiming to be both a thinker and, by making your account of thinking public, a public intellectual who has something to say about what social practices should look like and what form they should take. You have suddenly become potentially dangerous.

Public intellectuals

The idea of you as a public intellectual is important and worth considering further. A common understanding of intellectuals is that they are an elitist group who have something to say about high culture. While this may be the case in some quarters, it is different in others. Gramsci (1973) talked about organic intellectuals who are 'directly connected to classes or enterprises … to organize interests, gain more power, get more control' (Said, 1994: 3–4). Said also talks about public intellectuals, whose work is constantly to pose awkward questions about current social practices so that the status quo is interrogated and its discourses interrupted. Chomksy (1988) says that the responsibility of intellectuals is to tell the truth and expose lies. This also means digging beneath the propaganda systems that many elites put in place to keep ordinary people under control and prevent them from asking too many questions that might expose the real intentions of elites. These issues are especially relevant to you, because practitioners are often the targets of such propaganda systems. Messages communicated through public discourses systematically persuade practitioners that they cannot think for themselves, that they are not capable of talking intelligently about knowledge and that they should leave these matters to those who are publicly recognized as capable, that is, intellectuals (see Hammersley, 1993). More will be said about these issues in Chapter 17.

This also raises questions about who qualifies as an intellectual. An intellectual is someone who works with their intellect, not only their bodies. On this view, people in shops and on street corners who have something to say about social orders should be seen as intellectuals. As an action researcher you are special, because you show how working with your intellect is an embodied practice. Your work as an intellectual and as a practitioner is integrated. You are not an intellectual on Wednesday and a practitioner on Thursday. You are a thinker and a doer all the time.

So how to communicate this to those who believe that intellectuals working in publicly recognized research institutions are the only ones capable of advancing knowledge? How to persuade them that you also have something enormously valuable to say, that they can learn from you, and that they should consider regarding themselves as practitioners?

One of the ways is to show how you as a practitioner are contributing to others' learning. This involves showing the validity of the work, as discussed in the previous section. Another is to persuade intellectuals working in elite institutions to regard themselves as practitioners who are learning with and from other practitioners about how to improve their own work. This involves referring to those accounts by higher education personnel, who already regard themselves as practitioners, and explaining that a large body of knowledge already exists to show how and why they should do this. Large bodies of evidence go a long way to influencing public opinion and to persuading others to adopt similar practices.

Large bodies of knowledge do exist, produced by scholar-practitioners working in higher education. Here are some examples from recent contributions.

Karen Riding works in a secondary school working in modern foreign languages. See her PhD thesis 'How do I come to understand my shared living educational standards of judgement in the life I lead with others? Creating the space for intergenerational student-led research' (2008, retrieved 27 July 2010 from http://www.actionresearch. net/karenridingphd.shtml).

Simon Riding works as a deputy headteacher in a secondary school. See his PhD thesis 'How do I contribute to the education of myself and others through improving the quality of living educational space? The story of living myself through others as a practitioner-researcher' 2008, retrieved 27 July 2010 from http://www.actionresearch.net/simonridingphd.shtml).

Jocelyn Jones works as a consultant in social services. See her PhD thesis 'Thinking with stories of suffering: towards a living theory of response-ability' (2008, retrieved 27 July 2010 from http://www.actionresearch.net/jocelynjonesphd.shtml).

Joan Walton is the Director of the Centre for The Child and Family at Liverpool Hope University. See her PhD thesis 'Ways of knowing: can I find a way of knowing that satisfies my search for meaning?' (2008, retrieved 27 July 2010 from http://www.actionresearch.net/walton.shtml).

Jane Spiro works as an academic staff developer at Oxford Brookes University. See her PhD thesis 'How I have arrived at a notion of knowledge transformation, through understanding the story of myself as creative writer, creative educator, creative manager, and educational researcher' (2008, retrieved 27 July 2010 from http://www.actionresearch.net/janespirophd.shtml).

Chris Jones is a senior inclusion officer in Bath and North East Somerset. See her MA dissertation 'How do I improve my practice as an inclusion officer working in a children's service' (2008, retrieved 27 July 2010 from http://www.actionresearch.net/living/cjmaok/cjma.htm).

Another collection of accounts from Ireland is referenced in Chapter 17.

Many other stories exist, and their numbers are increasing by the day, as a visit to the living theory section and masters programme section at http://www.actionresearch.net and http://www.jeanmcniff.com will show. You can also see this burgeoning development of case studies in electronic journals such as the *Educational Journal of Living Theories*. Here are the contents for the July 2010 issue:

Contents: July 2010, Volume 3, Issue 1

Foreword (pp. i–iii), *Je Kan Adler Collins*

Engaging educators in representing their knowledge in complex ecologies and cultures of inquiry (pp. 1–38), *Jacqueline Delong*

Working towards a symbiotic practice (pp. 39–73), *Alex Sinclair*

On becoming an activist: a 'progress report' on a 37 year journey to date (pp. 74–104), *Philip J. Tattersall*

The transformative potential of living theory educational research (pp. 105–118), *Lesley Wood*

What is special about all these stories is how their authors position themselves as practitioners who are generating their living theories of practice. If you are on a programme leading to accreditation, your story of how you have improved your practice by improving your learning can stand with them. As someone who is studying for a degree, you are automatically positioned in higher education. This positioning would probably be contested, however, by those who regard themselves as specialists in knowledge, which returns us to the issue of power and politics. These issues are everywhere and should be treated seriously. You need to get on the inside of what the issues are, so that you can deal with them. This brings us to the next chapter about the politics of educational knowledge.

Summary

This chapter has dealt with ideas about establishing the legitimacy of your claim to knowledge, that is, getting it accepted in the public domain. Because you are claiming to have contributed both to new practices and to new theory, you have to secure the approval both of the community of practitioners and of the community of researchers. This second aspect is often more difficult than the first and can mean engaging with the politics of knowledge. This issue is dealt with in the next chapter.

Further reading

Habermas (1975) *Legitimation Crisis*, trans. T. McCarthy. Boston, MA: Beacon Press.
This classic text from Habermas engages with the idea of establishing legitimacy within new paradigms. See especially pages 2–3 where he sets out four criteria for social validity.

Jenkins, R. (1992) *Pierre Bourdieu*. London: Routledge.
Jenkins gives an accessible guide to the life and work of Bourdieu, a sociologist who was also much concerned with issues of power, privilege and legitimation. To read the man himself, have a look at

Bourdieu, P. (1992) *The Logic of Practice*: Cambridge: Polity.
Or, for a really wicked look at his debunking of academia, read:

Bourdieu, P. (1988) *Homo Academicus*. Cambridge: Polity.

Chomsky, N. and Foucault, M. (2006) *The Chomsky-Foucault Debate on Human Nature*. New York: The New Press.
The authors hold a sometimes hilarious debate in which they discuss issues to do with the politics of knowledge and the legitimation of knowers.

SEVENTEEN
Engaging with the Politics of Knowledge

Sometimes action researchers work in contexts that do not support their research. The lack of interest can range from apathy to outright hostility. In many cases, it is a matter of power and prestige, related to jobs and earnings. Those already in powerful positions make every effort to prevent others' voices from being heard. If you are in such a context, and want to continue doing your research, you need to be clear about how cultures of power operate, so that, as well as surviving, you can also transform hierarchical power into democratic power and go on to develop a culture of enquiry. This may take time, but it can be done.

This chapter is in two sections.

1 Understanding oppression
2 Strategies for transformation

1 Understanding oppression

The foundations of oppression lie in one person's wish to control the other, usually for their own self-promotion. People achieve this through strategies aimed at control and domination. They tend ontologically towards self-interest, using a form of thinking that sees the self as the centre of the universe, and all other entities, including people, as things that can be manipulated in order to serve their own interests. It was this kind of thinking that led to early experiments on animals, asserting that they were mechanical objects whose screams were caused by the movement of their limbs, and to a view of people as disposable (Bales, 1999). Practices that see a person as less than human stem from the assumption that one person has the right to make judgements about the potential value of another and to impose their will so that the other is made invisible if necessary. This can extend to controlling the entire environment. The planet is seen as a renewable resource to be exploited for cash.

Practices of domination and oppression are aspects of unilateral power. According to Foucault (1980), power is not a thing, but is in the relationships of people as they interact. It moves through their relationships like quicksilver, permeating personal boundaries and infiltrating attitudes and discourses.

In many organizational contexts, the person in power is the one who can exercise most control. In contemporary, post-industrial, knowledge-creating societies, where knowledge is the most prized possession, the person in power is the one who knows most. Because knowledge can be exchanged for cash, the person with the most knowledge gets the position and the money. Foucault (1980) knew this when he said that power and knowledge were inseparable.

In traditional organizational contexts, people tend to be organized in hierarchical structures, which are presented usually as hierarchies of responsibility but are actually hierarchies of power. Those at the top are publicly acknowledged as the best people. In knowledge contexts, they are the ones who know. It can be pleasant at the top, so they tend to resist any claim by pretenders, such as practitioners, that they also deserve to be seen as knowers. Sometimes those at the top go to extraordinary lengths to put down any rebellion or attempt to revolutionize the system that legitimizes their own position. They do this by using a range of strategies of control. This is where the discussion becomes significant for you.

Strategies of control differ according to the political nature of the context. For example, in a dictatorship, according to Chomsky (1988), in which human rights can be violated without fear of reprisal, it is commonplace to suppress insurgence by violent means. Those who protest are silenced by being made invisible, often by incarceration or death. In democratic societies, however, where laws protect citizens from violence, other means have to be sought. These, according to Chomsky, take the form of the control of the public mind, using strategies of persuasion. These strategies can range from gentle cajoling to forms of manipulation that have people colluding in their own subjugation and claiming that it was their idea in the first place.

In contexts of educational knowledge, the orthodoxy is that professional researchers are capable of doing research and generating theory, while practitioners are not. So commonplace is this view that many people, researchers and practitioners alike, come to believe it sincerely. Some researchers write books and articles that adopt a benevolent tone, as they explain how they will relieve practitioners of the responsibility of doing research (and presumably thinking for themselves). In practice contexts, the situation can become quite severe, when those in power refuse to allow practitioners to do their research because it may threaten the status quo.

It takes considerable skill and goodwill to avoid or overcome these relationships of oppression, yet this is what you are aiming to do as an action researcher. Because you would hold values around a desire for stable working relationships and thoughtful interactions, you would try to avoid confrontation or hostility, and find ways through potentially problematic situations.

Here is an example that shows how one group of people managed to do this. It is a true story, though the author has requested anonymity because of the sensitive nature of the context.

Action research in an acute psychiatric unit

The events I speak about in this story happened some years ago, but they have, I believe, lasting relevance for explaining how collaborative working between different groups in an organization, based on a willingness to understand the talent and capacity for knowledge generation of all, can contribute to organizational growth and human flourishing through knowledge production. It is also significant for me that, at the time this story took place, I had never heard of action research. It is only now, in retrospect, when I am officially retired and embarked on my higher degree programme, that I can see how the story itself constitutes the telling of an action enquiry, so I am delighted to be able to write it up formally as such. The story deals with issues of identifying a potentially problematic issue, asking appropriate and relevant questions, gathering data and generating evidence, working collaboratively with a range of stakeholders and participants, testing the validity of provisional conclusions, and changing practice in light of the evaluation.

My context at the time was that I was nursing manager of an acute psychiatric unit in a large hospital. My responsibilities were to ensure the smooth running of the unit for the well-being of patients and staff. Many aspects of organizational matters were quite routine, but one always potentially problematic issue was about who was best positioned to make informed judgements about patients' well-being. The situation was that different groups of staff had different responsibilities in patient care, informed by different kinds of knowledge. While nurses' practical knowledge was as respected as the medical staff's specialized medical knowledge, questions were still asked about the values and epistemological base from which care should be given and therefore whose contribution was seen as most valuable and should be sought first. On the one hand, nurses had day-to-day contact with patients, so could build up a personal relationship with them and develop insights into their state of mind as well as health, while medical staff had specific knowledge and responsibility for patients' treatments. Also, there were differences between the values and epistemological frameworks from which the two parties worked. Nurses tended to work from an inclusional epistemology that was grounded in human relationships, so they saw multiple responses to human dilemmas; while medical staff tended to work from a technical epistemology that was grounded in a medical model and pointed them to one specific outcome. The dilemma for me was always how, as nursing manager, I could arrange for nurses and medical staff, working collaboratively, to maximize their separate and joint knowledge and expertise for patients' benefit. This issue of finding ways to celebrate different forms of knowledge and experience was a regular feature of the unit's life, and became apparent on many occasions. I can think of many cases that illustrate the dilemma yet also indicate how it may be resolved, provided individuals are open to recognizing other people's capabilities. My research issue at the time was therefore always about how I could find ways to nurture people's goodwill so that they could work together collaboratively to provide the right response to individual cases.

For example, a common event was that a patient would be referred by their general practitioner to a consultant for treatment. The consultant would visit the patient and make a decision about the best way to deal with their situation. Many patients were admitted to the unit with a provisional diagnosis of depression, and appropriate medications were prescribed and administered. However, it would sometimes emerge, during conversations with nurses, that the patient was not clinically depressed but was reacting to other circumstances such as recent bereavement. The irony then became that, because the root of the patient's problems was not acknowledged, the patient was then in danger of really becoming depressed, compounded sometimes by inappropriate medications.

This made us think carefully about whether we were always handling individual cases appropriately. We began to wonder whether patients could in fact be prevented from going into a full-scale depression by dealing with the more human aspects of their reaction to circumstances, such as the loss of a loved one. This approach, however, fell somewhat outside the medical model and there was reluctance by some psychiatrists to accept that an immediate diagnosis was not the appropriate response. Others wished to avoid pathologizing normal human responses, such as profound grief in response to loss. There was general agreement that no situation was ever clear-cut, and no one person's opinions could be deemed as the correct solution, so each patient's case needed to be seen as unique and deserving of all carers' pooled knowledge and expertise.

My response to our staff's developing awareness of these dilemmas, and their desire to offer the best possible care to patients, was to arrange for meetings and discussions among nursing staff, and with medical staff, to develop a working response to the complexity of situations with which we were faced on a daily basis. We made overtures to outside organizations and support groups to increase our knowledge of different circumstances such as bereavement, but the response of those groups was patchy and localized. Working as a team, therefore, we began to research what was known about different circumstances such as bereavement, and contacted acknowledged experts in the area who shared their knowledge with us. We then put on further training for all unit staff, which inspired greater confidence in our overall ability to respond in a more encompassing and situation-sensitive form than a straightforward medical model.

We put together our own body of literature out of the experience, and shared this with our patients, drawing on their understanding of their own conditions. We were therefore able to offer support to all patients from a position of confidence in our capacity as a team to be flexible and imaginative in working with unpredictable and constantly shifting human scenarios. The shared growth of our understanding and respect for one another's capacities meant the enhanced ability of medical and nursing staff to work together without anyone feeling that roles were being threatened or professional values disrespected.

Our records showed that our work was recognized as contributing to the quality assurance of our unit, and that patients' well-being was enhanced, as was the job satisfaction of the majority of staff. We wrote up and published our findings, which were well received nationally and internationally. We all took great satisfaction out of our experience of a job well done together.

2 Strategies for transformation

As the nursing manager in the example above discovered, complex difficulties can be addressed and transformed, albeit that they need to be approached with sensitivity and awareness of possible fallout. It is in your power to influence the dynamics of whatever situation you are in. Your aim is to transform a situation in which your values are being denied into one in which they are realized. This usually involves developing a range of strategies to be used according to the situation. Not all strategies are appropriate to all circumstances, so it is important to develop some political sophistication in knowing how to deal with each situation as it arises, in as useful a way as possible. Here are some strategies you can consider.

Confrontation

This is seldom the best strategy, but it is sometimes the only option, especially when you are in a situation that is damaging to you or someone else, such as when you are in the company of a bully. Sometimes it is necessary to fight fire with fire. Confrontation is not the best, because it involves bringing a situation to complete closure, where one side wins and the other loses, with no way out for either party. This is a strategy of containment, not of potential development, because development means that the conversation remains open so that everyone can return to the issue and find a way forward without losing face. This is important, because people seldom adopt new practices when they feel disgruntled or begrudging. Avoid confrontation where possible, but if it is a case of stopping a potentially destructive situation, such as bullying, don't hesitate. Just be aware of the potential fallout if you do.

Negotiation

This is usually a better option, because it leaves opportunities for new conversations and new practices. Negotiation can be far more difficult than confrontation, because negotiation means compromise. It can also seem like hypocrisy, when you find yourself dealing with someone who for example, enjoys cruelty. Negotiation is however essential if you are to create new opportunities for the exercise of your influence. You are in fact trying to persuade people to change their minds, and your attitude of openness in negotiation will in most cases be far more effective than the finality of confrontation. Negotiation means always leaving a loophole for the other to change their mind publicly, without damage to their image and self-esteem. Be sure that they, and you, know what is going on, but in situations of conflict it is essential that you both play a politically strategic game so that both emerge as winners.

Creative compliance

In 1987, Barry MacDonald spoke about the need for creative compliance, that is, a form of resistance that recognizes the constraints of a current situation, and finds ways of working within the constraints in order to achieve one's own aims. This does not mean giving in to dominant systems. It means being pliable and bending with the prevailing wind, but not breaking; adapting to imposed systems but working creatively from the inside. This can be a most creative experience. The aim is not to change the external 'system' so much as influence people within the system, so that individual practices realize their potential for transforming wider thinking.

Build your own power base

This is a wise and powerful strategy. Building your own power base means that you can act from a position of publicly recognized strength, and you have resources behind you to back up what you say. These resources come in the form of people and profile.

Remember that the currency you are using is knowledge. You are dealing with people who are vying for power in the form of knowledge. They wish to be acclaimed publicly as knowers and often they are seeking to establish their own power base at the expense of others, by refusing to acknowledge them as knowers. Aim to engage from a position of strength in your own knowledge. Your best strategy is to secure as much public legitimation as possible for yourself. You can do this in the following ways.

Get accreditation

The academy is still the highest body for the recognition and legitimation of knowledge. If you want to engage politically, the more accreditation you have, the better. As well as offering opportunities for your own intellectual development, programmes leading to awards are also pathways to acknowledgement. Once you have a degree, no one can take it away. You are acknowledged publicly for ever. People know that it takes disciplined scholarship to get a degree, so they will regard you with respect, if not affection.

Get published

Publication is one of the most powerful resources, especially if your work proves popular. Nowadays, in initiatives such as the UK Research Excellence Framework, the numbers of books sold contribute to the 'impact factor' of the research. If people know that you can write, and also have access to print, they will treat you with respect. You do not necessarily need their friendship, but you do need them to allow you untrammelled freedom to exercise your influence.

Get the ear of policymakers

If policymakers perceive that you are a person with clout, they will make room for you. It is easier to gain access to them if you have some public standing. They will also look with interest at what you are doing, to see whether opportunities exist for their own self advancement. We are all human, and we all do what we can to further our own ambitions. If your ambition is to influence individual and collective thinking in such a way that systems will change to allow others access, you need to find ways of doing this. Furthermore, your work may come directly to influence policymakers. The contemporary focus on action research has arisen directly out of the early work of pioneers in action research, many of whom have now retired or gone on to do other things. Influencing the public mind can take a long time and we often do not see the benefits in our lifetime, but this should not stop us from building for a better future for others.

Get popular

You are working with practitioners and persuading them to find ways of improving their work, and also to improve their own capacity for publishing work and contributing to new theory. The kind of theory they produce is practical theory grounded in practice. This new form of theory is contributing to the knowledge base that influences policy (Chapter 22). You can popularize your own ideas by making them accessible to others, and encouraging others to see that what you are advocating is well within their grasp. Once people can see that they can achieve on their own terms, they will have more confidence to stand up for themselves and mobilize. Mobilization is essential, because collective voices are stronger than a lone one. If possible, you can then show people how they can become active in their own interests.

Mind yourself

Be aware of your own capacity at all times. While you can probably do more than you believe yourself capable of doing, you are also still human and can do only so much. Do not take on the worries of the world. Do what you can, from your own position. Often people find that they fight so hard that they have little energy left after the battle to begin reconstruction. It is important to pace yourself and stay reasonably within your own capacity. You are less use to people dead, but while alive you can achieve much. Find allies, develop economical strategies, be shrewd. Your own energy is limited, so use it with care. Find ways of supporting yourself, with caring people and the affirmation of your own productive work. You need others, but at the same time, never underestimate the power of your own voice of passion, and your own capacity for influence.

Summary

This chapter has set out ideas about the politics of educational knowledge and how to deal with them. Dealing with power begins by understanding its nature clearly. Power and oppression are not 'things', but aspects of the practices of real people, who aim to meet their own interests. It is important to be imaginative in finding strategies for survival, and also strategies that will help you transform negative situations into life-affirming ones.

One of the ways you can develop your own strategies for transformation is by making your work widely available and showing its significance for developing learning in order to improve practice. This is the focus of the next part.

Further reading

The theme of engaging with the politics of knowledge continues with these texts.

Chomsky, N. (2002) *Understanding Power: The Indispensable Chomsky* (ed. P.R. Mitchell and J. Schoffel). New York: The New Press.
As with all Chomsky's work, he dissects relationships of power, whether on a world stage or in individual settings.

Foucault, M. (1980) 'Truth and power', in C. Gordon (ed.) *Power/Knowledge: Selected Interviews and Other Writings, 1972–1977*. Brighton: Harvester.
Foucault is one of the best for analysing issues of power and its relationship to practitioners.

Whitehead, J. (1993) *The Growth of Educational Knowledge: Creating Your Own Living Educational Theory*. Bournemouth: Hyde Publications. Retrieved 1 August 2010 from http://www.actionresearch.net/writings/jwgek93.htm
This text documents some of Jack's responses to engaging with the politics of educational knowledge in the first 20 years of his work at the University of Bath.

PART VI

How Do I Represent and Disseminate My Knowledge?

This part is about sharing and disseminating your work. Communicating the value of your work to different audiences involves learning their languages and organizing your ideas in ways that will speak to their experience. The chapters give practical advice about how to do this.

This part contains the following chapters.

At this point in your enquiry into action research you are asking, 'How do I communicate the significance of my research?' 'How do I show the value of studying my learning in order to improve my practice?' Your interest is now developing into how you can best show the importance of your research for your own and other people's learning.

EIGHTEEN

Telling Your Research Story

You now need to tell others about your research. This means producing a text in written, oral or visual form. However, producing a text can be complex, because speaking about experience is different from the experience itself, which is a personal thing. Your task is to communicate what is 'in here', at an implicit personal level, to someone 'out there' at an explicit public level: you have to make the implicit explicit.

Aim to produce a text of high quality. Like it or not, what people know about you is what they see on the page, so your work is going to be judged in terms of the quality of your text. People are more likely to listen to you if they can see immediately what you are doing and what the significance of your work is, so your job is to tell them. If they have to struggle to understand you, they may put your text down, or worse, read someone else's. This carries big responsibilities for you. You have to use a language that your reader can easily comprehend, and make sure your message captivates their imagination even though some of the ideas may be complex and need disciplined study to understand fully. You can choose a written, oral or visual form for your text, but any form of expression has to communicate the reality of your experience, both what you did and what you learned, and the potential significance of your work for the learning of others.

To achieve this you have to tell your story in a way that people will want to listen to you, see immediately what you are getting at, and understand why they should read you.

This chapter therefore asks two questions.

1 How do you get people to listen to you?
2 How do you show them what you are getting at?

1 How do you get people to listen to you?

Habermas (1987) tells us that ideally we should:

- speak comprehensibly;
- speak truthfully;

- speak authentically;
- speak appropriately.

This has implications for you. How do you tell your story in a way that is comprehensible, truthful, authentic and appropriate? (Note: You can read detailed advice about these and other aspects of writing in McNiff and Whitehead [2009], *Doing and Writing Action Research* and McNiff [2011a], *Writing for Publication in Action Research*.)

Speaking comprehensibly

When you speak, you speak to a listener. When you write, you write for a reader. You may speak and write for yourself when you are preparing your text, but when you present it publicly you do so for someone else. This means you have to grip their imagination through language.

Here are some ideas to help you do this.

Get passionate

Getting people to engage with you and maintaining their interest means you have to show your own enthusiasm for your work. Encourage them to believe that if you can do it, they can too.

Show that you believe in your work, yourself and others. Believing in your work means you know how important it is. Say this. Believing in yourself means you had the courage of your convictions to do the research. Explain how you had to draw on your own inner strength and on the support of allies, and how you got there eventually. Audiences love to hear victory stories, but the most authentic ones are those that tell of the struggles involved. Do not present yourself as a victim. You are a responsible practitioner who has made a choice to speak for yourself and enable others to do so too. You drew on your commitment to individuals' capacity to think for themselves and make their own decisions. Be up front in saying to people, 'You can do this too. Believe in yourself.'

Get personal

Speak in a way that your audience can understand. Do not use unfamiliar words. If you have to use professional jargon, explain what it means in ordinary language. (The first edition of this book contained jargon. We acted on feedback for the second edition and stripped the jargon out – we hope!)

Do not tell people what to do. Adopt throughout an invitational stance. This means relating well to your audience. If you are speaking, establish eye contact. If you are writing, establish mind contact. Draw your reader into your text. Invite them to consider ideas, rather than impose them. Keep a light touch throughout. If you have some serious critique to make, do it in a constructive way, and move on. Never alienate your audience by talking down or up at them, and make the case that you also can be mistaken.

Use the language of the community you are addressing. If you are writing a scholarly document, use a scholarly language. If you are talking to a group of parents, use a language that relates to their experience. You have to become fluent in your audience's language, not the other way round (see below 'Speaking appropriately').

Get clarity

Say what you mean to say, clearly and directly. Never use two words when one will do. In your case, less is more. Producing a text that is simple and straightforward without jeopardizing the quality of ideas is difficult, and takes time and concentration. In a written text, you will spend 10 times as long editing as producing a first draft. For every book that is published, many more go in the recycling bin. Do not expect to get a text right in one go. The most experienced authors often spend days working on a few pages. This is what it takes to produce a quality text.

Get working

Get on with it. Do not spend time and energy finding other jobs to do. It is easy to put things off indefinitely. What can you do tomorrow that you cannot do today? If you are finding it hard to get started, write anything. You do not have to begin at the beginning. Begin half way through, or at the end. You are going to edit the text anyhow, and achieving a few sentences, even of lesser quality, is an achievement that will inspire greater achievement. Do not think you are the only one who is struggling. Everyone struggles. If you want to do it, just do it.

Speaking truthfully

You show that people can believe what you say by demonstrating your credibility. Whatever you claim to have happened, you show it to be true by producing evidence and also by saying that you are doing so. People will believe you because you are prepared to subject your claims to critique and not hide behind anything. You explain that this is your original work and you demonstrate consistently your capacity for critical engagement.

Speaking authentically

Throughout use your practitioner-researcher voice, not the voice you may normally use as a psychiatrist or primary teacher. Your practitioner voice is incorporated into your research voice (see also next paragraph). As a researcher you explain how you have aimed to live by the beliefs you hold as a practitioner through doing your research. You explain how the conduct of your research programme itself is consistent with your beliefs. Your participative and relational methodology demonstrates participation and relationship in practice, and your willingness to subject your provisional findings to critique demonstrates your commitment to holding your findings lightly and resisting the idea of a final truth.

Speaking appropriately

Sometimes researchers find it difficult to speak in a researcher's voice, especially when they are with, say, primary children for most of the working day. Bear in mind which community of practice you are with at different times. When you are in your primary classroom you are with your community of primary school practice. When you write your report you write it for your community of scholarly practice, so you leave your primary teacher's voice in your primary classroom, although you are telling a story about your practice in your primary classroom. Each community has its own language. Speaking appropriately means using language in a way that shows you are aware of the normative assumptions that you are making. Many practitioner-researchers have to learn the language of scholarship; this can take some time. Again, do not think you are the only one. Practice makes perfect. If you are unfamiliar with scholarly language, read other works, such as dissertations and journals, to see the kind of language used, and note it carefully. Do not copy or model your work directly on exemplars, but do aim to develop a language that is appropriate to the task of producing a research report. Always produce your own original text, but make sure it will be received well by the audience for which you are writing. When you go on to write your textbooks, you will use a different voice again. We authors are writing this book using a different voice to the one we use in some of our scholarly articles, which are written for a different audience. We are deliberately positioning ourselves as practitioner-researchers, and using practitioner-researcher language. This does not mean we are avoiding scholarly issues. The book has dealt throughout with scholarly issues, but we are using a form of expression that is, we hope, appropriate for the audience we wish to reach.

2   How do you show what you are getting at?

We said above that texts may be presented in different forms. In the next two chapters advice is given about the content and form of written reports, because print-based text is still the most common form of expression, and is expected by accrediting institutions. However, many higher education institutions now accept multimedia forms as part of degree submissions. While they would probably not accept extreme forms such as graphic novellas, or video narratives as entire theses, they would certainly accept those forms as supplementary to the main text. Also a printed text may be incorporated into a visual narrative to guide the reader through the interconnections of meanings.

Many high quality examples of these approaches are available to show the potentials of multimedia forms of representation. Seminal texts are Jack Whitehead's (2004c) 'Action research expeditions: do action researchers' expeditions carry hope for the future of humanity? How do we know? An enquiry into reconstructing educational theory and educating social formations'. Part II of this account takes you into Jack's (2004b) multimedia account: 'How valid are multimedia communications of my embodied values in living theories and standards of educational judgement and practice?' One of the most impressive achievements is by Ray O'Neill who, for his PhD award, produced a thesis both in print-based form (O'Neill, 2008) and in multimedia form (see http://www.ictaspoliticalaction.com/). Similarly, new electronic journals enable practitioners to show the realities they are speaking about through multimedia forms of communication: see for example *The Electronic Journal of Living Theories* at http://ejolts.net/ and *The Turkish Online Journal of Qualitative Inquiry* at http://www.tojqi.net. Practitioners are able to publish their work in forms that do justice to the relational and dynamic nature of the work.

The form of these works is extraordinary, because the form communicates their message, which is perhaps one of the most important for contemporary societies. This is that people need to work together for their own and their planet's survival, as well as to ensure the quality of life while they are surviving. They do this by showing how they are forming communities of enquiry, where like-minded people can come together, on an equal footing, to debate and decide the kinds of societies they wish to live in. The communities sustain and develop themselves by showing how they are consistent with their underpinning values and commitments to dynamic and relational forms of living. In research terms, they offer explanations for what they are doing and how and why they are doing it. Multimedia accounts show the dynamic processes involved as they do this. They also show a core commitment to creating new futures through purposeful social interaction. Each community has the potential to influence other communities, by sharing and critiquing what they are doing and thinking and through forming interconnecting branching networks, a global network that connects networks to one another in multiple innovative ways.

These networks have special features. At a surface, physical level they show 'the patterns that connect' (Bateson, 1979), as groupings of people connected to other groupings, where each grouping can connect with any other anywhere in the world. At a deep level of commitment they are held together by bonds of common purpose. Their underlying ontological commitments are the 'ties that bind' (Bateson, 1972). These ontological commitments emerge as epistemological standards (see page 84), when members of communities tell one another what they know and how they have come to know by generating their claims to knowledge and testing them against the critical insights and practices of themselves and others. These 'ties that bind' and 'patterns that connect' form an unseen web of interconnection, what O'Donohue (2003) calls a 'web of betweenness', similar to Capra's (2003) idea that the invisible threads between the networks are what power the creation and sustaining of the networks themselves.

As noted earlier, Foucault (1980) wrote about power and power relationships. He said that power was not a 'thing', which one person had and often used to dominate the other, but was in relationships. He spoke about 'capillary action', as power moved back and forth along the invisible strands that connect parties in relationship. This idea sits well with the idea of interconnected branching networks of global communication through education (Whitehead and McNiff, 2003). The form of these networks is not centre-to-periphery, but multidimensional, each network forming a node, which itself is a dynamic network of shifting relationships. There is no central point anywhere. The power of influence is in the people and their relationships, in their own contexts. No one manages these networks. They manage themselves, and are self-sustaining and self-regenerating. Power is everywhere. It is in the relationships that hold the networks together and enable them to develop at both a practical and a theoretical level. Each person within each network has the power of influence. Each has the capacity to influence their own learning and the learning of others. Each has to learn to exercise their influence in such a way that others will also learn to exercise their power for influence for educational sustainability.

It is easy to become part of the networks. Wherever you are, whatever your context, you can link with other practitioner-researchers who are asking, like you, 'How do I improve what I am doing?', and make your story public so that they can respond critically; so they influence your learning, as you are hoping to influence theirs. You are already a participant in physical space, in your own workplace, where you can share your reports, and you can connect virtually, through sharing your ideas electronically. There is simply nothing to stop you. This brave new world of educational influence has come into being through the commitments of people like you. You need to tell your story of what you are doing to develop it even further.

--------------------------- Summary ---------------------------

This chapter has offered ideas about how you can get people to listen to you, and how to explain clearly what you are getting at. It has used Habermas's ideas of speaking comprehensibly, truthfully, authentically and appropriately as the basis for your own communicative action. The chapter has gone on to suggest how you can get involved in networks of communication, and has offered ideas about the nature and formation of these networks.

The next chapter moves on to the practical business of writing a report.

Further reading

In writing for action research, it is important to appreciate what to write, why to write it and how to write it. The following texts give advice and examples.

Clandinin, D.J. and Connelly, F.M. (2000) *Narrative Inquiry: Experience and Story in Qualitative Research*. San Francisco, CA: Jossey-Bass.
A seminal text that speaks about the principles and practices of narrative inquiry.

Levin, P. (2005) *Excellent Dissertations!* Maidenhead: Open University Press.
An accessible book, packed full of useful ideas and advice.

McNiff, J. (2007) 'My story is my living educational theory', in D.J. Clandinin (ed.), *Handbook of Narrative Inquiry: Mapping a Methodology*. Thousand Oaks, CA: Sage. pp. 308–29.
This chapter is a living example of what to write about in action research and how to write it.

McNiff, J. (2011a) *Writing for Publication in Action Research*. Poole: September Books. [In preparation.]
An accessible book that explains what, why and how to write in action research.

NINETEEN
Writing a Workplace Report

This chapter gives advice on possible frameworks and contents for an action research report about workplace learning. The next chapter is about reports submitted for higher degree accreditation. Please note that this division of chapters is for emphasis of content only. Many workplace reports come to stand as reports submitted for degree accreditation. Therefore, what is said in this chapter is also relevant to submitting a report for accreditation.

It is important also to bear in mind that the ideas presented here are suggestions only. You should decide what is right for you, and then, if appropriate, adapt the ideas to your own purposes and in your own way. Many people, including those whose work is cited in this book, used ideas like these to get them started, and then modified them as they created their own narratives. Others organized their ideas into their own frameworks and representations. It does not matter how you organize your ideas, provided you meet all the criteria for writing a quality research report that shows how you have met the criteria for doing a quality action research project. The chapter is presented to show, first, how you can organize your ideas using a formal structure such as the one presented here and, second, how you can organize your ideas in your own innovative way. The chapter is in two parts to set out these different approaches.

1 Organizing your ideas as a formal framework
2 Organizing your ideas in your own innovative way

It should also be noted that the examples cited here are from a range of professions. While action research is most strongly developed in the teaching profession, other professions use action research approaches and high quality reports are forming a new body of professional development literature that will have significant influence.

1 Organizing your ideas as a formal framework

All action research reports, regardless of audience, should contain the following:

- Descriptions of practice – what you did.
- Explanations for practice – why you did what you did and what you hoped to achieve.
- An articulation of your theory of practice – saying that you understand how your descriptions and explanations constitute your personal theory of practice, and why it is important.

Your report will therefore be a narrative of your own learning from practice: an ongoing analysis in the form of a reflective commentary on its potential value and significance.

You can use the action plan you drew up at the beginning of your project as the main structure for your report (see pages 8–9). When you drew up your action plan you were looking forward to what you might do, so you told it in the future tense. You are now looking back on what you have done, so you tell it in the past tense. Possible section headings would therefore be as follows.

- What was my concern?
- Why was I concerned?
- What kind of data and evidence could I produce to show the reasons for my concern?
- What did I think I could do about it?
- What did I do about it?
- What kind of data and evidence did I produce to show the situation as it unfolded?
- How did I test the validity of my claim to knowledge?
- How did I ensure that any conclusions I came to were reasonably fair and accurate?
- How did I modify my practice in the light of my evaluation?

What was my concern?

Say what your research was about. Did you want to find better ways of working with people? Did you want to replace a hierarchical management system with flatter structures? Explain how this concern led you to decide to research the issue. Articulate your question as 'How do I …?', for example, 'How do I improve relationships?' or 'How do I introduce flatter structures into my organization?'

Why was I concerned?

Explain how the situation could be seen as a realization of, or a denial of, your values. Doing this means articulating the values that inspire your work, such as justice, freedom and care for the other. Explain that you undertook the research in order to stay consistent with your values. You may have experienced the situation as a problem needing a solution or you may have been just trying to understand the situation and finding ways of living with it.

What kind of data and evidence could I describe to show the reasons for my concern?

Explain that you undertook your research by first undertaking some reconnaissance (Elliott, 1991) to establish what the situation was like. You did this by gathering data using different techniques. You interviewed people and used excerpts from your transcripts, or you had a conversation with a trusted colleague about how you both felt about the situation. You kept a record of the conversation. Paint a word picture for your reader so that they can see clearly what you and others were thinking and doing, and why you felt dissatisfied with the current situation. If you are using multimedia you could paint a real picture, or represent the situation using a range of still or moving images.

What did I think I could do about it?

What were your options? How did you arrive at them? Perhaps you had conversations with critical friends? Did you invite ideas about what you could do? Explain here how you thought about the situation, and how you thought you could address it. Did you see yourself doing it alone or in company with others? Did you understand this as a process of testing out possible strategies? How did you feel about this kind of open-ended enquiry? Were you looking for final solutions, or testing out possible ways forward?

At this point also say that you were aware of the ethical considerations of involving others and also of working in a social context where your proposed action may have implications for others. How could you safeguard your own and their well-being?

What did I do about it?

Say what course of action you decided to follow. Explain that this was only one possible way forward, and that it was provisional. You were ready to change if necessary according to the changing situation. Say whether it was problematic to go forward like this.

Set out here some of the practicalities involved. Who would be your research participants? How did you select them? How long did you think the research would last? What resources did you need?

Also set out how you intended to ensure good ethical conduct. Say that you produced ethics statements and letters requesting permission to do the research, and put these letters, together with letters granting permission, in your appendices.

What kind of data and evidence did I produce to show the situation as it unfolded?

Recall the word or visual picture you painted to show the situation as it was, and now paint a new picture to show the situation as it developed, again drawing on the data you gathered. Explain that you used the same, or possibly different, data gathering techniques. Aim to describe what happened and also aim to explain why you think it happened and what was achieved. What was your part in the change? How did you influence people's learning, so that they changed their own ways of working together? Remember that the focus of the research is you and your learning, and you are monitoring and recording other people's learning in relation to your own, as you ask, 'How do I improve …?' You are helping people to change things for themselves.

How did I test the validity of my claim to knowledge?

Say that you took care in all methodological procedures involved in making your claim to knowledge. Say what your criteria and standards of judgement were and that you were aware of their significance for evaluating and testing the validity of your knowledge claim. Say that you specifically drew these matters to the attention of your critical friends and validation groups, and that you emphasized how you were producing explanatory accounts of learning and not only descriptive accounts of activities.

How did I ensure that any conclusions I came to were reasonably fair and accurate?

Say that you were aware of the need to test and critique your provisional conclusions at all steps of the research. This means explaining how you put procedures in place to deal with this. You arranged for key people to be critical friends. You negotiated with them and others to form a validation group, who would convene at regular intervals to listen to your research account and offer critical feedback on your provisional findings. Say whether they agreed, requested further and more quality-controlled evidence or asked you to go back and think again. Explain why you chose those people and not others and also how you ensured that you made clear that you were testing your ideas throughout and not presenting them as established fact. Set out the main recommendations of your validation group and include their reports as an appendix to your report. Say also whether you took or rejected their advice, and whether and how you adapted it to suit your own needs.

How did I modify my practice in light of my evaluation?

Set our how doing your research has led to the development of new practices and new thinking (theorizing). Whose practice has changed, yours or other people's or both? How can you show that this new practice is an improvement on previous practices? Are your values now being at least part-realized? On reflection, could/should you have done things differently?

Explain that although this may appear to be the end point of one research cycle, it is not the end of your enquiry. You now need to test the new practice, which means undertaking a new project that will help you to evaluate what you are doing and how to improve it where necessary. You will generate new practices and new thinking, and you will evaluate them so that you can say that these are an improvement on the previous situation. Do not feel you have to aim for an end point or final answer, because there is not one. You are looking for provisional answers that describe and explain the journey so far. Your story is about making the journey, not about arriving, because we never actually arrive, and often have to be satisfied with 'nearly there'. However, nearly to somewhere is a new beginning, and new beginnings carry with them their own intent. Set out what your new beginnings involve, and how you intend to live for the time being.

Examples of the framework in use

Many examples exist to show how people have used this framework. Some providers and supporters have put together inspiring collections of case study material. Here are examples from the collections of work supported by Jacqueline Delong in Ontario, Canada; Moira Laidlaw in Guyuan, China; and Jean McNiff, Qatar.

Collection 1

Jacqueline and her colleagues have produced eight volumes of *Passion in Professional Practice*, containing dozens of case studies from teachers across a range of levels. Here are some. These stories of scholarly practice are in the public domain and accessible to all. For workplace accounts see http://schools.gedsb.net/ar/passion/index.html; for higher degree accounts see http://schools.gedsb.net/ar/theses/index.html. See also http://www.spanglefish.com/ActionResearchCanada/

Sandy Fulford asks: How can I use electronic portfolios to create a reflective record of the highlights of my students' school year?

Her abstract says: I worked with George Neeb to develop student electronic portfolios that combine computer technology with traditional portfolios. Students collected

---

examples of their work, digital photos and reflective evaluations to create a record of the highlights of their school year. Working with colleague and mentor George Neeb, various techniques and approaches were developed to have students complete personal portfolios using Corel Presentations for the school year.

Dan Mattka and Heather Knill-Griesser ask: How can we support primary teachers to implement a Balanced Literacy Program to improve student learning based on the Provincial Ministry initiative, 'Schools in Need of Extra Help', as an administrator and teacher consultant?

Their abstract says: Princess Elizabeth School is a Junior Kindergarten to Grade 6 school with a student population of 260. It exists in a mixed residential area in Brantford where Ontario Housing provides residence to a significant number of students, where one in four families are single parent households. Grade 3 and 6 Education Quality and Accountability Office (EQAO) provincial testing results have placed many of the students below the provincial standards. The authors examine their educative influence as administrator and teacher consultant as they answer the question, 'How can we support primary teachers to implement a Balanced Literacy Program to improve student learning?'

Lindsey Huyge asks: How can I improve my effectiveness as a learning resource teacher (LRT) through the development of partnerships with my colleagues so that the specific needs of my students can be met or accommodated?

Her abstract says: The student population at Walsh Public School, from junior kindergarten to grade eight, is 434. It is situated in a rural area where farming is an important source of income for many families either directly or indirectly. At this school students are very diverse and require a community where they can actively participate in their education and can gain the necessary skills for success in a challenging world. Teachers at Walsh P.S. take every opportunity to create a uniform atmosphere and appreciate open communication.

Collection 2

The collection of case stories compiled by Moira Laidlaw and colleagues can be downloaded from http://www.actionresearch.net/writings/moira.shtml.

This collection includes the following accounts.

Liu Binyou asks: How can I cultivate my non-English students' interests in English?

Her abstract says: In my case study I reveal how I changed my methods to enable students to take a more active part in lessons. I found new ways to attract their interest and helped to motivate them. These methods consisted of introducing issues of personal interest to the students, and paying attention to the learning needs of individuals. I also describe in detail the responses of one student to a new method of teaching, in which his own talents as a poet are harnessed to motivate him to study English. I show how changing my methodology has helped my students to become better learners.

Li Peidong asks: How can I improve my students' self-confidence in their class work?

His abstract says: This paper is an account of what I have done in the very first cycle of my educational action research, which lasted about one year. I have struggled and explored myself within this long duration with the question: How can I help my students to improve their self-confidence in their classwork? I reasoned this as the extrinsic cause influencing learners' conversational performance and communicative motivation. The article records the process of how I came to my present action research questions with see-sawing inquiry and evaluation of my imagined solutions, all of this with respect to humanistic approaches and educational values based on my insights and learning about the New English Curriculum. I used questionnaires, interviews and my own observations to triangulate and draw conclusions.

Cao Yong asks: How can I improve the pronunciation and intonation of the first-year English Majors to meet the demand of the New English Curriculum?

His abstract says: In my report, I present my [action research] work on how I used action research in teaching pronunciation and intonation for the first-English majors. My concern reveals itself to be closely associated with the bases of the four language skills of speaking, listening, reading and writing. I put forward a case that the effort to master the sound system and to pronounce correctly, are key aspects of learning a second language. As clarification I give some technical details on aspects of sounds of speech, including articulation, vowel formation, accent, inflection, and intonation, with reference to the correctness or acceptability of the speech sounds. I also provide some descriptions of new classroom teaching-methods for pronunciation and intonation. I include comments from students, reveal statistics of their scores, quote from expert sources in linguistics, and show the results of a questionnaire. I conclude that by researching my practice in terms of targets for the New Curriculum for the teaching of English in China, there is the potential for my work and similar enquiries to be of educational benefit for schools and other colleges in China.

Collection 3

The collection of case stories compiled by Jean McNiff can be downloaded from http://www.jeanmcniff.com/userfiles/file/qatar/Qatar_Action_Research_booklet_email.pdf. Jean and others worked with Tribal Education UK on an intensive professional education course for teachers in Qatar from 2009–2010, and some of the work was put together as a Teacher Enquiry Bulletin (Tribal 2010: available from http://jeanmcniff.com/qatar.asp). The work is having significant influence in the Gulf States and elsewhere. In a new collection new voices speak.

Abeer Mukhtar asks: How can I help my students to differentiate between natural materials and manufactured materials?

He writes: Having attended the Action Research Course for Teachers, I decided to undertake my action enquiry into how I could help my students learn to differentiate between natural and manufactured materials. I tried different pedagogical strategies that required them to undertake their own action enquiries. This involved our foraging expeditions into the playground and, as supervised groups, into the desert. I carried out extensive reflections on my pedagogical and organizational practices, and specifically focused on writing them as part of my systematic reflective practices. I have come to clear understandings about the need to make my professional learning explicit, and I encourage my colleagues and students to do the same.

Noora Al-Mansoori asks: How can I help teachers to develop the capacity for professional critique in self-evaluation?

She writes: As a professional developer in my school, and as part of our national framework of Education for a New Era, I was responsible for encouraging all teachers to engage in processes of professional self-evaluation. This involved my observing them in class, and offering my responses to their practice, which we then negotiated. Many teachers initially found this experience threatening, especially given a cultural legacy of hierarchical forms of inspection. I therefore undertook my action enquiry into how I could help the teachers to feel comfortable with the process. This involved the teachers and me working together to plan observation visits, negotiate the outcomes, and develop a community of practice-based enquiry. Progress towards a culture of dialogical interaction in our school has been rapid and is influencing new approaches to teaching and learning.

Mohammed Ayoub asks: 'How can I encourage students to do their independent and original research?

He writes: Copying from the Internet is a problem iinternationally. Too many students simply copy work from the web or go to a bookstore and purchase ready-made answers to assignments. My research focused on how I could encourage students to do research for themselves, which would involve their developing an appreciation of what doing original research means as well as using resources critically to support their enquiries. As the Learning Resource Coordinator, I decided to use our school Knowledge-Net to encourage students to undertake independent enquiries and to reflect on the purposes and significance of doing so in order to advance their learning.

2 Organizing your ideas in your own innovative way

We said at the beginning of this chapter that you should feel free to organize your ideas in a way that is right for you. We encourage you to experiment and find your own way, while bearing in mind the need for methodological rigour. Here is an example of how Kathryn Yeaman has done so, in a masters module in research methods, It is from the introductory section of her report, 'Creating educative dialogues in an infant classroom', which can be downloaded from http://www.actionresearch.net/writings/module/kathy.htm.

A living educational theory!

Kathryn Yeaman

I am not used to the idea of theory being something which can be alive. So often it is something once studied, perhaps partly assimilated into one's teaching then long forgotten. The view that educational theory can be something less abstract and more meaningful is an exciting one.

I have found action research to be an empowering process. It has led me to what is right or educational and in doing so it has empowered me to follow this path. It is empowering in that it shows your actions to be the right ones and in doing this you [demonstrate] to yourself that your ideas work. They then become more than ideas; they change into truths.

The following action research was undertaken as a single module towards an MA at the University of Bath. I chose action research as I wanted my study to have direct relevance to my work in the classroom as a teacher. It is possible to have what might be termed a 'good knowledge' of educational theory without actually using it in one's own situation. It could then be argued that this superficial learning is not in fact knowledge at all. In doing my action research I have discovered for myself the relevance to me of some traditional, propositional theories and also discovered gaps and contradictions in the field of educational theory.

The 'living educational theory' for me is not an alternative one or indeed a subversive one as some might suggest (see Newby, 1994), but one which combines traditional theories with practice to form a new understanding and in doing so provides new theories which may have some generalizability to the profession as a whole.

'Critical research is praxis. Praxis involves the inseparability of theory and practice – i.e., informed practice. We must understand theoretical notions in terms of their relationship to the lived world, not simply as objects of abstract contemplation' (Kincheloe, 1991).

Schön stresses the need for such research to be 'I'-based. Such research can construct a new theory of a unique case. My action research report is written in the first person, as this is how it was. The research was done by me. 'I' was at the centre of my research question. If others as they read wish to propose what might happen to others in a similar situation, that is for them to imagine. I am concerned with the specifics of my research, not, in the report itself, with generalities or indeed with relevance to other situations. I will however consider these points after the report. I have also chosen not to write an introduction for readers, as I would like them to read the report and find significant points themselves.

My reasons for presenting this report are many. I am making public my action learning. I am presenting it as evidence of my own professional development. I would like fellow professionals to learn from it. In presenting my findings my intention is not to be prescriptive but to demonstrate some insights into the subject of educational dialogue. I hope too, that by revealing the self-educative nature of action research I will inspire others to become involved. I would like others to question and research for themselves my findings and those of others; I would like others to become involved in creating their own educational theory. As teacher-researchers, by focusing our enquiry on our children's learning and integrating the insights of existing theories into our enquiry we can make a significant contribution to educational knowledge.

By adopting this stance, Kathryn seems to be inviting her readers to draw from her research report those aspects that speak to their own experience. She uses her capacity for originality and critical engagement in order to encourage others to do the same.

Highly innovative work is now available in the form of multimedia accounts. We have already referred to the thesis of Ray O'Neill (2008) (page 195). Another inspiring account is from Christine Jones (2008), for her master's dissertation. This was the first multimedia living theory dissertation to be legitimated by Bath Spa University in 2009.

Title: How do I improve my practice as an inclusion officer working in a children's service?

Abstract

This dissertation examines my embodied knowledge and development as an Inclusion Officer working in a Children's Service as I focus on making a contribution to educational knowledge. In making this contribution, I have used visual narratives. This dissertation focuses on my personal knowledge and experience as an Inclusion Officer as I inquire into my question, 'How do I improve my practice as an Inclusion Officer?' In making my personal knowledge public, I believe that I am contributing to educational knowledge by using a living theory methodology for exploring the implications of questions such as, 'How do I improve my practice?' and by clarifying the meanings of inclusional standards of judgement from a perspective of inclusionality. Inclusionality (Rayner, 2004) may be described as a relationally dynamic and responsive awareness of others which flows with a desire to live values of care, compassion, love, justice and democracy. I explicate the inclusional way in which I like to work with others, how my practice is based on the values I hold and how this is reflected in my relationship with other educators working in a Children's Service and schools.

In undertaking my inquiry, I have adopted a living theory methodology (Whitehead, 2008a) in the sense that I am bringing my embodied knowledge into the public domain as an explanation of my educational influences in my own learning, in the learning of others and in the learning of social formations. Using video, I clarify the meanings of my inclusional values and how they are formed into living standards of judgement, whereby I and others can judge the validity of my claim to knowledge.

The dissertation may be downloaded from http://www.actionresearch.net/living/cjmaok/cjma.htm A distinctive feature is the videoclips, submitted at part of the Appendices.

If your dissertation or thesis is the first multimedia, living theory narrative to be legitimated in the institution with which you are registered it can take a lot of courage to break new ground, especially if your supervisors are not used to supervising living theory accounts. Christine Jones broke new ground in her master's submission to Bath Spa University when she submitted her living theory in the form of the multimedia narrative above, and set precedents that will enable others to have their multimedia work legitimated too.

Bear in mind that you are at liberty to create the report that most clearly communicates your experience. Provided you show the rigorous process of conducting the research and articulating the development of your own living theory, you can have confidence that you have done what it takes to achieve recognition.

Summary

This chapter has offered ideas about writing a workplace report. It has offered a basic framework, and given examples to show how this can work in practice. It has however emphasized that you should develop your framework to suit your own purposes as you tell your story. Further examples have been presented to show how this can be achieved.

The next chapter considers how to write a report for formal accreditation.

Further reading

Beard, R., Myhill, D., Riley, J. and Nystrand, M. (eds) (2009) *The SAGE Handbook of Writing Development*. London: Sage.
A comprehensive guide to writing and a valuable sourcebook.

McNiff, J. and Whitehead, J. (2009) *Doing and Writing Action Research*. London: Sage.
Covering most aspects of doing and writing action research, this book is an essential guide to the field.

Turley, R.M. (2000) *Writing Essays*. London: Routledge.
Another helpful and accessible book on academic writing.

Woods, P. (1999) *Successful Writing for Qualitative Researchers*. London: Routledge.
A useful guide this, well worth a read.

TWENTY

Writing a Report for Higher Degree Accreditation

If you are on an award-bearing course, you may prefer the framework outlined in this chapter. It is tried and tested, and if you use it you will not go far wrong. It deals with the same issues as in Chapter 19, but also covers different ground. For a degree, especially a higher degree, you would be expected to engage with the literature and to be clear about conceptual frameworks and more theoretical issues. This framework has proved useful to many practitioners as a starting point for their writing. Most have then adapted it for their own purposes and contexts.

The chapter is in two parts.

1 Outlining the framework
2 Examples of the framework in action

1 Outlining the framework

The framework uses the following chapter/section headings.

- Abstract
- Introduction
- Background
- Contexts for the research
- Methodology
- Monitoring practice, gathering and interpreting data, and generating evidence
- Main findings
- Significance
- Implications

Here is an outline of how you can use this framework and what should go into each chapter.

Abstract

This is a summary of what the research was about and its main findings. The abstract is about 200–300 words in length. It is not the place to put in quotations or descriptions of practice, unless these are directly relevant to your argument. It sets out what the claim to knowledge is and shows how the claim can be seen as valid through the production of validated evidence. It is important to say that you are presenting your work as work in progress, which you are now offering for public testing and critique.

Introduction

Introduce yourself and your research. Say who you are and where you work. Include anything special that will help your reader to see the significance of your work and why they should read this document. Immediately tell your reader what you believe you have achieved. Do this in terms of stating your claim to knowledge, probably in terms of having generated your living theory of practice. Explain why you wanted to do the research and why this may have been problematic, possibly in terms of your experience of yourself as a living contradiction and how you wanted to find ways of living more fully in the direction of your values. Say why it was important to adopt an action research approach, but do not go into detail here because you will develop these ideas in your methodology chapter. Feel free to cross-reference to your different chapters and sections within your report. If this is a scholarly document, set out what your conceptual frameworks are, that is, the main fields of enquiry or key ideas that informed your research, such as issues of justice, gender or ecological sustainability. These issues will be related to your values. Explain how your research enables you to participate in and contribute to these debates in terms of how you are contributing to new practices and new theory.

Give a brief summary of your chapters and explain whether the reader should read the whole as a beginning-to-end story, or whether they can move around the work without losing the thread. Always tell your reader what you want them to know and help them to see how they are coming to know it.

Background to the research

This is where you set out the background to the research in terms of what inspired you to do it. Some researchers like to combine their background chapter and introduction. Most find that it can be helpful to treat the background as a separate issue, especially as it relates to the values that underpinned the work. For example, you may have experienced bullying or marginalization in the home or the workplace, of yourself or someone else, and this has led you to find ways of overcoming the pain and creating new life-affirming ways of working. Or perhaps you wanted to evaluate your practice and see whether you were living in accordance with your own rhetoric.

Contexts for the research

This is your opportunity to set out in detail the contexts for your research. You may want to analyse them in terms of specific categories such as the following.

Personal contexts

What was going on in your personal/professional life that inspired you to do the research? Were you dissatisfied with or simply curious about the situation you were in? Why? How can your reader see your situation clearly?

Theoretical contexts

How could you relate your research issue to what you were reading in the literature? Could you see issues of injustice that you could relate to the work of Paulo Freire (1972), issues of freedom in the work of Isaiah Berlin (1998) or issues of ecological sustainability in the work of Zimmerman et al. (2001)? Were gender issues, issues of 'difference' or political action important? Aim to establish a link between your own ideas and the ideas in the literature. Show how you drew on the literature to help you develop and test your own thinking. The concepts you are dealing with come to form your conceptual frameworks.

Policy contexts

What was happening in the contexts of policy formation and implementation? Did this affect you and your research? Did policy enable you to work in a way that was consistent with your values? Or not? Did policy allocate funding to privileged groupings rather than the underprivileged groupings you were supporting? Was there a policy on assessment that used benchmarking and standardized testing, which were inappropriate for the kind of work you were doing? Did policy require you to practise in a way that was not consistent with your own preferred way of working? Could you do anything about it? Did you feel that you could contribute to policy by doing your research?

Any other relevant contexts

Mention here any other contexts that may be relevant. Perhaps you are a member of a wildlife trust, which may be significant if you are finding ways of protecting the environment; or you may be in the police service, which will be relevant to exploring how you can improve working practices in rehabilitation centres. Whatever is particularly relevant should be mentioned here. If you work with sexual offenders, are partially sighted or a member of a political action group, say so. Let your reader see why your contexts are important to your research.

Methodology

In this section you outline how you planned and carried out your research. Give details of the following (you may prefer to swap the plan/design and methodology sections if it suits your purposes).

- The research plan and design in terms of the following:

  o What was the time scale?
  o Where was the research conducted?
  o Who were your research participants? Why did you invite these people and not others?
  o What resources did you need?
  o Whose permission did you need to get? Did you get permission? If so, where can your reader see letters asking and granting permission? If not, why not?

- The methodology you used:

  o Why action research? Why self-study?
  o How did you monitor your actions and your learning, in relation to other people's action and learning?
  o How did you plan to gather data and interpret it?

- Ensuring ethical conduct:

  o Say that you were aware of the need for ethical considerations, and sought and obtained permission at all stages of your research as necessary.
  o Say where your reader can find your ethics statements and letters of permission.

Gathering and interpreting data and generating evidence

Set out here how you gathered the data, which data gathering techniques you used and why you used those and not others. Say that you were looking for data in relation to your research issue. Make it clear that you gathered data about your action and your learning.

Explain clearly how you gathered data systematically, so that you could track changes in the ongoing action and possibly see an improvement in terms of the realization of your values. Explain how you sorted your data into categories of analysis, such as conversations and transcripts, and that you began to focus progressively as the data began to form patterns about how you were beginning to influence other people's learning. Also explain how you decided to interpret the data in terms of your values and the extent to which these values were being realized, and that the values began to emerge as the standards by which you made judgements about your work. Show that you understand the differ-ence between data and evidence, by explaining how you pulled out of the data those pieces that you wished to stand as evidence in support of your claim to knowledge.

Remember that you may find disconfirming data that show that something is not going as you wish, so you have to rethink the situation. In this case, the data could generate powerful evidence for your claim that you have learned from experience.

Let your reader know that you were aware of the need to submit your data and evidence to the critical scrutiny of others. Say how you negotiated with colleagues to become your critical friends and validation group, how often you met and what kind of feedback they offered on your work. Say whether you acted on the feedback, or not, and why.

Main findings

At this point, set out what you believe you have found out. This should be both about substantive issues, such as how to manage your budget more efficiently, and also about your learning, such as the insights you developed about the need for budgeting. Link your findings with your claim to knowledge. You are saying that you know something that was not known before. You have created your own living theory of practice. You can show how you have incorporated ideas from others in the literature, and how you have reconfigured that knowledge in terms of your own context. Do not present your findings as final answers so much as tentative theories, which you are now subjecting to testing and critique. This is the spirit of research, when you always regard a solution as provisional and open to refutation and modification.

One of the most important claims you can make is that you have influenced learning for improving practice. This claim can be presented in terms of the following.

- Your own learning: you have learned through the process of being aware of your own capacity for learning.
- Your colleagues in your workplace: perhaps they have learned from you and are trying things out for themselves.
- The learning of wider social formations: people in different professions have learned from you how to work together so that they too can influence learning.

Say that you have contributed to new practices in terms of showing how it is possible for people to change their own situations. You can say that you have contributed to new theory by explaining how your own thinking and ideas have improved; how you have deepened your insights around the issue you have been investigating. By focusing on your learning you have come to know differently, and you are making your theory of practice public in order to test and validate your theory and have it accepted as a valuable contribution to the existing body of knowledge. Be confident about saying that people should listen to you and learn from what you have done, both in terms of practice and of knowledge generation. At this point also be clear about how you have drawn attention to your awareness of the need for methodological rigour in presenting your account of learning. Be clear that whenever you have made a claim to knowledge, you have also articulated the criteria and standards of judgement you have identified. It is as important to say that you have done these things as to have done them.

Implications

What might be the implications of your research for other people? Perhaps they will learn to see things differently, because you have made them think about things in new ways. Perhaps they will begin to think differently, because they will see the world through new eyes. Perhaps they will act differently, because their new thinking will inspire them to develop new practices.

One of the most valuable (and difficult) things to do is persuade people to begin to question their own prejudices. If you can do this, your research will have been most worthwhile. Just as important is to lead people to be aware of their own capacity for learning, where they come to see themselves always as in process, on the edge, never at a point of closure. Perhaps one of the most valuable things action researchers can do is to allow their work to promote new perspectives that celebrate open-endedness, lack of certainty and a tentative view towards the planet and the life it supports.

2   Examples of the framework in action

Here are some examples to show these ideas in action. Our own collections of work can be accessed through our published papers and books, and also via our websites: see http://www.actionresearch.net and http://www.jeanmcniff.com.

Jean has supported masters studies in Ireland from 1994–2000, accredited by the University of the West of England, and doctoral studies at the University of Limerick, from 2000–2007. Examples of accounts are available on her website, and show how the above framework has enabled practitioners to organize their ideas in relation to their own contexts.

In the first example, the contents of the chapters are given in expanded form. In the following examples, chapter headings only are given.

Example 1   Marian Nugent

Title: How can I raise the level of self-esteem of second year Junior Certificate School Programme students and create a better learning environment? (Nugent 2000)

Here is the abstract from Marian's dissertation and a summary of her chapters. You can access the entire dissertation from http://www.jeanmcniff.com/items.asp?id=53.

Abstract

This study shows, I believe, an improvement in my teaching of the Junior Certificate Schools Programme (JCSP) students. The philosophy of the JCSP is that every student is capable of success. It describes the shift in my thinking and practice from a view of reality as objectified to a view of reality as holistic and integrated. Carr and Kemmis (1986: 24) state: A humanistic perspective emphasizes that education is a human encounter whose aim is the development of the unique potential of each individual.

I believe my practice demonstrates this quality. The question which informed my research is: How can I raise the level of self-esteem of second year JCSP students and create a better learning environment? I set out to explore this question in a number of ways: in terms of my own professional development as a reflective practitioner and in terms of the students' development.

In my work with the students I have attempted to develop their respect for one another, to managing behaviour and classroom discipline. I have fostered a climate of mutual respect between the students and myself as year head. The research was in the overall context of classroom management and I followed an action research methodology to locate my research.

A problem which I encountered was that as an authority figure it is easy to maintain the status quo but it is difficult to imagine how things could be different. I have implemented practices, which can be used in order to show a move to a different style of discipline, to teaching and care for the students.

Action research aims to improve our practice and our understanding of that practice. For me, my educational journey has evolved as a result of participation on the MA in Education programme, and I am now further towards my goals of being more understanding of the students and their needs and of encouraging students to believe in their own powers of learning.

Contents

Introduction To the research project.

Chapter 1 Reasons for doing the research

Here I reflect upon the values I hold that inform my practice as an educator. This chapter also deals with why I want to research this topic and my values underpinning my research. It explains the aims and objectives of the research.

Chapter 2 Contextualization

This chapter deals with my present context as class teacher, year head and the JCSP co-ordinator in an inner city school designated disadvantaged. It allows the reader to connect with the relevant background of the school. The descriptions here will act as the background for the research and indicate the reasons I give for the course of action taken during the research project.

Chapter 3 Methodology

This chapter deals with issues of methodology and epistemology. I describe the three main educational research paradigms and compare and contrast the advantages and limitations of each paradigm. I show my responsibility as a researcher by providing an analysis of the main research paradigms, which will include a short history of their origins, and I explain my methodology stating why I have chosen action research and the problematics of action research. I describe in this chapter how important ethical values are to my work and how I maintained them throughout the research. I aim to support my claim that an action research methodology was the best form of research for me to use while I researched this question.

Chapter 4   The project

Here I tell the story of the project. My research question is: How can I raise the level of self-esteem of second year JCSP students and create a better learning environment? This chapter describes how I set about researching this question and how I discovered through critical reflection and moved on and explored alternative ways of improving my practice, such as encouraging more student participation. I have also described the data gathering methods I used and their value to me, and I supported my descriptions with evidence and validation to show that the claim to improvement in my practice can be reasonably justified. This chapter is built on an action research plan:

- I experienced a problem.
- I sought a solution.
- I implemented the solution.
- I evaluated the outcomes of my actions.
- I re-formulated the problem in the light of my evaluation …

I present my findings as a result of this analysis, and show the evidence of my findings.

Chapter 5   Significance of the research

This chapter deals with the significance of my research for the JCSP class and myself. I hope to show the relevance and significance of the study, show my own professional learning and what it has done for my workplace and me. I hope to do this by reflecting on observing and evaluating the feedback from the students.

Conclusion

I hope to show progress of how I changed my practice and moved from using an authoritarian teaching style to a more caring teaching style. By implementing a class code of good behaviour I have learned the importance that a positive approach can have on the students and how they can benefit from this approach. I will return to my aims and objectives and see how far I have fulfilled them. I will critically review the limitations of the study, and indicate avenues for further possible research.

Example 2   Sally McGinley

Title: How can I help the primary school children I teach to develop their self-esteem? (McGinley 2000)

Here is the abstract from Sally's dissertation and a summary of her chapters. The entire dissertation can be downloaded from http://www.jeanmcniff.com/items.asp?id=55.

Abstract

This dissertation tells the story of a study I carried out in my primary classroom in answer to the research question, how do I help the primary school children I teach to develop their self-esteem? Through the process of doing this research, I learned that focusing on care in relationships and care in the learning process can impact positively on the children's self-esteem.

In undertaking this study I had two aims:

- To understand the ways that self-esteem develops and the impact of the classroom experience on that self-esteem.
- To reflect on and improve my own practice with a view to creating an atmosphere where the children could be enabled to view themselves in a more positive light.

I used an action research methodology, because my intention was to improve my own practice and to involve and learn from the participants in order to enhance the learning experience for all. Through the process of doing the research I learned to reflect on my values, attitudes and relationships with the children as they impacted on my practice and on the children's view of themselves.

In doing the research I developed an enhanced awareness of the emotional needs of the children in my class and a greater understanding of their individuality. I came to understand the impact of self-esteem on learning and I developed a respect for the children's capacity to make decisions about their own learning and for the level of trust they place in me as their class teacher.

In the course of the research I developed an awareness of the need to create a caring practice centred on values of gentleness, respect, kindness and awareness of individual needs. This has implications for the ways I organize learning, attend to individual needs and help the children to manage their relationships with each other and, most importantly, for the way I as teacher show respect for each child.

Summary of chapters

Of particular note is the collection of five doctoral theses Jean supported from the University of Limerick. These have been acknowledged as of outstanding methodological quality, each demonstrating commitments to social justice. Each followed roughly the organization of ideas above. Jean had supervised the masters programmes of four of the group, and, with others, they formed an independent study group based in Dublin. This arrangement continued for a year, voluntarily and unfunded, while Jean found an Irish university that would accredit the work. Eventually she negotiated with the University of Limerick that they would accommodate the group. From an original group of eight partici-pants, five completed. Each thesis follows the guidelines given in this chapter. The theses are as follows.

Cahill, M. (2007) 'My living educational theory of inclusional practice'. PhD thesis, University of Limerick. Retrieved 9 January 2008 from http://www.jeanmcniff. com/margaretcahill/index.html

Glenn, M. (2006) 'Working with collaborative projects: my living theory of a holistic educational practice'. PhD thesis, University of Limerick. Retrieved 9 January 2008 from http://www.jeanmcniff.com/glennabstract.html

McDonagh, C. (2007) 'My living theory of learning to teach for social justice: how do I enable primary school children with specific learning disability (dyslexia) and myself as their teacher to realise our learning potentials?'. PhD thesis, University of Limerick. Retrieved 9 January 2008 from http://www.jeanmcniff.com/mcdonagh abstract.html

Roche, M. (2007) 'Towards a living theory of caring pedagogy: interrogating my practice to nurture a critical, emancipatory and just community of enquiry'. PhD thesis, University of Limerick. Retrieved 9 January 2008 from http://www.jeanmcniff. com/MaryRoche/index.html

Sullivan, B. (2006) 'A living theory of a practice of social justice: realising the right of Traveller children to educational equality'. PhD thesis, University of Limerick. Retrieved 9 January 2008 from http://www.jeanmcniff.com/bernieabstract.html

To give an example of how they found the guidelines helpful in structuring their work, here are the chapter headings from Mairín Glenn's thesis.

Introduction

Chapter One What were my concerns? Examining the background and contexts of the research

Chapter Two Why was I concerned? Examining my understanding of my practice as I clarified my ontological values

Chapter Three What could I do about my concerns? Examining issues around methodology

Chapter Four What did I do about my concerns? Developing key insights around my research in terms of am emergent understanding of my practice

Chapter Five How do I use technology to enhance a dialogical and inclusional epistemology? Examining how technology and holistic approaches to education can merge

Chapter Six Developing epistemological justification – demonstrating validity

Chapter Seven How do I contribute to new practices and theory and to the education of social formations? Examining how I show the significance and potentials of my work

Bibliography

Appendices

Jack supports doctoral studies at the University of Bath. Here are two examples of recently completed studies.

Simon and Karen Riding's doctoral theses

Simon and Karen Riding are the only husband and wife that Jack has supervised for their doctoral theses. They both graduated in 2009 from the University of Bath.

Simon focused on the creation of a living educational space to support the development of school-based teacher-researcher groups. Karen focused on supporting the development of intergenerational groups of pupils as researchers. In the creation of their living educational theories both Simon and Karen recognized the significance of their relationally dynamic awareness of inclusionality in generating their original contributions to educational knowledge with action research.

Simon Riding's doctoral thesis

How do I contribute to the education of myself and others through improving the quality of living educational space? The story of living myself through others as a practitioner-researcher

Abstract

Within this text I propose and demonstrate an original relationally dynamic standard of judgement within my practice of Living Myself Through Others. I explore the ongoing nature of transition between living educational spaces upon myself and how this process of change is addressed as I move through different stages of my career and life. I argue that I am able to improve the quality of the living educational space because of the relationships and experiences that I have had, alongside the living core values that I hold. This thesis reflects on the potential impact of enabling teachers to engage as teacher-researchers within their own school and accounts for the process I went through in order to make this happen. I further argue for the need to consider how practitioner accounts are assessed in order to ensure that the future of education is driven forward through the development of teachers as researchers influencing what educational knowledge is and how it is produced. The following text is a living educational theory action research enquiry that utilizes autobiography as a way of accounting for one educator's transitions from being a classroom teacher, through middle leadership and finally into senior school leadership. I argue that I am the educator that I am because of the life I have led and the life that I am currently leading. This thesis addresses the vastly important influence of relationships within education and explores how these relationships impact on my practice as an educator. The text incorporates and captures these relationships through enabling these others to speak through their own voice. This thesis explores how I was able to create the shared living educational space necessary to enable teacher-research to occur and flourish.

Accessible from http://www.actionresearch.net/living/simonridingphd.shtml

Karen Riding' doctoral thesis

How do I come to understand my shared living educational standards of judgement in the life I lead with others? Creating the space for intergenerational student-led research

Abstract

In this account I explain the shared life that I lead with my husband Simon transforms itself into a loving energy that emerges in our educational practice. This loving way of being emerges as the energy that drives me to transform the social formation of the school to work alongside student researchers in an intergenerational and sustainable way.

These living and loving standards of judgment are shared between us, asking the other to be the best that s/he can be and valuing the contribution that s/he makes. I live out an inclusional way of being that extends across the professional and personal domain, asking me to be responsive to the others with whom I share this life. This account attempts to explicate the emergence and significance of these standards between those in my life.

The boundaries shared between participants on this journey are fluid and dynamic. They are permeable, yet also recognise the limitations of certain relationships into impermeable boundaries. In the current debate about personalised learning within education, I see a new language of education emerging, shared between school and student researchers that places learning at its heart. I am supporting Schön's (1995) call for the emergence of a new epistemology for educational knowledge with the expression and clarification of new living standards of judgment that can contribute to enhancing educational space.

Accessible from http://www.actionresearch.net/living/karenridingphd.shtml

--- Summary ---

This chapter has outlined basic frameworks for writing a report for accreditation. Examples from a range of settings are offered. The chapter has also emphasized that, while the ideas here can act as a guide, individual people have adapted them to their own needs, producing reports of outstanding quality for higher degree accreditation. Examples are given to show the range and variety.

The next chapter deals with issues of further dissemination.

Further reading

As the idea of academic literacies takes hold, more and more books are appearing about writing for accreditation. Here are some of them.

Murray, R. (2002) *How to Write a Thesis*. Buckingham: Open University Press.
A valuable textbook for explaining about the writing process for higher degree accreditation.

Crème, P. and Lea, M. (2008) *Writing at University*. Maidenhead: Open University Press.
Full of valuable advice about writing and the expectations of universities.

Hartley, J. (1997) 'Writing the thesis', in N. Graves and V. Varma (eds), *Working for a Doctorate*. London: Routledge. Chapter 6.
A really helpful chapter on writing up a PhD thesis.

Herr, K. and Anderson, G. (2005) *The Action Research Dissertation*. Thousand Oaks, CA: Sage.
One of the most useful books for writing in action research, with lots of practical advice. A good read.

Phillips, E. and Pugh, D. (2005) *How to Get a PhD*. Maidenhead: Open University Press. Another helpful book that will help you get your PhD.

TWENTY ONE

Publishing and Disseminating Your Research

You have completed your research and produced your report. Now what? Your report is not much use locked away. You have to put it to use and let it serve your purposes. This chapter gives ideas about how you can do this, and why. It contains these sections.

1 Publishing and disseminating your research
2 Contributing to the knowledge base
3 An example of a significant contribution

1   Publishing and disseminating your research

You can disseminate your work to an increasingly wide audience – workplace, professional, global – and in a variety of forms – written, oral, multimedia.

Potential audiences

Your workplace

Throughout your project you have kept your workplace colleagues informed. Now you need to tell them your findings, and why these may be important for them (see Chapter 22 for the significance of your work). Get permission from your manager to disseminate your work, certainly in the workplace, if not for wider audiences. Try to get your manager's active support by asking them to mention your work at a staff meeting or write a cover note to endorse the report. Aim to communicate to colleagues how much you have learned and to suggest diplomatically that they could learn too.

Your professional field

Take and create opportunities to connect with wider professional circles, explaining the significance of your learning and its potential for their own. Emphasize that you are contributing to new professional practices and knowledge. They can do the same and can form new communities of practice that can link with wider global communities. Publishing your work may sound daunting, but it is achievable. Do not leave it to someone else to publish the ideas you have already thought about. Get on and do it yourself.

The wider public

Be bold in publishing your work for global dissemination. Write articles and books. Even the most widely published authors had to start somewhere. Learn how to write for the market (see next section). Study journals and see the kind of articles that are accepted, and the language they use. Learn how to write a book proposal. Many publishing houses have websites that give guidelines on submitting proposals. Editors are constantly on the lookout for promising proposals, and most are prepared to work with you to refine your proposal and get your book published. It is a competitive market, so basic advice is to take your work seriously and professionally, learn how to write for the market and be prepared to work hard.

Form of publication

You can publish your work in a range of forms.

Written reports

You can write reports, articles and books. Your initial publication will possibly be your research report, but you can adapt this for new outlets. Being serious about disseminating your work means studying the market. Where do other people like you publish? Which journals and magazines? Which publishing houses? Look on the Internet. Library databases are great if you have access. The most important resource, as always, is yourself and your own passionate commitment that you have something to say that other people should hear.

The golden rule for publishing is to study and learn to write for a particular market. Writing is a job, the same as any other job that takes preparation and practice. Learn to accept critique and do not be dismayed if your work is rejected initially. Learn from the experience. What did you do right? What could you have done better? It can take a long time for work to get published, but if you have faith in your capabilities, you will succeed.

Oral presentations

Getting people to listen to you means engaging and sustaining their interest so that they will want to hear more. You can do this by developing specific presentation skills, including the following.

Believe in yourself and others

Let your passion show through. Say that you had a dream and you now want to share it. Let your audience know that they too can do similar things and can also contribute to other people's improved learning and practice.

Get maximum participation and involvement

Do not tell other people what to do. Suggest that they can do what you have done. Be inviting. Relate well and maintain eye contact. Keep a light but serious touch throughout. Get involvement. Set up instant pair work or conversations in threes. You can do this with an audience of hundreds, but negotiate beforehand that they will stop when you give the signal. Once people begin talking about something that interests them, they often do not want to stop.

Watch your language

Always talk in the language of the community you are addressing. If you use a new professional word, say so and explain it, but do not talk down to anyone. Engage them as educated participants who are interested in what you have to say. Keep it simple and accessible.

Organize your material

Plan in advance what you are going to say and then say it. Do not get sidetracked and stick to the topic. If someone raises a question, make sure you address it at some point. If you cannot, say so. People will respect your lack of knowledge but they will not respect you if you dodge the issue. If you are speaking from notes, do not read them but glance at them occasionally to keep you on track. Speak from the heart, not from notes.

Electronic communication

Electronic communication can put you in touch with virtually anyone anywhere. You can disseminate your work through your own or your organization's website or by sending it to an email list which you or others may compile. This is a wonderfully attractive and valuable form of dissemination because you can use multimedia, and also connect people to others by using live links, which relate your work to others in the field. You can immediately show the significance of your research by disseminating its relevance to the field, perhaps through social networking sites, and explaining how people can renegotiate their meanings so that practice and knowledge can advance. As with other forms of dissemination, you have to learn how to do this, which takes time and practice. One of the rewards of electronic communication is that you tend to get rapid feedback, so the sense of isolation that many writers experience in conventional print publication tends to be reduced.

2 Contributing to the knowledge base

A knowledge base refers to everything that is known in a particular field. The knowledge base is usually found in the publications of that field.

The idea of creating a new kind of knowledge base is well developed in the teaching profession. In 2001, Catherine Snow, then President of the American Educational Research Association, called for the development of a knowledge base that was created by teachers for teachers. This, she said, would enable teachers to access developments in the field and see what they had to do to advance it further. The work reported in this book is already making that contribution. It is also important to recognize and strengthen the idea that all practitioners in all professions, if engaged in contributing to people's learning, should regard themselves as involved in education, though not necessarily in the teaching profession, with important things to say about developing learning through the systematic testing of knowledge claims.

Bear in mind that one strong kind of knowledge base already exists, but not in the form that all practitioners can access, or that has direct relevance to everyday practice. This knowledge base resides in the publications of the professional elites that Schön (1983) mentioned. These publications usually take the form of the exposition and linguistic analysis of ideas, which are often unrelated to practice. The accumulation of articles and books tends to be written for peers in the professional elites, not for practitioners, and this reinforces the idea that one grouping is designated an elite who can understand these things, while another grouping is designated a learner group, some of whom are incapable of understanding, let alone contributing. We are saying in this book that all are capable of both understanding and contributing, and should contribute, and ways need to be found to communicate this message and show its truth.

One of the ways to communicate the message is to develop a knowledge base by practitioners for practitioners. This knowledge base should incorporate the ideas of professional elites and develop them through systematic critique, for example, by showing their relevance (or not) to practice. Similarly, the work of practitioners should be incorporated into the thinking of the elites and be tested for validity in relation to whether practitioners support their claims through stringent methodologies. This will take time, given the current situation, but it is already happening in many places. One of the outcomes that is already happening, as demonstrated in this book, is that previously artificial categorizations of elites and practitioners disappear from the culture and the language. People may work in different settings and have different responsibilities, but all are equal in status and in the recognition that they are valuable people who have the right to be listened to when they stake their claims about how they wish to conduct their lives.

Doing this can be risky for anyone who positions themselves in what is still seen as one camp or the other. It can be risky for those who regard themselves as belonging to an elite, because it means relinquishing the power that this positioning gives them and recognizing themselves as practitioners. It can be risky for practitioners, too, because it means leaving the security of subjugation. It is easy to grumble about a situation, but rather difficult to find the energy to do something about it. It is risky for all who run the gauntlet of the comments of peers, many of whom also wish to keep them in their place. Breaking down barriers and coming out from hiding takes energy and commitment, a willingness to move forward while accepting the hazards involved. This is demonstrated in the work of Joan Whitehead (2003), who speaks of 'making the probable possible'. Joan, and Bernie Fitzgerald, who are practitioners in higher education, have renegotiated roles and responsibilities with others whom they support on schools-based mentoring programmes, a practice that has involved the development of new relationships and ways of working between university staff and school-based mentors, and confronting the hierarchy which had previously existed (Joan, Whitehead and Fitzgerald, 2004). Such renegotiation is often not easy, because it means all have to unlearn what they have previously learned from the culture and change their language accordingly. It means developing new cultures that have to be tried out and developing new languages that often take time to learn. Joan and Bernie show how this can be done.

Contributing to the knowledge base takes time, energy and commitment. It takes the efforts of all to build up the publications and disseminate the work. This is essential if ideas are to be disseminated and take hold in the public mind. The position in contemporary work is that there are two knowledge bases, the traditional propositional one of those who still position themselves as professional elites and the newer person-centred one of those who position themselves as practitioner-researchers. Whereas these knowledge bases used to be in an asymmetrical relationship of power, they are now concurrent. It is well to bear this in mind, as well as the constant struggle involved, because a knowledge base is sustained through careful maintenance and constant regeneration. This means regular contributions from the community of practitioners whose ideas make up the knowledge base. If the energy flags, it is salutary to remember that practitioners in the other knowledge base are working hard to build their own platforms, from which they can speak with authority. This may be a game, but it is a seriously important game, in which there are winners and losers, some of whom are the people you work with now and future generations of practitioners. The future, it is hoped, will be that the two knowledge bases will merge: all will learn how to learn from the other, so that all work is regarded as potentially valuable and as contributing to a wider understanding of creating a better world. For the meantime, for the current practitioner-researcher knowledge base to remain intact, and grow, you have to become an active participant.

3   An example of a significant contribution

Here is an example of one such contribution. It is the entire accepted proposal for a keynote symposium at the 2009 British Educational Research Association

(BERA), one of the most prestigious educational research associations. The references are not with the individual papers but can be found in the main list of references at the end of the book. The proposal is significant in several senses. First, it shows how practitioner researchers are establishing a new epistemology for educational knowledge. Second, the symposium represents generative transformational capacity, both in terms of how the settings develop from individual classrooms to worldwide systems. Third it shows how ontological commitments can be transformed into epistemological standards of judgement, which in turn transform into social practices with potential for global influence.

We present this also as an example of how to submit a proposal. Submitting a proposal for a paper or a symposium is competitive, so you have to observe all protocols carefully and write to a high standard. BERA and other research organizations require proposals to be presented anonymously. Even citations from the literature should not give away the proposer's identity. In the example, we have put in the names and affiliations of the presenters, to honour them and their contributions. You can see other proposals also on our websites. They are there to help you organize your own proposal for successful submission, and contribute to the growing knowledge base yourself.

Explicating A New Epistemology For Educational Knowledge With Educational Responsibility

Convenor: Jack Whitehead, University of Bath
Chair: Margaret Farren, Dublin City University
Discussant: Christine Jones, Bath and North East Somerset Local Authority.

Papers of the Contributors: The papers can be accessed below or from education*online* at http://www.actionresearch.net/writings/bera/educationlinebera09keynote.pdf

Jean McNiff, York St John University: Learning for Action in Action
Marie Huxtable, Bath and North East Somerset Local Authority: How do I Improve What I am Doing in my Professional Practice and Make an Original Contribution to the Knowledge-Base of Education?
Jane Renowden, St Mary's College Twickenham: Linking Accountability with Professional Identity: How Do I Develop My Living Theory of Educationally Responsible Practice?
Jack Whitehead, University of Bath: Generating Educational Theories that can Explain Educational Influences in Learning

Successful Submission for the Keynote Symposium

Overview

The overall coherence of the symposium is in the explication of the epistemology transformation of educational knowledge under discussion in Open Dialogue in the 2008 issues 102, 103, 104 and 105 of *Research Intelligence*. The new epistemology has been created in the explanations that practitioner-researchers have produced for their educational influences in learning. These include explanations of their educational influences in their own learning, in the learning of others and in the learning of the social formations in which they are living, working and researching. The idea of living educational theories is introduced to distinguish these explanations from the explanations of education researchers who are making their contributions to knowledge in disciplines of education other than a discipline of educational enquiry. The database for the explication of the new epistemology will include over 30 doctorates that have been successfully completed between 1988–2009.

Epistemological coherence is provided by a new unit of appraisal, living standards of judgment and a living logic of inclusionality. The unit of appraisal is the individual's explanation of their educational influence in learning. The meanings of living standards of judgment are clarified in the course of their emergence in the practice of educational enquiries in doctoral and other research programmes. The clarification includes the use of principles of rigour and personal and social validity. A living logic of inclusionality forms the epistemological coherence through integrating insights from propositional and dialectical theories without the usual problem arising between adherents of propositional and dialectical logic denying the rationality of the other's logic.

Methodological coherence is provided by narratives that integrate action reflection cycles in enquiries of the kind, 'How do I improve my practice?' Some of the narratives will include video-data, from educational relationships, to clarify ostensively and develop meanings of living standards of judgment. These standards include the value of educational responsibility for distinguishing the research as educational.

Conceptual coherence is provided by a view of educational research that is distinguished by the expression of educational responsibility in educational relationships in educational spaces. In this view of educational research the contributions of education researchers provide insights for the generation of educational theory.

Evidence will be presented to show the demonstrable international significance of living theory educational research upon practice, policy and theory in the UK, the Republic of Ireland, China, Japan, Canada, Croatia, India and South Africa.

Supporting Statement

In the sense that educational researchers are seeking to contribute to educational knowledge it is always timely to present ideas that claim to be contributing to the reconstruction of what counts as educational theory. The contributions to the symposium can be understood as an answer to the call made in 1995 by Donald Schön to develop a new epistemology for educational knowledge from action research into teachers' professional practice. The contributions can also be understood as a response to Snow's 2001 call in her Presidential Address to AERA to develop procedures for systematizing and making public the knowledge-base of practitioners. The presentations are also consistent with current ideas that show how narratives can communicate explanations of educational influence in living educational theories. In this symposium educational researchers are viewed as distinct from education researchers in seeking to contribute to forms of educational knowledge that can explain an individual's educational influence in their own learning, in the learning of others and in the learning of social formations.

To ensure the high quality of the research data as well as the quality of the analyses, the analyses include the research programmes of practitioner-researchers who have engaged in several years of educational enquiry into their practice for their successfully completed doctoral or other research degrees.

In focusing on learning for action with action, McNiff draws evidence from five living theory doctorate research programmes successfully completed at the University of Limerick over the past three years with the titles:

My living educational theory of inclusional practice.
Working with collaborative projects: my living theory of a holistic educational practice.
My living theory of learning to teach for social justice: how do I enable primary school children with specific learning disability (dyslexia) and myself as their teacher to realise our learning potentials?
Towards a living theory of caring pedagogy: interrogating my practice to nurture a critical, emancipatory and just community of enquiry.
A living theory of a practice of social justice: realising the right of Traveller children to educational equality.

Each practitioner-researcher expresses educational responsibility in distinguishing his or her research as educational. As part of this educational responsibility they produce research narratives in which they hold themselves to account for living their ontological values as fully as they can.

Each contributor to the symposium recognizes the importance of addressing the sociocultural influences of postcolonialism and Renowden focuses on this in researching accountability with professional identity in her enquiry, 'How do I develop my postcolonial living theory of educationally responsible practice?'

Practitioner researchers cannot do anything without expressing energy. An assumption that gives coherence to the symposium, and that is open to question, is the belief that educational relationships involve the expression of a life-affirming energy with values. Huxtable focuses on forms of representation that can communicate such flows of energy with values of educational responsibility, loving recognition and respectful connectedness in her educational enquiry, 'How do I improve what I am doing in my professional practice and make an original contribution to the knowledge-base of education?'

From the ground of the expression of educational responsibility in educational relationships, the practitioner-researchers contributing to the symposium, as well as the successfully completed living theory doctorates drawn on in the analyses, use new units of appraisal, living logics and standards of judgment in their claims to educational knowledge. Whitehead explicates these units, logics and standards in his analysis of educational theories and a living theory methodology that can be used in explaining educational influences in learning.

Individual contributions

Learning for action in action

Jean McNiff, York St John University, UK

Background to the research

This paper explains how I hold myself accountable for my professional learning as I seek to influence the development of new institutional epistemologies that are grounded in a commitment to personal accountability in professional practice. It traces the educational journey of five teacher-researchers and myself as their supervisor. Having completed their masters studies with me through a British university, using a self-study action research methodology, the teachers now wished collectively to undertake their doctoral studies at an Irish university, eventually locating at the University of Limerick. Six years on, the successful completions of all five doctorates (Appendix 1) provide a strong evidence base for the legitimation of a new epistemology of educational knowledge in Ireland, with potential global significance.

Focus of the enquiry

The project was marked by a focus on reciprocal learning in the pursuit of social justice. For the teachers, it was for social justice on behalf of marginalized children. For me, it was for educational justice in relation to legitimating the teachers as educational theorists, and also for epistemological justice in legitimating their workplace-based knowledge as valid theory. This involved strengthening new institutional epistemologies (Schön 1995) that accepted personal ways of knowing, informed by living logics and values (Whitehead and McNiff 2006). Over time, we researched our practices as a group who could demonstrate the realization of educational influence in our own and one another's learning. Each thesis shows this value of learning for action through action, some using a multimedia form. My enquiry focused on explaining my pedagogical practices in relation to influencing the professional learning of my colleagues and myself, by interrogating our own and one another's normative assumptions, in order to challenge unwarranted truth claims in the public sphere.

My interactive presentation makes a case for the development of relational and transformational epistemologies that can promote sustainable social and cultural practices. It also raises questions about the responsibilities of intellectuals in demonstrating their accountability for social well-being through the development of appropriate institutional epistemologies for the production of the kind of knowledge and form of educational theory that can contribute to human well-being. The presentation will also include some of the research being undertaken at York St John University that is contributing to current debates in the area.

Research methods

Our individual and collective research methodologies became transformational action enquiries, grounded in a view of history as an infinite process of new beginnings (Said 1997). We came to appreciate ourselves as actively making history by improving present practice for future sustainability, through developing cultures of enquiry focused on dialogically constituted communicative action (Habermas 1987). We came to appreciate that we were learning for action through action. Furthermore, we began to ask, 'What kind of action? Action for what?' and, since we all aimed for justice for the people in our care, we effectively transformed the university motto, *Eagna chun Gnímh* (Learning for Action), into the living realization of our living values and logics.

Theoretical frameworks

We tested the validity of our work against the ideas of action theorists, such as Taylor (1992), linking justice with political philosophy; of political philosophers such as Said (1997) and Chomsky (1986), linking personal accountability with social sustainability;

and Polanyi (1958), positioning personal knowledge as the basis of social action. We demonstrated methodological rigour (Winter 1989) in our accounts. The content of each thesis explains the processes of transformative action, the communicability of which is strengthened by its transformational form. Each text demonstrates ironic validity (Lather 2004), by interrogating its unarticulated assumptions, and subjecting its findings and evidence base to rigorous social validation.

Evidence base

The five theses comprise an evidence base with several functions. It demonstrates the values-based knowledge of the teachers, and a focus on achieving social justice for children. It is evidence of my educational influence in the teachers' learning; and evidence of the development of new institutional epistemologies for a new scholarship of educational knowledge. In each case, the validity of the evidence may be tested against the values that informed the practice, as living standards of judgement. Testing the validity of the evidence base points to the educational significance of the research.

Contribution to new educational knowledge

The educational significance of the research lies in the capacity of all participants to explain their accountability for their practices, and so contribute to the development of new institutional epistemologies grounded in the values of justice and the exercise of originality and critical engagement. The idea of 'learning for action through action' takes on new meaning, as the work of our group shows how the linguistic form becomes live, and so returns education to its living practitioners.

References

Please see main references list.

Appendix 1

Cahill, M. (2007) 'My living educational theory of inclusional practice'. PhD thesis, University of Limerick. Retrieved 9 January 2008 from http://www.jeanmcniff.com/margaretcahill/index.html

Glenn, M. (2006) 'Working with collaborative projects: my living theory of a holistic educational practice'. PhD thesis, University of Limerick. Retrieved 9th January 2008 from http://www.jeanmcniff.com/glennabstract.html

McDonagh, C. (2007) 'My living theory of learning to teach for social justice: how do I enable primary school children with specific learning disability (dyslexia) and myself as their teacher to realise our learning potentials?'. PhD thesis, University of Limerick. Retrieved 9 January 2008 from http://www.jeanmcniff.com/mcdonaghabstract.html

Roche, M. (2007) 'Towards a living theory of caring pedagogy: interrogating my practice to nurture a critical, emancipatory and just community of enquiry'. PhD thesis, University of Limerick. Retrieved 9 January 2008 from http://www.jeanmcniff.com/MaryRoche/index.html

Sullivan, B. (2006) 'A living theory of a practice of social justice: realising the right of Traveller children to educational equality'. PhD thesis, University of Limerick. Retrieved 9 January 2008 from http://www.jeanmcniff.com/bernieabstract.html

Linking accountability with professional identity: how do I develop my postcolonial living theory of educationally responsible practice?

Jane Renowden, St Mary's University College, UK

Background to the research

In this paper I explore the potentials of my research as a senior lecturer in a higher education supervisory position for the development of a new epistemology of educational knowledge with social responsibility. I trace the development of my postcolonial commitments through the experience of my transition from mainly content-based classroom teaching to knowledge-creating higher education pedagogies, and I link this with Foucault's (1977) ideas of the development from specific and universal intellectual (see below). My professional learning journey, now at doctoral level, has been characterized by an increasingly strong link between a desire to demonstrate professional accountability and the creation of my professional identity as fulfilling my potentials for a dialogically-constituted practice that honours the other's capacity for original thinking and creative engagement. I theorize my practice as a form of public accountability through demonstrating the validity of my claims to be influencing my own and others' learning for good.

Focus of the enquiry

The focus of the enquiry is therefore my practice as I interrogate what I am doing and produce evidence against which I test the validity of my claims to be acting in the public good. My understanding of 'the good' is that it resides in the living practices of people as they work collaboratively for social sustainability. Sustainability implies that a process contains its own capacity for infinitely renewable self-transformation. My practice therefore focuses on how I can support student teachers and myself as their supervisor to develop relational forms that encourage independent thinking through rational debate and stringent critique, within a caring dialogically-constituted context of critically reflective practice.

Research methods

I adopt a self-study action research approach to enquiring into my practice, as I encourage student teachers and myself to interrogate the normative epistemologies and cultural assumptions of our social contexts and our own thinking. This involves drawing on the work of critical deconstruction and action theorists, such as Derrida (1976) and Butler (1999), who explain the futility of working within the regulatory strictures of an imaginary Law. My methodologies are grounded in a view of identity as continually self-transforming, as a realization of the values of growth through unfettered freedom and the practice of freedom as development (Sen 1999). My data gathering focuses on those episodes that show the development of critical thinking and critically reflective practices through the problematization of normative cultural assumptions and organizational epistemologies. I continually subject my data and evidence to the critique of others, to ensure that I do not fall into the trap of self-deception through believing in the stable nature of my capacity for self-critique while using a form of logic that is grounded in assumptions about the inviolable nature of normative epistemologies.

Theoretical frameworks

My theoretical frameworks are to do with the politics of knowledge generation, within a postcolonialist frame of intellectual and social emancipation, grounded in a politics of deconstruction. To fulfil my values of accountability in exercising my own freedom, and encouraging others to do the same, I draw on the work of Freire (1993) and Memmi (2003), which enables me to realize that my professional narrative contains examples of how, in my knowledge creating practices, I have been both the oppressor and the oppressed. I strengthen my understanding of how to free myself from the crippling limitations of such colonialist practices through drawing on Foucault's ideas of the archaeology of knowledge-power, and I strengthen my professional identity in relation to his (1977) insights about the transformational processes involved in moving from specific to universal intellectual.

Evidence base

As evidence to test the claims above, I look to the assignments of my students together with my own reflective journal and writings, using my values as my living standards of judgment (Whitehead and McNiff 2006). I trace the development of our reciprocal learning, as I encourage them to become independent thinkers, while their feedback on my practice encourages me to do the same. Collectively, our storied accounts show the development of dialogically-constituted communities of practice (Wenger 1998), whose aims are to engage in communicative action (Habermas 1988) for personal and social well-being.

Contribution to new educational knowledge

The educational significance of my research is in the demonstration of my educational influence in my students' and my own learning, and my claim to have developed a critical emancipatory epistemology of practice. By developing emancipatory intellectual and social practices, I claim that I am contributing to a new epistemology of educational knowledge through my practice of emancipatory critical pedagogy that values the inclusion of the other (Habermas 2002) as a prerequisite for social sustainability.

References

Please see main references list.

How do I improve what I am doing in my professional practice and make an original contribution to the knowledge-base of education?

Marie Huxtable, University of Bath, UK

Background to the research

There has been much discussion in BERA and AERA about the appropriate forms of representation for the educational theories generating by practitioner-researchers in their educational research (Eisner, 1988, 1993, 1997, 2005; Bruce Ferguson, Whitehead 2008a, Laidlaw, 2008; Adler Collins, 2008). Recent discussions in 2008 issues 102, 103, 104 and 105 of *Research Intelligence* have suggested that an epistemological transformation in what counts as educational knowledge is underway in the living educational theories being produced by practitioner-researchers.

Focus of the enquiry

In my work as a senior educational psychologist in Bath and North East Somerset Authority I have a systemic responsibility to organize both the APEX (Able Pupils Extending Opportunities) programme on extending educational opportunities for children and young people and the leadership programme on Gifts and Talents in Education. In this self-study of my professional practice I make a contribution to educational knowledge through explicating the relationally dynamic standards of judgment that can be used to validate and legitimate my embodied educational knowledge in the Academy.

The explanations of educational influence in my own learning, in the learning of others and in the learning of social formations include the narratives of the teachers and pupils whose work I have supported. They include analyses of, and creative educational responses to, government and local government policies on gifts and talents in education. The explanations of educational influence I present include the recognition, expression, clarification and communication of energy flowing values of loving recognition, respectful connectedness and educational responsibility.

Research methods

The living theory methodology (Whitehead, 2008b) developed in this thesis draws insights from a range of methods from phenomenological, ethnographic, case study, grounded theory and narrative approaches to educational research (Cresswell, 2007). It includes a multimedia narrative to explicate the meanings of the energy flowing values and understandings that constitute the explanatory principles of educational influences in the thesis. Rigour is enhanced using the methods advocated by Winter (1989) and social validity is enhanced using the principles advocated by Habermas (1976, 2002).

Theoretical frameworks

The paper draws on:

- Whitehead's (1989, 2008a) living theory and living theory methodology.
- Hymer's (2007) generative-transformational framework for gift creation.
- Rayner's (2005) idea of inclusionality.
- Biesta's (2006) ideas on moving beyond a language of learning into a language of education through the exercise of educational responsibility.

Contribution to new educational knowledge

The significance of the paper is in the contribution it makes to an educational knowledge-base of practice, theory and systemic influence, in the development of a new, inclusional educational epistemology.

References

Please see main references list.

Generating educational theories that can explain educational influences in learning

Jack Whitehead, University of Bath, UK

Background to the research

There has been much discussion in BERA and AERA about the appropriate standards of judgment for evaluating the quality and validity of the educational knowledge generated by practitioner-researchers.

The 1988 BERA Presidential Address focused on the development of a research-based approach to professionalism in education through the generation of living educational theories. By 2008 over 30 living theory doctorates had been legitimated in the Academy with new units of appraisal, living logics and standards of judgment, in explanations of educational influences in learning.

The research answers the call made by Schön (1995) for the development of a new epistemology for the scholarship of teaching and by Snow (2001) to develop methodologies for making public the professional knowledge of teachers.

Foci of the enquiries

There are three research questions addressed in this presentation:

1 Can the explanations produced by individuals to explain their educational influences in learning be used as appropriate units of appraisal in the generation of educational theory?
2 What are the logics of the explanations that individuals produce for their educational influences in their own learning?
3 Which living standards of judgment for evaluating the validity of explanations of educational influences in learning have been legitimated in the academy?

Research methods

The appropriateness of the action reflection cycles used in the generation and development of living educational theories rests in showing their usefulness in clarifying the meanings of ontological values in educational relationships and in forming these values into living epistemological standards of judgment.

Visual narratives are used in multimedia explanations of educational influences in learning.

The methods for enhancing the robustness of the validity and rigour of the explanations include the use of Habermas' (1976) four criteria of social validity and Winter's (1989) six criteria for enhancing rigour.

Lather's (1991) catalytic validity is used to justify claims about the educational influence of the ideas generated in one context for individuals working and researching in different contexts in the UK, Ireland, Canada, Croatia, India, China, Japan and South Africa.

Theoretical frameworks

Answers to the research questions include the following analytic frames.

Adler-Collins' (2000) safe space; Bernstein's (2000) mythological discourse; Biesta's (2006) language of education; Bourdieu's (1990) ideas of habitus and social formation;

Charles' (2007) guiltless recognition and societal reidentification; Delong's (2002) culture of inquiry; Farren's (2005) pedagogy of the unique and web of betweenness; Habermas' (1976, 1987, 2002) notions of social validity, learning and the inclusion of the other; Hymer's (2007) idea of giftedness; Ilyenkov's (1977) dialectical logic; Lohr's (2006) love at work; McNiff's (2007) my story is my living educational theory; Merleau-Ponty's (1972) notion of embodiment; Rayner's (2005) idea of inclusionality; Vasilyuk's (1996) psychology of experiencing; Whitehead's (1989) idea of living educational theories; Laidlaw's (1996) idea of living standards of judgement; Winter's (1989) criteria of rigour;

Contribution to new educational knowledge

1 The generation of a new epistemology for educational knowledge (Whitehead, 2008a, 2008b).
2 The explication of a living theory methodology for making public the embodied knowledge of professional practitioners.
3 An understanding of educational theory as the explanations that individuals produce for their educational influences in learning.

References

Please see main references list.

Summary

This chapter has talked about how you can publish and disseminate your research for a range of different audiences. The chapter has also made the point that your report now contributes to the knowledge base, so others may access your work and learn from it. In this sense, your report represents a contribution that has profound significance. An example is given of such a significant contribution.

The next part goes on to explain the nature of that significance and how it can contribute to the education of social formations for the development of good social orders.

Further reading

If you are writing for publication in academic books or journals, the best source for advice is from the publishers themselves. Go to the websites of major publishers and read the advice they give there about how to submit proposals and papers. Perhaps the most relevant journal is *EJOLTS* (see below).

Murray, R. (2005) *Writing for Academic Journals*. Maidenhead: Open University Press.
A most helpful book for offering advice for writing for academic journals.

Educational Journal of Living Theories (*EJOLTS*) (2010) Retrieved 1 August 2010 from
  http://ejolt.net/
See the submission guidelines for this online journal, which offers the opportunity for including multimedia narratives in the publishing and disseminating of your action research.

PART VI

How Do I Show the Significance of My Knowledge?

Part VII explains how you can communicate the significance of what you have done and learned through engaging in your action enquiry. It contains the following chapters.

Chapter 22   Explaining the Significance of Your Research
Chapter 23   Developing New Epistemologies for Workplace Cultures of Enquiry

These chapters show how a personal action enquiry has the generative transformational potential to influence thinking and practices in a wide range of organizational cultures of enquiry and potentially with global influence.

In terms of your own action enquiry, you are now asking, 'How do I use what I have learned for my own and others' benefit?' 'How do I explain the significance of my learning and my practice for encouraging the kind of learning that will transform my own and wider organizational social practices?'

TWENTY TWO
Explaining the Significance of Your Research

Frequently, when you tell someone about what you are doing and why you are excited about it they say, 'So what?' This is an important question, because it means, 'Tell me what is special about your work.' 'Why is it significant?' 'What is in it for me?' 'Why should I listen to you and not someone else?' This chapter gives advice about how you can respond to these questions, and why. You need to appreciate the significance of what you have done so that you can communicate it properly in your broader aim of influencing individuals' and collectives' thinking and practices.

The overall significance of action research as a methodology is in relation to its capacity to generate and test theory to improve learning in order to improve practice. In other words, it is possible through action research to offer explanations for processes of improving learning. The significance of your action enquiry is that you are able to generate and test your living theory of improving learning, in relation to your own learning, the learning of others in workplaces and social situations, and the education of social formations. This chapter discusses these issues. It is in three parts.

1 The significance of your research for your own education
2 The significance of your research for the workplace-based education of others
3 The significance of your research for the education of social formations

1 The significance of your research for your own education

You are claiming that you have improved your practice in an identifiable way. This did not happen by accident. It happened because you studied what you were doing, and made specific decisions in relation to possible choices. You became aware that your learning was the grounds for your practice. As you began to critique and modify your existing practice, you became aware of how you could do things differently. You tried out new ways, and tested your provisional thinking about their effectiveness in informing other people's learning by listening to what those people said about you and how they were responding to you. You are able to stand back and comment on those processes that involved your own and other people's learning.

Here are some examples of how people have done this, taken from work submitted for higher degrees. The examples are from the work of Thérèse Burke in teaching, Marian Naidoo in health care, JeKan Adler-Collins in nursing and Graham van Tuyl in business. There is urgent need for practitioners across the professions to make their stories of learning public, so that others may learn from them.

Thérèse Burke (1997) writes the following abstract for her masters dissertation:

> My research recounts the steps I took to address my professional concerns that my belief in the values of education as emancipatory and the uniqueness of the individual were denied. It shows how I attempted to develop a theory of learning difference through action and reflection, as I researched the question, 'How can I improve my practice as a learning support teacher?' ...
>
> In my dissertation I intend to show how I moved from a deficit model of learning remediation to a theory of learning difference. I investigated new methods of learning support, which I believe resulted in the development of a more collaborative consultative model of practice.
>
> Finally, I hope my dissertation demonstrates that I have taken my first tentative steps towards the development of an emancipatory theory of learning difference.

Reflecting on the significance of her work, she says:

> Most importantly the critical self-reflective aspect of my work required me to look at who I was and where I was situated, both personally and professionally as I approached my twenty-fifth year of teaching. ... This recognition of my own professional development complements my own theory of learning difference. I no longer view the child as the sum of all her parts, but as an individual with her own ontological and epistemological needs, a person who can engage with others and use her potential to learn at this moment. ... I am now conscious of what I would like to name as an 'epistemological equality' between myself and my students. I do not have a monopoly on knowledge: mine is not the only way of knowing. ... This was a significant learning experience for me as a practising teacher. There can be a smugness about those in education, myself included, who suggest that the values of the school system are the only values that matter, and that what it offers is the only way to be. I challenge this assumption. I believe the theory of individuality which is at the basis of an understanding of learning difference makes a nonsense of this. When I reflect on who and how I was in the past, I realise that I would always have paid lip service to this theory, but now I know its truth and I claim it as an educational value of my own.

Marian Naidoo in her 2005 PhD thesis entitled 'I am because we are (a never ending story). The emergence of a living theory of inclusional and responsive practice', which is available at http://www.actionresearch.net/living/naidoo.shtml, writes:

Abstract

I believe that this original account of my emerging practice demonstrates how I have been able to turn my ontological commitment to a passion for compassion into a living epistemological standard of judgement by which my inclusional and responsive practice may be held accountable. I am a story teller and the focus of this narrative is on my learning and the development of my living educational theory as I have engaged with others in a creative and critical practice over a sustained period of time. This narrative self-study demonstrates how I have encouraged people to work creatively and critically in order to improve the way we relate and communicate in a multi-professional and multi-agency healthcare setting in order to improve both the quality of care provided and the well being of the system. In telling the story of the unique development of my inclusional and responsive practice I will show how I have been influenced by the work of theatre practitioners such as Augusto Boal, educational theorists such as Paulo Freire and drawn on, incorporated and developed ideas from complexity theory and living theory action research. I will also describe how my engagement with the thinking of others has enabled my own practice to develop and from that to develop a living, inclusional and responsive theory of my practice. Through this research and the writing of this thesis, I now also understand that my ontological commitment to a passion for compassion has its roots in significant events in my past.

JeKan Adler- Collins in his 2007 PhD thesis entitled 'Developing an inclusional pedagogy of the unique: how do I clarify, live and explain my educational influences in my learning as I pedagogise my healing nurse curriculum in a Japanese university?', which is available at http://www.actionresearch.net/living/jekan.shtml, writes:

Abstract

The social context of this thesis is embedded in the processes and reflections experienced during the development, implementation and evaluation of a healing nurse curriculum, using action research enquiry on my teaching practice, in a Japanese rural university in the years 2003–2007. These processes include the evolution of my ontology and the creation of an inclusional pedagogy of the unique with transitional certainty as a living epistemological standard of judgment. An energy-flowing, living standard of inclusionality as a space creator for engaged listening and informed learning is offered as an original contribution to knowledge. Two major strands of enquiry are interwoven and inseparable in this thesis. The first is my lifelong self study of my own learning and the values and practices that embrace all the different facets of my life, including being a nurse, educator, and Buddhist priest. The second extends the first, putting them firmly in the context of a specific time frame, weaving a textual narrative that passes between the different aspects of my multiple selves, building a picture for my readers that is grounded in my actual praxis. This narrative gives insights to the growth of my educational knowledge as I research the unique position I hold of being the only white, male nurse, foreign educator in a culture that is so completely different from that of my birth and early education. Finally, I use the analysis of the voices of my students' experience of my teaching and curriculum to mirror back to me my own values as they were seen through the eyes of others in their emergence in praxis. Such usage brought about fundamental ontological changes in me and my practices as a teacher.

Graham van Tuyl in his 2009 doctoral thesis 'From engineer to co-creative catalyst; an inclusional and transformational journey. An inquiry into the epistemology of how traditional management "tools and theory" can be used and evolved in enhancing organizational effectiveness in an industrial setting, and how to value and evaluate change', which is available at http://www.actionresearch.net/living/gvt.shtml, writes:

Abstract

This thesis is motivated by my desire to understand what it is a Change Agent actually does. Change Agents work in a variety of ways, and have a variety of organizational experiences in helping to create change. Over the years I have become more aware that there is no single body of theory that combines and explains the practical and theoretical approaches that can be taken in Change Management. In this thesis I will show how I use my current and past practice to improve my understanding of my ontology as a Change Agent and develop an inclusional epistemology, based on my evolving practice. This ontology transforms the way Change Management within an industrial setting can be approached, by creating fluidity across boundaries and a receptive co-creative space. In this way I create my own Living Theory. This thesis demonstrates through the narrative of my personal journey how being an Engineer and a Co-Creative Catalyst in generating organizational change can be an inclusional and transformational journey. Co-Creative Catalyst(s) use their own professional and personal values to help generate a creative space at the 'Edge of Fluidity', a space of embodied and emergent viewpoints on what change should be. This thesis will demonstrate how an inclusional practice can be used to help create change, while also demonstrating that current economic practice needs to be understood as a fundamentally important barrier to fluidity of ideas across boundaries. This thesis demonstrates how inclusional change can incorporate social, technical as well as economic models to be truly sustainable. A further element that this thesis shows is that the language used needs to change in order to generate an inclusional and transformational journey. The language used in this narrative changes with the development of my epistemology.

2   The significance of your research for the workplace-based learning of others

You can explain how your work has influenced the learning of others so that they have been inspired to investigate how their learning can improve practice. Your theory of practice is yours alone, yet it has the transformative potential to influence new theories, that is, the ones that your colleagues and others in wider fields will create to account for their own practices. Those new theories will contain descriptions of what people did, what aspects of practice they changed, and also explanations for why they did what they did and for what purpose. Your theory of practice therefore has the potential for transformative influence in relation to practice (what is done to improve learning), and also in relation to theory (how explanations can be offered for the learning processes involved).

Here is an example to show how this can be done. Karen O'Shea (2000), a human rights educator, writes the following abstract for her masters dissertation that sets out the aims of her research:

> This research is rooted in the act of reflective enquiry and focuses on my prac-tice. [I am] a human rights educator who is concerned that students of all ages and abilities have access to an education that includes a strong commitment to human rights and citizenship education … it illustrates how I set about influ-encing a national curriculum. It aims to contribute to the field of human rights and citizenship education by illuminating the curriculum development process and highlighting how it can benefit from personal reflection and collaboration.
>
> It also documents how I, by seeking to become an agent of change in my own con-text, was drawn into a deeper exploration of my values, which in turn challenged me to explore my understanding of my practice. I reached a stage in my research where I describe my educational practice as a reflective, value-based community activity that seeks to encourage the development of a more just society within which all can reach their fullest potential. Thus the research highlights how understanding can be generated through the process of action and reflection. …
>
> From my research I suggest that educational practice is generative in nature in that it is in a continual state of growth and development. In conclusion, I explore the implications of my learning for educational theory and practice, in particular for the development of communities of learning and ongoing teacher education. I suggest that teacher education is a lifelong process and that developing an understanding of one's practice provides an ideal starting point for ongoing professional development.

Commenting on the significance of her work, Karen says:

> As a result of my research I would now suggest that my practice is a reflective, value-based community activity, which seeks to encourage the development of a more just society within which all can reach their fullest potential. As both a human rights educator and curriculum developer my practice is con-cerned with the betterment not only of the educational experience of young people in the classroom, but also with the development of educational experi-ences for teachers and others. My practice is therefore a hopeful activity.
>
> In relation to my emerging understanding of my own practice I would suggest that reflectivity is concerned with remaining attentive to what is going on within myself as a practitioner, how I am responding to people and events within my everyday practice. My practice does not exist outside of the relationship I live

every day. It exists in relationship to my co-workers, my colleagues, teachers with whom I work on a number of curriculum development projects. The idea of being a reflective practitioner is core to how I develop these relationships in ways which are just and respectful. The idea of reflectivity is also important as it challenges me to go to the heart of what I do. To be willing to ask questions about myself, my motives, and to regularly confront such as questions as 'what is really going on here?' … From the evidence I have provided this understanding is more than simply a theory of practice but is a living theory (Whitehead 1989). It resides in me and emerges through my reflection and action.

3   The significance of your research for the education of social formations

By 'the education of social formations' we mean changes in the rules that regulate social organizations and that move the social formation in the direction of values that carry hope for the future of humanity. This involves the learning processes that people engage in when they decide to improve their collective capacity for generating theory for improving learning. This is a crucial aspect of social renewal, and has deep implications for policy formation and implementation (see Chapter 23). Most theories of social renewal are grounded in bodies of propositional work that tell how social renewal can come about: the development literatures are frequently grounded in analyses of the flow of economic capital; the literatures of peace education tend to be grounded in analyses of the distribution of justice and entitlement; and the literatures of social renewal are often grounded in analyses of social interactions and activities. While these literatures are enormously valuable, they tend to stay at the level of grand narrative, offering solutions to problems, on the assumption that theory can be applied to practice. What is needed is a complementary body of small local narratives, which show how people thought about what they were doing in relation with one another, in order to improve their own personal and social lives as they lived and worked together. We need not only advice about the development of communities of practice (Wenger, 1998), but also stories that show the living processes of people negotiating their meanings so that the freedom of all is safeguarded to make their contribution and be listened to when they say they wish to live their lives in ways of their own choosing.

Here are two examples that show how this can be done. Swaroop Rawal in her 2006 doctoral thesis 'The role of drama in enhancing life skills in children with specific learning difficulties in a Mumbai school: my reflective account', which is available at http://www.actionresearch.net/living/rawal.shtml, writes:

Abstract

This thesis is a reflective account of an action research project set in a drama classroom. It is a multi-voiced patchwork text which is created and built imaginatively to re-present my students and my experience in the drama classroom. On one level it deals with the question 'How can drama be used to enhance life skills in children with specific learning disabilities studying in a school in Mumbai?' On the second level it is related to the question 'How can I improve my practice?' This research is concerned with a teacher's capacity to recognise and realise the opportunity of an alternate reality in teaching. The reality of loving and caring for the students. The reality of an empathetic, compassionate, just and democratic classroom. The foundation of this study was laid when I saw the children in need suffer due to insensitive teaching practices and uncooperative peers and family. I was concerned with the trauma faced by students in the prevalent educational setting in India. I believe that what I do in education should help make changes for the better in our society. Life skills enhancement, in my understanding, was a way to alleviate the stress the children experienced seeing that life skill education promotes mental well-being in young people and behavioural preparedness. As a drama teacher I see drama as a tool for education. It is a natural vehicle for explorative and experiential learning. The aim of my thesis is to describe and reflect on the learning process and the context in which it occurs. I present the critical points with close analysis of the choices made by me as I taught my pupils using drama as a learning medium. Additionally, this study investigates the influences of action research on my practice and the impact of engaging in the stages of action research which provided me with a methodical structure for implementing and analysing the teaching and the learning process. This defined structure guided me through systematic and conscious data collection, data analysis, and reflection. The data is composed of classroom observations and transcripts, a collection of the students' and my work and interviews with their schoolteachers and parents. The main objective of this research was to enable a gain in positive behavioural intentions and improved psychosocial competence in children. This was accomplished through augmentation of creativity, emotional understanding and development, improved self-esteem and a notion of the joy of autonomy to enable the students to deal effectively with the demands and challenges of everyday life.

Jocelyn Jones in her 2008 doctoral thesis 'Thinking with stories of suffering: towards a living theory of response-ability', which is available at http://www. actionresearch.net/living/jocelynjonesphd.shtml, writes:

Abstract

In the thesis I develop a living theory of responsibility, movement, engagement, withdrawal, and self care with a living standard of judgement of response-ability toward the other. I use a hermeneutic phenomenological approach to develop a dynamic, relational understanding, where social constructions are discussed and refined using cycles of loose and strict thinking, an inter-play of emotion and intellect, and a combination of intuitive and analytic reasoning. This is underpinned by an extended epistemology embracing experiential learning, documentary and textual analysis, presentational knowing, dialogue, narrative and photographic inquiry. I address the essence of inquiry with people who have difficult stories to tell and for us to comprehend: narratives which emerge from episodes of chaos and suffering, interspersed with occasional glimpses of the inter-human. Within this context I explore responsibility [response-ability] to 'the Other' as subject, and the ethical obligations implied in that relationship. My and others' narratives, through space and over time, are researched using an extended epistemology and inquiry cycles across two interwoven strands. I look back over a long career and 'epiphanous' moments as a social worker and academic in the field of child protection and children and families work; and as the child of a war veteran, I reflect on World War II narratives of suffering, changing identity, and the inter-human. This first and second person inquiry extends outwards through cycles of dialogue with ex-European prisoners of war and relation with landscape across Europe and Russia. In these reflections I clarify my meanings of chaos, suffering and responsibility [response-ability]. The learning from this extended inquiry and the contribution to knowledge are reflected on within my current practice as a participative researcher who is expressing response-ability toward the other. Finally, I consider implications for improving practice and organizational climate in children and families work.

Summary

This chapter addresses ideas about the significance of your claim to have improved learning. You are placing your account of learning in the public domain to test the validity of your claims that you have influenced the learning of yourself, of others in your workplace, and wider groupings who wish to learn how to act in ways that recognize others as able to think for themselves. You are showing how new learning can inform new practices that can influence sustainable forms of social growth.

Further reading

A key aspect of your research is your capacity to say in what way it is significant. Here are some texts that help you to understand how and why you should be able to do so.

Foucault, M. (2001) *Fearless Speech*. Los Angeles, CA: Semiotext(e).
Foucault makes the point that people can, and should, speak for themselves.

Tidwell, D.L., Heston, L. and Fitzgerald, M.L. (eds) (2009) *Research Methods for the Self-Study of Practice*. Dordrecht: Springer.
An excellent text in which the contributors relate the significance of their research to the self-study methods they have used to enquire into their teacher education practices.

Zinn, H. (1997) *The Zinn Reader: Writings on Disobedience and Democracy*. New York: Seven Stories Press.
If you are ever in any doubt about the importance of speaking for yourself, go to Howard Zinn, where you will soon become convinced of the importance of speaking out against all kinds of tyranny and wrong-headedness. Similarly, go back to

Chomsky, N. (1989) *Necessary Illusions: Thought Control in Democratic Societies*. London: Pluto.
For a chilling analysis of what can happen when you do not explain the significance of your own ideas and practices.

TWENTY THREE
Developing New Epistemologies for Workplace Cultures of Enquiry

We have said throughout that what we know and how we come to know it influences what we do. In more formal terms, our epistemologies influence our practices. So, if you want to influence how other people act, you need first to influence what they know; and, even before that, you need to influence how they think (their logics) and what they see as important (their values). If this is what you aim to do, you have to have a sense of vision yourself about (1) what you hope to achieve, (2) why you want to achieve it and (3) how you think you can achieve it.

We have also said throughout that the world is caught in a debate about what counts as knowledge and who counts as a knower: this is a debate about the epistemological underpinnings of personal and social practices. Therefore, if you want to influence what people think, know and do, you have first to encourage them to think and make decisions about these things for themselves: get them to think critically about what they know and how they have come to know it, and whether this knowledge is right for themselves and others, or whether they should do things differently. This also means you have to persuade them that you are the right person to listen to and to believe when you say that they can do it.

This chapter is organized as three sections that address these questions.

1 Are you contributing to new epistemologies for new cultures of enquiry?
2 Influencing thinking and discourses in the workplace
3 Influencing policy formation and implementation

1 Are you contributing to new epistemologies for new cultures of enquiry?

Recall the ideas of Donald Schön (in the Introduction and Chapter 2). In 1995 he spoke about the epistemological battle currently going on, especially in many institutional settings and especially in higher education. Traditional views, he said, regarded theory (a body of explanations) as a reified accumulation of abstract knowledge, which could be applied to practice. It was held that abstract ideas about how to do things represented the best kind of knowledge; they were better than practice-based forms of knowledge, which were considered good practice but not good knowledge. Consequently, even though abstract knowledge was divorced from reality, it was still considered the best kind of knowledge. These abstract ideas, taken together, made up a body of literature, and this is still held today as the 'best' body of literature that represents the best that has ever been discovered or known.

You are an instructor in a drama school. Your job is to teach trainees how to dance traditional jive. How to do this? Do you give your trainees worksheets that explain how they should dance the steps and how they should communicate their passion for dance; or do you encourage them to try out the steps and find their own way of communicating their passion? Where does the knowledge lie: in worksheets or in their bodies and feelings? You probably encourage them to try out the steps themselves, and perhaps later work with the worksheets to make sure they are doing the steps in the right order. Which epistemologies are you prioritizing?

Furthermore, said Schön, there was an expectation that the literatures would contain an answer, which could be applied to practice in all appropriate situations. He made the point that, although this body of literature contains useful information from which practitioners could take ideas, the ideas were presented in a propositional form, that is, as words about abstract ideas. Practitioners could relate to the ideas and see how they could be useful to their own practices, but they were not allowed in turn to put forward their own ideas about practice as legitimate theory, because the practice that informed the epistemology that informed the theory was not taken seriously as a form of enquiry: practice was always seen as something you do, rather than something you think about and explain.

Jo is a golf instructor. He works with his clients to develop their swing. He takes videos of the clients and encourages them to watch themselves on video, to feel their swing as they watch. He also invites them to take books out of the library to see what are the correct techniques. One client finds it impossible to execute her swing as the books say, yet she still manages to hit a hole in one. She has developed confidence in her understanding of her own practice and in explaining it to herself; she does not worry if she is not doing it exactly as the books say she should.

Schön spoke about the need for a new epistemology, to see practice as a form of enquiry, to be investigated and explained. He said that what we know and how we come to know should be understood as grounded primarily in practice, not only in conceptual ideas. Since the 1970s, Whitehead has also spoken about the need for a new epistemology. This would involve practitioners studying their practices as the grounds for the generation of their own living theories of practice. Therefore, theory would be seen as not necessarily static, as in traditional abstract forms, but also as embodied in the real lives of real people – hence the idea of living theory. Schön's idea was that the development of a new epistemology would be part of the development of a new scholarship – in his and others' terms, a culture of enquiry. The new scholarship would be different from traditional scholarship: instead of focusing on the measurement of outcomes, the new scholarship would focus on the negotiation of personal and social meanings. Whitehead's (1999) idea of an epistemology of educational enquiry is that practitioners would offer their explanations of how they have learned to improve practice with educational intent.

The question therefore arises of whether you are contributing to the new scholarship and, if so, what is special about your work that enables you to do so. Here are some ideas about how you are already doing this. In the next section are some ideas about how you can do it in a way that will encourage the evolution of new cultures of enquiry in everyday workplaces.

Look at what you are already doing.

2   Influencing thinking and discourses in the workplace

Through making your work public, and explaining how and why you are doing so, you are sharing workable ideas that encourages others in workplaces to say, 'I can do this too.' Perhaps the greatest gift you can give to others is both the encouragement to develop a new vision and also the idea that a new vision is possible. You are saying to people, 'It doesn't have to be like this. You are capable of rethinking the way things are and changing them.' You are showing your faith in yourself and them that you can exercise your imagination to create your own new futures. By providing your account of practice you are giving others ideas about how they can do so too.

If you are in any doubt that encouraging a sense of vision and providing the means to realize it is the overall purpose of your work, stop and think about the relationship between your action research and the Holocaust. The Holocaust and other catastrophic events of pain and suffering were the direct outcome of lack of acceptance of the Other, a monumental hubris that allowed some people to think they were more deserving of life than others. Holocausts are historical events. The people who are part of them are real people. Some of the people from the Holocaust are still alive. Other people in other contexts of horror are very much alive. Read any newspaper, or the literature of Amnesty International, for copious evidence. See how relationships of power and their outcomes of pain spread themselves across the pages. Listen to the rhetoric of politicians and read between the lines. 'We want people to be free', you hear. Free for what? Free to continue serving power? Go into your workplace. See how relationships of power permeate discourses. In which direction does the power lie? Who tells others what to do? How do they do this? Do they blatantly coerce, or do they manage to get people to perform appropriately, and even come to believe that performing appropriately was their own idea?

Things do not need to be the way they are. The most amazing thing about you is that, by even considering the possibility of doing your action research, you hang onto your sense of vision that there is another way. By doing your action research you exercise your imagination to find that way. By making your account public you are saying to people, 'You can do this too.'

However, you live in the real world, and are also part of those organizational relationships of power. You are not a fly on the wall. You are part of it. Therefore, if you want to influence trajectories of change, you have to understand what keeps this real world ticking over, and find ways of disrupting the hidden assumptions in the standard thinking. Even when your piece of the world appears to be entirely satisfactory, you still need to dig beneath the surface to reveal those hidden assumptions and ensure that they are life-affirming rather than life-destroying. You want to disrupt the current social order and put a new one in its place, not only the social order of how people are, but also the social order of the way people think, and how the way they think influences what they do. Most importantly, you also need to encourage other people to become aware of these things, and develop their own political sophistication in finding ways to rethink what they are doing and ensure that the means are in place to help them to do it.

3   Influencing policy formation and implementation

How to do this? You need to do two things.

- First, you need to influence people so that they realize that they too can exercise their sense of vision and create new futures. What you have read so far has offered advice about how to influence others by showing how you are contributing to new practices and new theory and persuading them that they can do this too.
- Second, you need to influence policymakers so that they recognize the benefit of these new ways of working, so that they will put in place the basic means to enable people to continue creating their new futures.

These two aspects are interlinked. If policymakers can see that there is popular demand for new ways of working, and the demand is credible, they are more likely to put the basic means in place and ensure their continuation.

Therefore you and your colleagues need to develop your political sophistication in understanding how policy formation and implementation works, in order to ensure that your own political action will be effective.

Understanding policy formation and implementation

Policy does not come into existence by itself. It is the creation of policymakers, real people, some of whom become policymakers as a job, not necessarily because they have expertise in a particular discipline. In governments, people can go from one department to another overnight. Some politicians are deeply committed, and have extensive knowledge of the field, but not all. It is important to remember that policy formation and implementation is not a given fact, but a human practice, which, like all human practices, is grounded in different interests.

Different people analyse human interests in different ways. Habermas (1972, 1987) sets out three main forms of human interest.

- *Technical interests* focus on the production of technical rational knowledge, with the aim of controlling the environment. Knowledge becomes instrumental activity.
- *Practical interests* focus on meaning-making and interpretation, with the intention of understanding the social life-world and with an awareness of its historical and political emergence.
- *Emancipatory interests* enable people to understand the influences that lead them to think and act as they do, and to liberate their own thinking in order to resist closure of any kind.

From an action research perspective, these three interests are supplemented by a fourth:

- *Educational interest*, which focuses on establishing relational practices that are grounded in people's capacity and desire for relationship and attachment, and self-government in communitarian work.

Which interests drive your individual and collective work? What do you hope to achieve and why? Which interests drive the work of policy makers, and why? Give this some thought, because understanding what drives policy formation will help you to find ways of appealing to the interests of policymakers. It will also help you see how you can develop a culture of enquiry in your workplace, through the development of relational epistemologies.

Here are some ideas about how you can do this.

Show the value of your work for organizational renewal

In your workplace, show how your research has implications for improving practice. Explain that improved practice will raise your organization's standing in the eyes of the peer community. Raising profile meets the organizational interests of self-promotion.

It also meets your own interests of promoting personal and social well-being through relationship. In wider contexts, explain how improving practice needs to be high on policy agendas, and how this will benefit the community as a whole.

Work all levels of the system

It is not enough to appeal only to the interests of other practitioners. It may be enough when the focus is on improving practice only, but not if you are aiming to influence policy for improving practice. Managers and organizational elites need to know what you are doing, and you need to let them see that it is in their interests to support your work. You can get their commitment by sending them copies of your reports and inviting their critical feedback. Invite them to be members of your validation groups. Ask them to attend seminars and workshops. Point out the implications of your work for organizational benefit.

Find allies

You cannot do it alone. While you may have the original vision of how things can be improved, you must find others who share your commitment. You need allies both to support you, and also to form a critical mass that will have political clout. Your single voice may be heard, but a collective voice is stronger.

Contribute to the knowledge base

Scholarly accounts of practice are still seen as the most powerful way to contribute to the knowledge base. Publishing your account will provide you with a prestigious platform from which you can speak with authority, and which will also bring kudos to any organization with which you are associated. Find outlets for publishing. Research the market to see what journals are appropriate for you and spend some time and energy in getting published. Set up your own website and make your work available on it. Set up discussion forums so that you can get instant feedback and promote your own and others' learning. Link with other websites and set up global conversations, which is easy with electronic networking. If you work in higher education, use the various Research Frameworks to promote your work. Although much of what is published is controlled by journal editors with a traditional bent, many new places for scholarly papers about self-study action research have become available. The journals *Action Research* and *Reflective Practice* are available. New e-journals such as the *Educational Journal of Living Theories, Educational Action Research Expeditions* and *Action Research International* as well as the well-established *Journal of Interactive Media in Education* are now regarded as legitimate sources for citation. Many traditional journals are rushing to go online. Aim to create a demand, and then supply whatever will keep the demand going.

Get accreditation

It is in your political interest to achieve status for yourself. One way of doing this is to get accreditation for your work. It is possible to get the whole range of accreditation for workplace learning, from certificates to doctorates. Your accreditation will in turn reinforce a new conceptualization of what counts as knowledge. Practitioners' accounts enter the knowledge base, and stand alongside traditional propositional accounts. Doctoral theses with titles such as 'An investigation into the relationship between leadership and organizational effectiveness' stand alongside those with titles such as 'How do I improve my practice as an educational leader?' These theses are there and will not go away. The knowledge base is changed for ever, in the same way that organizational practices and systems change for ever when new practices are established.

Become a participant in the debates

Above all, if you really want to influence policy, you need to gain access to the debates, and then demonstrate that you are competent to take part. This means having the right credentials, which involves showing that you know what you are talking about, in relation both to practice and to theory. Advisors to policymakers are people who have the credentials. They have built up considerable expertise as practitioners who are able to discuss practice in theoretical terms. You have an advantage. You are not only competent to discuss practice, but can also show how you theorize practice itself. This is no small achievement, and you need to refine it to a high level of sophistication.

We are back to the Introduction. Practitioners need to position themselves as researchers and theorists if they are to have a say in what counts as good practice and which directions their professions should go and for what purposes. There are no short cuts. It is hard work, but achievable. And achievement is essential, if practitioners are to have a voice in what kind of society they wish to create for the future. The stakes could not be higher.

The positioning of managers and educational leaders

The positioning of managers and educational leaders is especially important. In traditional forms of scholarship, managers and leaders are positioned as responsible for policy formation and implementation. The job of managers and leaders is to move people and practices around, like pieces on a chessboard.

In the new scholarship, with its focus on emancipatory learning and democratic participation, managers and leaders are positioned as practitioners who are learning how to support their own and others' professional learning. 'Management' and 'leadership' turn from abstract concepts into real human practices, what people do when they decide to encourage others to manage their own affairs and lead one another.

> Chris Glavey, working in Northern Ireland, has encouraged young people to regard themselves as educational leaders in schools and colleges. Chris and the young people have brought communities together in strife-torn contexts. In a leadership position himself, he regards his work as 'leading others to

places where they have not yet been' (Donovan 1978). His PhD study was commended as of outstanding excellence. (Glavey 2008, retrieved 1 August 2010 from http://www.jeanmcniff.com/items.asp?id=44)

Séamus Lillis is a rural community development officer, also in Ireland. He also brings communities from the North and South together. Through engaging in his action enquiry into his own learning, Séamus sees himself as a practitioner who is supporting the development of his own and other people's understanding of management and leadership practice. In the abstract to his PhD thesis, a slightly edited version of which appears here, he writes:

In this study I research my practice in rural community development with a view to improving it.

The study reconceptualises the nature of rural community development by shifting perceptions of development as an externalised focus of study, which may be theorised about by detached 'outside' experts, to focusing on the insights from participants' experiences. These experiential insights facilitate a process where practitioners, other stakeholders and I can generate our own theories of how rural community development is enhanced.

Long-established empirical approaches are effective in probing traditional technical, economic, practical, social and political characteristics of rural community development. But I wish to investigate the full range of the factors affecting rural communities, particularly ethical, aesthetic, spiritual, cultural and ecological influences. Here empirically based methodologies are less effective. ... I therefore chose action research as my methodology [as] sensitive to the emergent nature of community development, to its contextual, practice-based and relational characteristics.

The study's findings question the appropriateness of traditional approaches to training in community development, and highlight the 'knowledge in community' or wisdom shared by established communities' participants. As a teacher and advisor in horticulture [which is my professional positioning], I [previously] mediated prescriptive technical expertise to farming clients. This approach did not help advance rural community development. This was a key discovery. I recount how, as a consequence, I changed and became a learning practitioner-researcher and how that stance advances my practice. In modelling the experience through examining my own practice, I provide an imitable pattern for other practitioners. (Lillis 2001, retrieved 1 August 2010 from http://www.jeanmcniff.com/items.asp?id=51)

Taking this position can be especially difficult, because personal identity is often related to professional identity, so what a person does professionally can become who a person is personally. It takes a special kind of courage and commitment to position oneself as a learner, rather than as a role. Many people hide behind their roles. Those in senior positions in organizations who get rid of the role and position themselves as part of a community of enquiry are special people who need to publish their accounts of work, in order to influence others in relation to practice and about how management and leadership should be theorized.

What do you need to avoid doing?

It is important to know what you have to do, but also be clear about what you need to avoid doing. Primarily, you need to avoid closure of any kind. By closure we mean believing you have found the final answers. This means becoming aware of any influences that may persuade you to aim for closure in the following areas.

Avoid epistemological closure

Never believe that your knowledge is complete or there is no more to learn. Some traditional academic practitioners aim to find a definitive answer to a specified problem. Instead, focus on transformational enquiry, and see all answers as provisional and open to critique and change within complex and shifting contexts.

Sometimes institutions actually encourage epistemological closure in order to maintain the status quo. They use a range of ways to encourage practitioners to close down their thinking and not question norms. This can take the form of straightforward bullying and threat, to more insidious forms including persuasion and flattery. Be aware of what is happening to you and avoid giving in through persisting in the face of pressure. This can be difficult, because human tendencies are to conserve energy by not taking action (Taylor, 2004) and it takes real energy to question and resist complacency. Many of the case studies in this book are from people who are fortunate to work in institutions that do encourage change or those who find groups of allies within their institutions to work with. The question for you then becomes, how to influence peers and managers so that they will keep their options open and see the importance of enquiry and the kind of epistemologies that encourage it.

Avoid professional closure

It is easy to slip into professional complacency by adopting a role or internalizing messages that tell you to go to sleep. Most people prefer to let someone else question practices or blow a whistle, knowing also what penalties may be incurred (Alford, 2001). The need to belong, and to be seen as belonging, is strong and raising questions means that individuals inevitably place themselves outside the normal frame. Said (1994) says that practitioners who position themselves as public intellectuals are always outsiders, because they insist on questioning their own and other people's assumptions. 'Never solidarity before criticism is the short answer,' says Said (1994: 24). Loneliness is preferable to selling one's soul. Some organizations however want your soul as well as your productive work, so you have to make choices about what you are going to keep as your own and the costs involved.

Avoid social closure

Fundamentalist practices develop because some people think that they are right and everyone else is wrong. Fundamentalist practices usually lead to what Popper (1966) calls a closed society, in which people devote their energies to maintaining the status quo through the perpetuation of established regimes and apparatuses. This can be dangerous for people who step outside the norm, such as action researchers, who always look for ways of improving existing situations by encouraging new thinking. Fundamentalists do not believe their practices need improving, so they try to silence those who do. Fundamentalism in any form is anathema to the creation of open societies and the idea of social renewal. This is of course what action research is about.

Achieving your vision

So, what is the relationship between your action research and the creation of good social orders? The relationship is that future social orders begin here and now, where you are. Because of the inherent generative transformational nature of human processes, new practices, influenced by new thinking and forms of knowledge, will develop out of old ones. You can influence your own contexts and your contexts can influence increasingly wider contexts. You really do have the capacity for global influence.

Just to show how this is possible, look at this extract from a conversation between primary school teacher Mary Roche and her five-year-old children (Roche 2007).

Eoin: I am going home with so, so, so many questions in my head today!
Mary: Good, that's what school is for, asking questions and thinking about possible answers.
Aoife: Anyway, if you go home with a question and you get an answer, you can always question the answer.

Renewable futures lie in the capacity of all practitioners to question the answer and encourage others to do the same. Practitioners do not take 'no' for an answer, but they do not take 'yes' either. The possibilities of this life end only with death, and there is a lot of living to do before that. How do people learn to live in a way that ensures not just survival, but intense and complete joy in the experience of life itself? Perhaps you have some ideas about this. If you do, tell others.

——————————————— Summary ———————————————

This chapter has set out the potentials of your action research for influencing ideas and practices at global level. Realizing this potential involves (1) developing an understanding of the interrelated nature of public discourses and policy formation, and (2) developing the political sophistication to appeal to the interests of policy makers, primarily by showing the value of your work and its potential for new policy. The chapter sets out some strategies for how this can be done, and also makes the point that some practices are to be avoided. The overall point is however that you can succeed in realizing your vision, and need to exercise your tenacity and imagination to find ways of doing so.

Further reading

And finally …

Here are some texts on the importance of your work for new ways of thinking and knowing for developing cultures of enquiry in everyday workplaces and organizations.

BERA (2009) 'Explicating a new epistemology for educational knowledge with educational responsibility'. Keynote symposium at the British Educational Research Association Annual Conference, University of Manchester, 3 September 2010. Retrieved 1 August 2010 from http://www.actionresearch.net/writings/bera/bera09keyprop.htm

Schön, D. (1995) 'Knowing-in-action: the new scholarship requires a new epistemology', *Change*, November–December: 27–32.
Although this article appeared in a relatively low-key journal, it is probably the best available in setting out the idea of developing a new epistemology for the new scholarship.

Senge, P. (1990) *The Fifth Discipline: The Art and Practice of the Learning Organization.* New York, Doubleday.
Peter Senge sets out his vision of organizational learning from a person-centred, practice-based perspective.

Wheatley, M. (1992) *Leadership and the New Science: Learning about Organization from an Orderly Universe.* San Francisco, CA: Berrett-Koehler.
This lovely book explains organizational learning in terms of chaos and complexity theory. A must read for anyone.

References

Abbey, D. (2002) 'Teacher consultant's role in developing and facilitating an interdisciplinary studies course'. MEd dissertation, Brock University. Retrieved 21 January 2005 from http://schools.gedsb.net/ar/theses/index.html.

Adler-Collins, J. (2000) 'A scholarship of enquiry'. MA dissertation, University of Bath.

Adler-Collins, J.-K. (2007) 'Developing an inclusional pedagogy of the unique: how do I clarify, live and explain my educational influences in my learning as I pedagogise my healing nurse curriculum in a Japanese university?'. Retrieved 1 August 2010 from http://www.action research.net/living/jekan.shtml.

Adler-Collins, J.P. (2008) 'Creating new forms of living educational theories through collaborative educational research from eastern and western contexts: a response to Jack Whitehead', *Research Intelligence*, 104: 17–18. Retrieved 11 January 2008 from http://www.action research.net/writings/bera/16&18RI104.pdf.

Alford, C.F. (2001) *Whistleblowers: Broken Lives and Organizational Power*. Ithaca, NY: Cornell University Press.

Alvesson, M. and Deetz, S. (2000) *Doing Critical Management Research*. London: Sage.

Ashley, J. (1994) *Acts of Defiance*. London: Penguin.

Bales, K. (1999) *Disposable People: New Slavery in the Global Economy*. Berkeley, CA: University of California Press.

Bassey, M. (1999) *Case Study Research in Educational Settings*. Buckingham: Open University Press.

Bateson, G. (1972) *Steps to an Ecology of Mind*. New York: Ballantine.

Bateson, G. (1979) *Mind and Nature: A Necessary Unity*. New York: Dutton.

Bergson, H. (1998) *Creative Evolution*. New York: Dover.

Belenkey, M.F., Clinchy, B.M., Goldberger, N.R. and Tarule, J.M. (1986) *Women's Ways of Knowing*. New York: Basic Books.

Berlin, I. (1998) *The Proper Study of Mankind: An Anthology of Essays*. London: Pimlico.

Bernstein, R. (2000) *Pedagogy, Symbolic Control and Identity: Theory, Research, Critique*. Lanham, MD: Rowman & Littlefield.

Biesta, G.J.J. (2006) *Beyond Learning: Democratic Education for a Human Future*. Boulder, CO: Paradigm Publishers.

Bortoft, H. (1996) *The Wholeness of Nature: Goethe's Way of Science*. Edinburgh: Floris.

Bourdieu, P. (1990) *The Logic Of Practice*. Stanford, CA: Stanford University Press.

Boyer, E. (1990) *Scholarship Reconsidered: Priorities of the Professoriate*. Carnegie Foundation for the Advancement of Teaching. San Francisco, CA: Jossey-Bass.

Bruce-Ferguson, P. (1999) 'Developing a research culture in a polytechnic: an action research case study'. PhD thesis, University of Waikato. Retrieved 26 November 2004 from http://www.twp.ac.nz/research.

Bruce-Ferguson, P. (2008) 'Increasing inclusion in educational research: reflections from New Zealand', *Research Intelligence*, 102: 24–25. Retrieved 11 January 2008 from http://www.actionresearch.net/writings/bera/24&25RI102.pdf.

Bullough, R. and Pinnegar, S. (2001) 'Guidelines for quality in autobiographical forms of self-study research', *Educational Researcher*, 30 (3): 13–21.

Bullough, R. and Pinnegar, S. (2004) 'Thinking about thinking about self-study: an analysis of eight chapters', in J.J. Lougran, M.J. Hamilton, V.K. Labosky and T. Russell (eds), *International Handbook of Teaching and Teacher-Education Practices*. Dordrecht: Kluwer.

Burke, T. (1997) 'How can I improve my practice as a learning support teacher?'. MA dissertation, Dublin, University of the West of England. Retrieved 27 November 2004 from http://www.jeanmcniff.com.

Butler, J. (1999) *Gender Trouble*. London: Routledge.

Cahill, M. (2007) 'My living theory of inclusional practice'. PhD thesis, University of Limerick. Retrieved 1 August 2010 from http://www.jeanmcniff.com/items.asp?id=49.

Callahan, R. (1962) *Education and the Cult of Efficiency*. Chicago, IL: University of Chicago Press.

Capra, F. (2003) *The Hidden Connections*. London: Flamingo.

Carr, W. and Kemmis, S. (1986) *Becoming Critical: Education, Knowledge and Action Research*. London: Falmer.

Charles, E. (2007) 'How do I improve my practice? Creating a decolonising living educational theory that embraces and extends our humanity into new relationships that carry hope for humanity'. PhD thesis, University of Bath.

Chomsky, N. (1965) *Aspects of the Theory of Syntax*. Cambridge, MA: MIT Press.

Chomsky, N. (1986) *Knowledge of Language: Its Nature, Origin and Use*. New York: Praeger.

Chomsky, N. (1988) *The Chomksy Reader* (ed. J. Peck). London: Serpent's Tail.

Chomsky, N. (1991) *Media Control: The Spectacular Achievements of Propaganda*. New York: Seven Stories Press.

Cockerell, L. (2008) *Creating Magic*. London: Vermilion.

Cohen, L., Manion, L. and Morrison, K. (2007) *Research Methods in Education* (6th edn). London: Routledge.

Corey, S. (1953) *Action Research to Improve School Practices*. New York: Teachers College Press.

Cousins, J.B. and Earl, L. (eds) (1995) *Participatory Evaluation in Education*. London: Falmer.

Cresswell, J.W. (2007) *Qualitative Inquiry and Research Design: Choosing Among Five Approaches*. Thousand Oaks, CA: Sage.

Dadds, M. (2008) 'Empathetic validity in practitioner research', *Educational Action Research*, 16 (2): 279–90.

Dadds, M. and Hart, S. (2001) *Doing Practitioner Research Differently*. London: Routledge.

Delong, J. (2002) 'How can i improve my practice as a superintendent of schools and create my own living educational theory?'. PhD thesis, University of Bath.

Delong, J. (2010) 'Engaging educators in representing their knowledge in complex ecologies and cultures of inquiry', *Educational Journal of Living Theories*, 3 (1): 1–38. Retrieved 1 August 2010 from http://ejolts.net/node/174.

Delong, J. and Knill-Griesser, H. (2002) 'How do we integrate issues of power and ethics in valid explanations of our educative influence as a teacher-consultant and superintendent?', in J. Delong and C. Black (eds), *Passion in Professional Practice*, Vol. 2. Ontario: Grand Erie Board of Education. Retrieved 21 January 2005 from http://schools.gedsb.net/ar/passion/pppii/index.html.

Denzin, N. and Lincoln, Y. (eds) (2005) *The Sage Handbook of Qualitative Research* (3rd edition). Thousand Oaks, CA: Sage.

Derrida, J. (1976) *Of Grammatology*. Baltimore, MD: Johns Hopkins University Press.

Donovan, V. (1978) *Christianity Rediscovered*. London: SCM Press.

Eisner, E. (1988) 'The primacy of experience and the politics of method', *Educational Researcher*, 17 (5): 15–20.

Eisner, E. (1993) 'Forms of understanding and the future of educational research', *Educational Researcher*, 22 (7): 5–11.

Eisner, E. (1997) 'The promise and perils of alternative forms of data representation', *Educational Researcher*, 26 (6): 4–10.

Eisner, E. (2005) *Reimaging Schools: The selected works of Elliot W. Eisner.* Abingdon: Routledge.

Elliott, J. (1991) *Action Research for Educational Change.* Buckingham: Open University Press.

Farren, M. (2005) 'Creating my pedagogy of the unique through a web of betweenness'. PhD thesis, University of Bath.

Feldman, A. (2003) 'Validity and quality in self-study', *Educational Researcher*, 32 (3): 26–8.

Finnegan, J. (2000) 'How do I create my own educational theory in my educative relationships as an action researcher and as a teacher?'. PhD thesis, University of Bath. Retrieved 1 August 2010 from http://www.actionresearch.net/fin.shtml

Forrest, M. (1983) 'The teacher as researcher: the use of historical artefacts in primary schools'. MA dissertation, University of Bath.

Foucault, M. (1977) 'Intellectuals and power: a conversation between Michel Foucault and Gilles Deleuze', in D. Bouchard (ed.), *Language, Counter-Memory, Practice: Selected Essays and Interviews by Michel Foucault.* Ithaca, NY: Cornell University Press.

Foucault, M. (1980) 'Truth and power' in C. Gordon (ed.), *Power/Knowledge: Selected Interviews and Other Writings, 1972–1977.* Brighton: Harvester.

Foucault, M. (2001) *Fearless Speech.* Los Angeles, CA: Semiotext(e).

Frankl, V. (1963) *Man's Search for Meaning.* New York: Pocket.

Freire, P. (1972) *Pedagogy of the Oppressed.* New York: Seabury Press.

Freire, P. (1993) *Pedagogy of the Oppressed* (new revised 20th anniversary edn). New York: Continuum.

Fromm, E. (1956) *The Art of Loving. World Perspectives* (Vol. 9). New York: Harper & Row.

Furlong, J. (2000) *Higher Education and the New Professionalism for Teachers: Realising the Potential of Partnership.* London: CVCP/SCOP. Retrieved 26 November 2004 from http://www.edstud.ox.ac.uk/people/furlong.html.

Furlong, J. (2004) 'BERA at 30. Have we come of age?', *British Educational Research Journal*, 30 (3): 343–358. Presidential address to the British Educational Research Association, 2003. Retrieved 26 November 2004 from http://www.bera.ac.uk/publications.

Furlong, J. and Oancea, A. (2005) *Assessing Quality in Applied and Practice-Based Educational Research: A Framework for Discussion.* Oxford: Oxford University Department of Educational Studies.

Furlong, J., Barton, L., Miles, S., Whiting, C. and Whitty, G. (2000) *Teacher Education in Transition: Re-forming Professionalism?* Buckingham: Open University Press.

Gardner, H. (1983) *Frames of Mind: The Theory of Multiple Intelligences.* New York: Basic Books.

Garnett, J., Costley, C. and Workman, B. (eds) (2009) *Work Based Learning: Journeys to the Core of Higher Education.* Hendon: Middlesex University Press.

Geoghegan, M. (2000) 'Improving the quality of staff meetings'. MA dissertation, Dublin, University of the West of England, Bristol.

Glavey, C. (2008) 'Helping eagles fly – a living theory approach to student and young adult leadership development'. PhD thesis, University of Glamorgan. Retrieved 1 August 2010 from http://www.jeanmcniff.com/items.asp?id=44.

Glenn, M. (2007) 'Working with collaborative projects: my living theory of a holistic educational practice'. PhD thesis, University of Limerick. Retrieved 1 August 2010 from http://www.jeanmcniff.com/items.asp?id=50.

Goethe, W. ([1790] 1988) *Die Metamorphose der Pflanzen*, reproduced as 'The Metamorphosis of Plants', in D. Miller (ed.), *Goethe: Scientific Studies.* New York: Suhrkamp.

Gorard, S. (2002) 'The Future of Educational Research Post RAE 2001'. A paper presented at the British Educational Research Association Conference, Exeter, September.

Gramsci, A. (1973) *The Prison Notebooks: Selections* (trans. Q. Hoare and G. Nowell-Smith). London: Lawrence and Wishart.

Guba, E. and Lincoln, Y. (1989) *Fourth Generation Evaluation*. Thousand Oaks, CA: Sage.

Habermas, J. (1972) *Knowledge and Human Interests* (trans. J. J. Shapiro). London: Heinemann.

Habermas, J. (1974) *Theory and Practice* (trans. J. Viertel). London: Heinemann.

Habermas, J. (1975) *Legitimation Crisis* (trans. T. McCarthy). Boston, MA: Beacon Press.

Habermas, J. (1976) *Communication and the Evolution of Society*. London: Heinemann.

Habermas, J. (1987) *The Theory of Communicative Action Volume Two: The Critique of Functionalist Reason*. Oxford: Polity.

Habermas, J. (1988) *On the Logic of the Social Sciences*. Cambridge: Polity.

Habermas, J. (2002) *The Inclusion of the Other* (ed. C. Cronin and P. De Greiff). Cambridge, MA: MIT Press.

Hammersley, M. (1993) 'On the teacher as researcher' in M. Hammersley (ed.), *Educational Research: Current Issues*, Vol. 1. London: Paul Chapman.

Hartog, M. (2004) 'A self-study of a higher education tutor: how can i improve my practice?'. PhD thesis, University of Bath. Retrieved 26 November 2004 from http://www.bath.ac.uk/~edsajw/hartog.shtml.

Heron, J. (1998) *Sacred Science: Person-centred Inquiry into the Spiritual and the Subtle*. Ross-on-Wye: PCCS Books.

Heron, J. and Reason, P. (2001) 'The practice of co-operative inquiry: research 'with' rather than 'on' people', in P. Reason and H. Bradbury (eds), *Handbook of Action Research*. London: Sage.

Higgs, J. and Titchen, A. (2001) *Professional Practice in Health, Education and the Creative Arts*. Oxford: Blackwell.

Hignell, W. (2004) *Final Report*. Birmingham: Disability West Midlands.

Hillesum, E. (1983) *An Interrupted Life: The Diaries of Etty Hillesum* (trans. A. Pomerans). New York: Pantheon.

Hitchcock, G. and Hughes, D. (1995) *Research and the Teacher* (2nd edn). London: Routledge.

Huxtable, M. (2009) 'How do we contribute to an educational knowledge base? A response to Whitehead and a challenge to BERJ', *Research Intelligence*, 107: 25–6. Retrieved 10 August 2010 from http://www.actionresearch.net/writings/huxtable/mh2009beraRI107.pdf.

Hymer, B. (2007) 'How do I understand and communicate my values and beliefs in my work as an educator in the field of giftedness?'. EdD educational psychology thesis, University of Newcastle. Retrieved 1 August 2007 from http://www.actionresearch.net/living/hymer.shtml.

Ilyenkov, E. (1977) *Dialectical Logic*. Moscow: Progress Publishers.

Jenkins, R. (1992) *Pierre Bourdieu*. London: Routledge.

Jones, C. (2008) 'How do I improve my practice as an inclusion officer working in a children's service?'. MA dissertation, Bath Spa University. Retrieved 1 August 2010 from http://www.actionresearch.net/living/cjmaok/cjma.htm.

Jones, J. (2008) 'Thinking with stories of suffering: towards a living theory of response-ability'. PhD thesis, University of Bath. Retrieved 1 August 2010 from http://www.actionresearch.net/living/jocelynjonesphd.shtml.

Knill-Griesser, H. (2002) 'A vision quest of support to improve student learning: validating my living standards of practice'. MEd dissertation, Brock University. Retrieved 21 January 2005 from http://www.actionresearch.ca/.

Kuhling, C. and Keohane, K. (2007) *Cosmopolitan Ireland*. London: Pluto.

Kuhn, T. (1970) *The Structure of Scientific Revolutions* (2nd edn). Chicago, IL: University of Chicago Press.

Kushner, S. (2000) *Personalizing Evaluation*. London: Sage.

Laidlaw, M. (1996) 'How can I create my own living educational theory as I offer you an account of my own educational development?'. PhD thesis, University of Bath.

Laidlaw, M. (2002) 'How can I promote sustainable development at Guyuan Teachers' College?'. Retrieved 14 January 2005 from http://www.actionresearch.net/moira.shtml.

Laidlaw, M. (2008) 'Increasing inclusion in educational research: a response to Pip Bruce-Ferguson and Jack Whitehead', *Research Intelligence*, 104: 16–17. Retrieved 11 January 2008 from http://www.actionresearch.net/writings/bera/moira16-18RI104.pdf.

Lakatos, I. (1970) 'Falsification and the methodology of scientific research programmes', in I. Lakatos and A. Musgrave (eds), *Criticism and the Growth of Knowledge*. Cambridge: Cambridge University Press.

Lather, P. (1991) *Getting Smart: Feminism Research and Pedagogy With/in the Postmodern*. London: Routledge.

Lather, P. (1994) 'Textuality as praxis'. A paper presented at the American Educational Research Association annual meeting, New Orleans, April.

Lather, P. (2004) 'Getting lost: feminist efforts toward a double(d) science'. Paper presented at the American Educational Research Association annual meeting, San Diego, 12–16 April.

Law, J. (2004) *After Method: Mess in Social Science Research*. London: Routledge.

Lawlor, S. (1990) *Teachers Mistaught: Training Theories or Education in Subjects?* London: Centre for Policy Studies.

Lewin, K. (1946) 'Action research and minority problems', *Journal of Social Issues*, 2 (4): 34–46.

Lillis, S. (2001) 'An inquiry into the effectiveness of my practice as a learning practitioner-researcher in rural community development'. PhD thesis, Dublin, University College Dublin.

Lohr, E. (2004) Prologue to PhD submission to the University of Bath. Retrieved 16th January 2005 from http://www.jackwhitehead.com/elFront%202.htm.

Lohr, E. (2006) 'What is my lived experience of love and how may i become an instrument of love's purpose?'. PhD thesis, University of Bath.

Losee, J. (2004) *Theories of Scientific Progress*. New York: Routledge.

Loughran, J.J., Hamilton, M.L., LaBoskey, V.K. and Russell, T. (eds) (2004) *International Handbook of Self-Study of Teaching and Teacher Education Practices*. Dordrecht: Kluwer.

MacBeath, J. (1999) *Schools Must Speak for Themselves: The Case for School Self-evaluation*. London: Routledge.

MacClure, M. (1996) 'Narratives of becoming an action researcher', *British Journal of Educational Research*, 22 (3): 273–86.

MacDonald, B. (1987) 'The state of education today'. Record of the First C.A.R.E. Conference. Norwich, University of East Anglia.

MacRaild, D. (2010) *The Irish Diaspora in Britain, 1750–1939*. London: Palgrave Macmillan.

Marlin, R. (2002) *Propaganda and the Ethics of Persuasion*. Ontario: Broadview Press.

Marshall, J. (1999) 'Living life as inquiry', *Systemic Practice and Action Research*, 12 (2): 155–71.

Marshall, J. (2004) 'Living systemic thinking: exploring quality in first-person action research', *Action Research*, 2 (3): 309–29.

McDonagh, C. (2007) 'My living theory of learning to teach for social justice: how do I enable primary school children with specific learning disability (dyslexia) and myself as their teacher to realise our learning potentials?'. PhD thesis, University of Limerick. Retrieved 1 August 2010 from http://www.jeanmcniff.com/items.asp?id=48.

McGinley, S. (2000) 'How can I help the primary school children I teach to develop their self-esteem?'. MA dissertation, Dublin, University of the West of England, Bristol. Retrieved 27 November 2004 from http://www.jeanmcniff.com/theses.

McIntyre, D. (1997) 'The profession of educational research', *British Educational Research Journal*, 23 (2): 127–40.

McNiff, J. (2000) *Action Research in Organisations*. London: Routledge.

McNiff, J. (2002) *Action Research: Principles and Practice* (2nd edn). London: RoutledgeFalmer.

McNiff, J. (2005) 'Living with foxes: learning about home, self and the other'. Paper presented at the Peace Education SIG, American Educational Research Association annual meeting, Montreal, April. Retrieved 25 January 2005 from http://www.jeanmcniff.com/ jean'swritings.

McNiff, J. (2010a) *Action Research for Professional Development: Concise Advice for New (and Experienced) Action Researchers* (new rev. edn). Poole: September Books.

McNiff, J. (2010b) 'Supporting teachers personally and professionally in challenging environments', *Turkish Online Journal of Qualitative Inquiry*, 1 (1): 1–15. Retrieved 1 August 2010 from http:// www.tojqi.net/articles/TOJQI_1_1/TOJQI_1_1_Article_1.pdf.

McNiff, J. (2011a) *Writing for Publication in Action Research*. Poole: September Books. [In preparation.]

McNiff, J. (2011b) *Action Research in South Africa*. Dorset: September Books. [In preparation.]

McNiff, J. (2011c) 'Action research for troubled times and troubled places'. Paper presented at the American Educational Research Association Annual Conference, New Orleans, April'.

McNiff, J. and Whitehead, J. (2005) *Action Research for Teachers*. London: David Fulton.

McNiff, J. and Whitehead, J. (2009) *Doing and Writing Action Research*. London: Sage.

McNiff, J. and Whitehead, J. (2010) *You and Your Action Research Project* (3rd edn). London: Routledge.

McNiff, J., Whitehead, J. and Laidlaw, M. (1992) *Creating a Good Social Order through Action Research*. Bournemouth: Hyde.

Mellor, N. (1998) 'Notes from a method', *Educational Action Research*, 6 (3): 453–70.

Memmi, A. (2003) *The Colonizer and the Colonized*. London: Earthscan.

Merleau-Ponty, M. (1972) *Phenomenology of Perception*. London: Routledge.

Miller, R. (2002) *Free Schools, Free People: Education and Democracy after the 1960s*. Albany, NY: State University of New York Press.

Mitroff, I. and Kilman, R. (1978) *Methodological Approaches to Social Science*. San Francisco, CA: Jossey-Bass.

Muir, C. (2004) *The Establishment and Development of South East Birmingham Community Credit Union Ltd*. Birmingham: West Midlands Social Economy Partnership.

Morrison, T. (1999) *Paradise*. New York: Plume.

Naidoo, M. (2005) 'I am because we are. How can I improve my practice? The emergence of a living theory of responsive practice'. Paper presented at the interactive symposium 'Have we created a new epistemology for the new scholarship of educational enquiry through practitioner research? Developing sustainable global educational networks of communication', British Educational Research Association Annual Conference, UMIST, Manchester, September. Retrieved 16 January 2005 from http://www.bath.ac.uk/~edsajw//bera04/mnbera04.htm.

Ngumbe, L. (2008) 'How do I encourage my learners to take an active interest in historical studies?'. MA dissertation, University of Surrey.

Nixon, J. (2008) *Towards the Virtuous University: The Moral Bases of Academic Practice*. Abingdon: Routledge.

Noffke, S. (1997) 'Themes and tensions in US action research: towards historical analysis', in S. Hollingsworth (ed.), *International Action Research: A Casebook for Educational Reform*. London: Falmer.

Nugent, M. (2000) 'How can I raise the level of self-esteem of second year Junior Certificate School Programme students and create a better learning environment?'. MA dissertation, Dublin, University of the West of England, Bristol. Retrieved 30 November 2004 from http:// www.jeanmcniff.com/theses.

O'Callaghan, I. (1997) 'Growing into principalship'. MEd dissertation, Dublin, University of the West of England, Bristol.

O'Donohue, J. (2003) *Divine Beauty*. London: Bantam Press.

O'Neill, R. (2008) 'ICT as political action'. PhD thesis, University of Glamorgan. Retrieved 1 August 2010 at http://www.ictaspoliticalaction.com/.

O'Shea, K. (2000) 'Coming to know my own practice'. MA dissertation, Dublin, University of the West of England, Bristol.

Parlett, M. and Hamilton, D. (eds) (1977) *Beyond the Numbers Game*. Basingstoke: Macmillan Education.

Polanyi, M. (1958) *Personal Knowledge*. London: Routledge and Kegan Paul.

Popper, K. (1966) *The Open Society and its Enemies:* Vol. I *Plato,* Vol. II, *Hegel and Marx*. London: Routledge.

Pring, R. (2000) *Philosophy of Education*. London: Continuum.

Punia, R. (2004) 'My CV is my curriculum: the making of an international educator with spiritual values'. EdD thesis, University of Bath. Retrieved 21 January 2005 from http://www.bath.ac.uk/~edsajw/punia.shtml.

Raymond, P. (2010) 'Encouraging ecological creativity in schools and partnerships'. Proposal for PhD studies, York St John University.

Rawal, S. (2008) 'The role of drama in enhancing life skills in children with specific learning difficulties in a Mumbai school: my reflective account'. PhD thesis, University of Bath. Retrieved 1 August 2010 from http://www.actionresearch.net/living/rawal.shtml.

Rayner, A. (2002) Video clip of Alan Rayner talking about inclusionality and severance. Retrieved 17 January 2005 from http://www.jackwhitehead.com/rayner1sor.mov.

Rayner, A. (2005) 'Essays and talks about "inclusionality" by Alan Rayner'. Retrieved 8 December 2008 from http://people.bath.ac.uk/bssadmr/inclusionality/.

Rayner, A. (2003) '"Nested Holeyness": the dynamic inclusional geometry of national space and boundaries'. Retrieved 17 January 2005 from http://www.bath.ac.uk/~bssadmr/inclusionality/nestedholeyness.htm.

Reason, J. and Bradbury, H. (2008) *The SAGE Handbook of Action Research*. London: Sage.

Reason, J. and Rowan, J. (1981) *Human Inquiry*. London: Wiley.

Reid, C. and Frisby, W. (2008) 'Continuing the journey: articulating dimensions of feminist participatory research (FPAR)', in P. Reason and H. Bradbury (eds) *The SAGE Handbook of Action Research*. London: Sage.

Riding, K. (2008) 'How do I come to understand my shared living educational standards of judgement in the life I lead with others? Creating the space for intergenerational student-led research'. PhD thesis, University of Bath. Retrieved 1 August 2010 from http://www.actionresearch.net/living/karenridingphd.shtml.

Rivers, M. (2003) 'How can I create an inclusive atmosphere to support an autistic student in my classroom?', in J. Delong, C. Black and H. Knill-Griesser (eds), *Passion in Professional Practice*, Vol. 3. Ontario: Grand Erie Board of Education. Retrieve 21 January 2005 from http://schools.gedsb.net/ar/passion/pppiii/index.html.

Roberts, P. (2003) 'Emerging selves in practice: how do I and others create my practice and how does my practice shape me and influence others?'. PhD thesis, University of Bath. Retrieved 20 January 2005 from http://www.bath.ac.uk/~edsajw/roberts.shtml.

Roche, M. (2007) 'Towards a living theory of caring pedagogy: interrogating my practice to nurture a critical, emancipatory and just community of enquiry'. PhD thesis, University of Limerick. Retrieved 1 August 2010 from http://www.jeanmcniff.com/items.asp?id=46.

Rowland, S. (2000) *The Enquiring University*. Milton Keynes: Open University Press/Society for Research in Higher Education.

Said, E. (1994) *Representations of the Intellectual: the 1993 Reith Lectures*. London: Vintage.

Said, E. (1997) *Beginnings: Intention and Method*. London: Granta.

Schön, D. (1983) *The Reflective Practitioner: How Professionals Think in Action*. New York: Basic Books.

Schön, D. (1995) 'Knowing-in-action: the new scholarship requires a new epistemology', *Change*, November–December: 27–34.

Scott, W.A.H. (2010) 'Developing the sustainable school: thinking the issues through'. Research report. Aylesford: South West Learning for Sustainability Coalition.

Sen, A. (1999) *Development as Freedom*. Oxford: Oxford University Press.

Senge, P. (1990) *The Fifth Discipline: The Art and Practice of the Learning Organization*. New York: Doubleday.

Senge, P., Cambron-McCabe, N., Lucas, T., Smith, B., Dutton, J. and Kleiner, A. (2000) *Schools That Learn: A Fifth Discipline Fieldbook for Educators, Parents, and Everyone Who Cares About Education*. New York: Doubleday/Currency.

Sinclair, A. (2010) 'Working towards a symbiotic practice', *Electronic Journal of Living Theories*, 3 (1): 39–73.

Snow, C. (2001) 'Knowing what we know: children, teachers, researchers', *Educational Researcher*, 30 (7): 3–9. Presidential Address to the American Educational Research Association Annual Meeting, Seattle.

Sowell, T. (1987) *A Conflict of Visions: Ideological Origins of Political Struggles*. New York: Morrow.

Spiro, J. (2008) 'How i have arrived at a notion of knowledge transformation, through understanding the story of myself as creative writer, creative educator, creative manager, and educational researcher'. PhD thesis, University of Bath. Retrieved 1 August 2010 from http://www.actionresearch.net/living/janespirophd.shtml.

Stenhouse, L. (1975) *An Introduction to Curriculum Research and Development*. London: Heinemann.

Suderman-Gladwell, G. (2001) 'The ethics of personal, narrative, subjective research'. MA dissertation, Brock University, Ontario. Retrieved 26 November 2004 from http://www.bath.ac.uk/~edsajw/values/gsgma.PDF.

Sullivan, B. (2006) 'A living theory of a practice of social justice: realising the right of Traveller children to educational quality'. PhD thesis, University of Limerick. Retrieved 11 August 2010 from http://www.jeanmcniff.com/items.asp?id=47.

Tattersall, P. (2010) 'On becoming an activist: a progress report on a 37 year journey to date', *Electronic Journal of Living Theories*, 3 (1): 74–104.

Taylor, C. (1992) *Sources of the Self*. Cambridge, MA: Harvard University Press.

Taylor, F. (1911) *The Principles of Scientific Management*. New York: Harper & brothers.

Taylor, K. (2004) *Brainwashing: The Science of Thought Control*. Oxford: Oxford University Press.

Thomas, G. (1998) 'The myth of rational research', *British Educational Research Journal*, 24 (2): 141–61.

Thomas, G. and Pring, R. (2004) *Evidence-Based Practice in Education*. Maidenhead: Open University Press.

Todorov, T. (1999) *Facing the Exteme: Moral Life in the Concentration Camps* (trans. A Denner and A. Pollack). London: Weidenfeld & Nicolson.

Tribal Education UK (2010) *Teacher Enquiry Bulletin: Action Research for Teachers* (ed. J. McNiff). London: Tribal.

Usher, R. (1996) 'A critique of the neglected epistemological assumptions of educational research', in R. Usher and D. Scott (eds), *Understanding Educational Research*. London: Routledge.

Van Tuyl, G. (2009) 'From engineer to co-creative catalyst; an inclusional and transformational journey. An inquiry into the epistemology of how traditional management "tools and theory" can be used and evolved in enhancing organizational effectiveness in an industrial setting, and how to value and evaluate change'. PhD thesis, University of Bath. Retrieved 1 August 2010 from http://www.actionresearch.net/living/gvt.shtml.

Varga, S. (2009) *Brilliant Pitch*. Harlow: Pearson Education.

Vasilyuk, F. (1996) *The Psychology of Experiencing: The Resolution of Life's Critical Situations*. Hemel Hempstead: Harvester Wheatsheaf.

Walsh, D. (2004) 'How do I improve my leadership as a team leader in vocational education in further education?'. MA dissertation, University of Bath. Retrieved 16 January 2005 from http://www.bath.ac.uk/~edsajw/walsh.shtml.

Walton, J. (2008) 'Ways of knowing: can I find a way of knowing that satisfies my search for meaning?'. PhD thesis, University of Bath. Retrieved 1 August 2010 from http://www.action research.net/living/walton.shtml.

Wenger, E. (1998) *Communities of Practice: Learning, Meaning, Identity*. Cambridge: Cambridge University Press.

Whitehead, Jack (1976) *Improving Learning for 11-14 year olds in Mixed Ability Science Groups*. Swindon: Wiltshire Curriculum Development Centre. Retrieved 26 November 2004 from http://www.actionresearch.net/writings/ilmagall.pdf.

Whitehead, Jack (1985) 'The analysis of an individual's educational development', in M. Shipman (ed.), *Educational Research: Principles, Policies and Practice*. London: Falmer. Retrieved 24 January 2005 from http://www.bath.ac.uk/~edsajw/bk93/5anal.pdf.

Whitehead, Jack (1989) 'Creating a living educational theory from questions of the kind, "How do I improve my practice?"', *Cambridge Journal of Education*, 19 (1): 137–53. Retrieved 26th November 2004 from http://www.bath.ac.uk/~edsajw/writings/livtheory.html.

Whitehead, Jack (1993) *The Growth of Educational Knowledge: Creating Your Own Living Educational Theories*. Bournemouth: Hyde Publications. Retrieved 21 January 2005 from http://www.bath. ac.uk/~edsajw/bk93/geki.htm

Whitehead, Jack (1999) 'How do I improve my practice? Creating a new discipline of educational enquiry'. PhD thesis, University of Bath. Retrieved 23 January 2005 from http://www. bath.ac.uk/~edsajw/jack.shtml.

Whitehead, Jack (2003) 'Creating our living educational theories in teaching and learning to care: using multi-media to communication the meanings and influence of our embodied educational values', *Teaching Today for Tomorrow*, 19: 17–20. Retrieved 26 November 2004 from http://www.7oaks.org/ttt/ttt19.htm.

Whitehead, Jack (2004a) 'What counts as evidence in the self-studies of teacher education practices?', in J.J. Loughran, M.L. Hamilton, V.K. LaBoskey and T. Russell (eds), *International Handbook of Self-Study of Teaching and Teacher Education Practices*. Dordrecht: Kluwer.

Whitehead, Jack (2004b) 'How valid are multi-media communications of my embodied values in living theories and standards of educational judgement and practice'. Retrieved from http:// www.bath.ac.uk/~edsajw//multimedia/jimenomov/JIMEW98.html.

Whitehead, Jack (2004c) 'Action research expeditions: do action researchers' expeditions carry hope for the future of humanity? How do we know? An enquiry into reconstructing educational theory and educating social formations'. Retrieved 26 November 2004 from http://www.arexpeditions.montana.edu/articleviewer.php?AID=80.

Whitehead, Jack (2005) 'Developing the dynamic boundaries of living standards of judgement in educational enquiries of the kind. How do I improve what I am doing?'. Retrieved 17 January 2005 from http://www.jackwhitehead.com/jwartl141015web.htm.

Whitehead, Jack (2006) 'Living inclusional values in educational standards of practice and judgement', *Ontario Action Researcher*, 8.2.1. Retrieved 12 January 2007 from http://www.nipissingu. ca/oar/new_issue-V821E.htm

Whitehead, Jack (2008a) 'An epistemological transformation in what counts as educational knowledge: responses to Laidlaw and Adler-Collins', *Research Intelligence*, 105: 28–9.

Whitehead, Jack (2008b) 'Using a living theory methodology in improving practice and generating educational knowledge in living theories', *Educational Journal of Living Theories*, 1 (1): 103–26. Retrieved 8 December 2008 from http://ejolts.net/node/80.

Whitehead, Jack (2008c) 'Increasing inclusion in educational research: a response to Pip Bruce Ferguson', *Research Intelligence*, 103: 16–17. Retrieved 11 January 2008 from http://www. actionresearch.net/writings/bera/16&17RI103.pdf.

Whitehead, Jack and McNiff, J. (2003) Proposal to the American Educational Research Association for the symposium, 'The transformative potential of individuals' collaborative self-studies for sustainable global educational networks of communication', accepted November 2003 for presentation in April 2004. Retrieved 21 January 2005 from file://localhost/Volumes/LacieC233/public_html/multimedia/aera04sym.htm.

Whitehead, Jack and McNiff, J. (2006) *Action Research: Living Theory*. London: Sage.

Whitehead, Joan (2003) 'The future of teaching and teaching in the future: a vision of the future of the profession of teaching – making the possible probable'. Keynote address to the Standing Committee for the Education and Training of Teachers Annual Conference, Dunchurch, October. Retrieved 23 January 2005 from http://www.bath.ac.uk/~edsajw/evol/joanwfiles/joanw.htm.

Whitehead, Joan and Fitzgerald, B. (2004) 'new ways of working with mentors and trainees in a training school partnership as practitioner-researchers'. Paper presented at the symposium 'Have we created a new epistemology for the new scholarship of educational enquiry through practitioner research? Developing sustainable global educational networks of communication', presented at the British Educational Research Association annual meeting, UMIST, Manchester, September. Retrieved 23 January 2005 from http://www.bath.ac.uk/~edsajw//bera04/bera3.htm.

Wickham, J. (2009) 'Meet the dragons: how do i encourage physiotherapy students to engage in action research as part of life long learning?'. Proposal for Skills and Development. Unit Working Paper. York St John University.

Wickham, J. (2010) 'Tip toeing towards transforming transition: action research on an undergraduate programme'. A paper for the Seminar on Higher Education Action Research for Teaching, York St John University, 24 May 2010.

Williams, M. and Dick, B. (eds) (2004) *Write a Doctoral Thesis About Work: Professional Action Research – A Creative Reader Introducing Rich Modelling*. Cottesloe WA: Resource Press.

Winter, R. (1989) *Learning from Experience*. London: Falmer.

Winter, R. (1998) 'Managers, spectators and citizens: where does "theory" comes from in action research?', *Educational Action Research*, 6 (3): 361–76.

Wood, L. (2010) 'The transformative potential of living theory educational research', *Electronic Journal of Living Theories*, 3 (1): 105–18.

Yeaman, K. (1995) 'Creating educative dialogue in an infant classroom – my educational journey. Action research module'. University of Bath. Retrieved 16 January 2005 from http://www.bath.ac.uk/~edsajw/module/kathy.htm.

Yin, R. (2009) *Case Study Research: Design and Methods* (4th edn). Thousand Oaks, CA: Sage.

Zimmerman, M.E., Callicott, J.B., Sessions, G., Warren, K.J. and Clark, J. (2001) *Environmental Philosophy: From Animal Rights to Radical Ecology* (3rd edn). Upper Saddle River, NJ: Prentice Hall.

Index

Crème, P. and Lea, M. 221
Cresswell, J.W. 51
critical friends 93–4, 163–5
critical processes 3, 56
criteria: and standards of judgement
    151–2; in social sciences 32, 162;
    which ones? 152–3, 191–2
critical pedagogy 29
critical theory 46–7
critique: importance of 31, 34, 64; practice
    of 36, 161–2

Dadds, M. 29; and Hart, S. 35
data: different kinds of 124; disconfirming
    213; gathering it 92, 126, 140–7, 200,
    211; looking for it 133–9; selecting it
    154–5; sorting and storing it 147–9;
    sources of 135–7
Davies, M.B. 110, 149
Delong, J. 45, 178, 202; and Knill-Griesser,
    H. 174
democracy 53; models of 72
Denzin, N.K. and Lincoln, Y.S. 86
Derrida, J. 233
design 89–91
Dick, B. et al 77
Du Plessis, E. 48

Easterby-Smith, M. et al 119
Educational Journal of Living Theories
    (EJOLTS) 45, 147, 178, 195, 237
Eisner, E. 234
Elliott, J. 10, 16, 43, 77, 200
empathetic approaches 48
engaging with the literatures; see
    literatures, engaging with them
epistemological: issues 30–33; standards 84
epistemologies, new ones 249–57
ethical issues 95–8, 137
evaluating: practice 37; research 79–86;
    your own work 83–4, 127
evidence: different from data 150;
    generating it from the data 150–8;
    importance of 66; of learning 66–7
externalist stance to research 47

Fals Borda, O. 12
Farren, M. 228, 236
feasibility planning 91–3
Feldman, A. 86, 163
Finnegan, J. 50
first, second and third person research
    11–12, 27–8
Forrest, M. 168–9
Foucault, M. 2, 59, 73, 181, 187, 195, 233, 248

Frankl, V. 63
freedom 58; and responsibility 44, 53, 56
Freire, P. 12, 211, 234
Fromm, E. 73
Fulford, S. 202–3
Furlong, J. 60; and Oancea, A. 162;
    et al 61

Gardner, H. 57
Garnett, J. et al 37
generative transformational forms 2–3,
    36–8, 44
Geoghegan, M. 57
Ghaye, T. and Ghaye, K. 70
Glavey, C. 255
Glenn, M. 219, 232
Goethe, W. 44, 63
Gorard, S. 60
Gramsci, A. 177
Grix, J. 119
Guba, E. and Lincoln, Y. 81

Habermas, J. 3, 30, 63, 82, 170, 174, 179,
    191, 231–5, 253
Hamad Al-Hajri, S. 69
Hammersley, M. 177
Hartley, J. 221
Hartog, M. 20, 23, 50, 153
Henon, A. 139
Heron, J. 14
Heron, J. and Reason, P. 14
Herr, K. and Anderson, G. 222
Higgs, J. and Titchen, A. 10
Hignall, W. 58
Hillesum, E. 64
Hitchcock, G. and Hughes, D. 45
Hopkins, D. 130
How do I ...? 16, 31, 34, 44, 56, 83, 89,
    121, 134
human interests 253
Huyge, L. 203
Huxtable, M. 24
Hymer, B. 235–6; et al 78

'I' and others 32–3, 44, 62
Ilyenkov, E. 44, 236
improving learning for improving practice
    1, 37, 62, 213
influence 34, 62–3; educational
    64, 126, 136–7
interpretive forms of research 46

Jenkins, R. 19, 179
Jones, C. 178, 207
Jones, J. 178, 247–8

practitioners as researchers 55
practitioners' knowledge: importance of 21–5, 37, 55–6, 59
presentations 224–5
policy formation 252
power, issues of 5, 181
praxis 23, 29
Pring, R. 72
propaganda system 72, 177
public critique 85, 94–5
public intellectuals 34, 59, 176–7
publishing your work 185, 196
Punia, R. 155–7

Rawal, S. 246
Raymond, P. 65–6
Rayner, A. 22, 24, 235–6
reading as a writer 116–7
Reason, P.: and Bradbury, H. 12, 17; and Rowan, J. 75
records, keeping them 125–6
referencing correctly 117–9
reflective practice 13
reflection on practice 67
Reid, C. and Frisby, W. 13
relationships, nature of 30, 48; 64
reconnaissance phase 16
Renowden, J. 233
reports for publication 1
research: cycles 122–3; explanatory frameworks 121–2; outsider and insider forms 8, 12. 38; questions 121, 134; social science forms 8, 34
Resources 93–5
Riding, K. 177, 219–21
Riding, S. 178, 219–20
rigour, need for 83
risk in action research 35
Rivers, M. 174
Roberts, P. 143–4
Robson, C. 139
Roche, M. 29, 219, 232
Rowland, S. 114

Said, E. 34, 59, 61, 63, 70, 177, 231, 257
Scaife, J. 86
Schön, D. 18–20, 25, 56, 231, 249–51, 259
Scott, W. 14
Scott, D. and Usher, R. 40, 78
self-study perspectives 43
self-evaluation 85
Sen, A. 21, 34, 38, 56, 58, 61
Senge, P. 50, 82, 259
Significance of your research 172

Sinclair, A. 14, 178
Snow, C. 226
social formations, education of 174
social science approaches 58
social evolution 38
social justice 44, 79
social networking 225
social orders 38
social purposes of action research 36–9
Somekh, B. 61
Sowell, T. 58
speaking for yourself 73–4
Spiro, J. 20, 50, 178
S-STEP 13
standards of judgement 38, 151–3
Stenhouse, L. 42–3, 50
Stringer, E. 130; et al. 70
Suderman-Gladwell, G. 92, 171
Sullivan, B. 219, 232

targets, problematics of 36, 80, 82
Tattersall, P. 14, 178
Taylor, F. 80
technical rational forms of research 46
theory: accreditation of 45, 49–52; different kinds of 2, 12, 47; need to re-think 1–2; practical forms of 1–2
theories of practice 7; need to generate them 71
theory-practice gap 11
Thomas, G. 19, 46
Tidwell, D. et al 149, 248
Todorov, T. 64
triangulation 154
Tribal Education 67
truthfulness as a criterion 193
Turley, R.M. 208

Usher, R. 45

validation: groups 95, 165–6
validation meetings 165–6; briefing sheets for 166–7; examples of 168–9
validity: different kinds of 163; testing in relation to knowledge claims 23, 84, 127, 161–6, 201; of theories 23; significance of 177
values: and culture 28; as conceptual frameworks 113; as guiding principles 28, 73, 83–4, 123; as standards of judgement 38, 152–3, 212; conflict of 58, 60, 64; denied in practice 23; in action research 27; living towards them 22–3, 28, 73
Van Tuyl, G. 176, 244